the golden woman

dreaming as art

the golden woman

dreaming as art

J. GORDON SHILLINGFORD
PUBLISHING INC

KAY STONE

Cover and interior design by Relish Design Studios Ltd.

We acknowledge the financial support of the Manitoba Arts Council, The Canada Council for the Arts and the Government of Canada through the Book Publishing Industry Development Program (BPIDP) for our publishing program.

Printed and bound in Canada

Library and Archives Canada Cataloguing in Publication

Stone, Kay F., 1939-
The golden woman: dreaming as art/Kay Stone.

Includes bibliographical references and index.
ISBN 0-920486-77-0

1. Dreams and the arts. 2. Dream interpretation.

I. Title.

BF1078.S86 2004 154.6'34 C2004-904919-4

J. Gordon Shillingford Publishing Inc.
P.O. Box 86, RPO Corydon Avenue, Winnipeg, MB R3M 3S3

Table of Contents

Dreaming a Book

Some years ago I had a perplexing dream that I knew was deeply significant, but had no idea why this might be so. The entire brief dream, perhaps less than 30 seconds long, was of a pail dipping and rising by itself in an old stone well. Though I was not even a character in the dream, I could actually feel the pull of that pail in my chest, as I was dreaming and when I woke up. I pondered this image for a while before sensing that it was something about getting wisdom by following the unconscious mind as it dipped into its watery depths to bring up deeper knowledge of…what? Perhaps the fervent, two-hour conversation I had just had with my intense nephew; or the folklore class I would be teaching the next week; or any number of other issues that were occupying my mind at the time of the dream. But it goes further than that. The archetypal image of a pail rising and falling in a well continues to carry symbolic meaning for me, and I have come back to it again and again whenever I had a problem that I was grappling with. This book, for example. The water runs deep.

For several years I daydreamed about writing a book about the art of dreams and folktales, and their intriguing connections with biography. This dream finally came into the waking world in 1995 in an experimental English honours class I taught with five colleagues. We each spent two weeks engaging students in our works-in-progress and building assignments around these. It was a perfect opportunity to risk my dreamed-of dream book, and it turned out to be a very fine adventure. At this point I was still thinking of dreams as stories, but student discussions and written work revealed that dreams were also poetic, as well as pure abstract art. In their essays, some included poetry inspired by their own dreams, others did drawing and painting. We talked about how the imaginative energy of dreaming could just as easily be expressed in drama, dance, and other expressive forms. Someone mentioned culinary arts since she had created recipes in dreams. From their own direct experiences, they suggested that anything that arises from the imagination comes from the same place that gives birth to dreams—our unconscious artistic selves. Waiting tables? Answering the telephone? There was no end to it. We surprised ourselves constantly with what arose when we least expected it.

I was delighted to see how alive their dreams were, full of playful and profound language and imagery, rich with spontaneous symbol and metaphor. Their willingness to connect dream, biography, and art inspired me to continue working on this book. What began as a rhetorical exploration of dreams and stories opened out into a poetic gathering that included a wider variety of creative expressions. Their responses affirmed my intuitive sense of dreaming as an art, and since we all dream, whether we remember or not, that means we are artistic creatures, whether we admit it or not.

I found an unexpected gift in Tanis MacDonald, who was already a published poet. She wove her final student essay around poems inspired by class readings and by some of her dreams. I was intrigued with what she had done and asked if she was interested in contributing dream-inspired poems to my ongoing project, and she agreed to join the adventure. I had to allow my dreams to be whirled in different directions, of course, since any artistic expression needs liberty to evolve—in this case a lot of poetic license. Tanis described the challenge from her own perspective:

> Writing poems from other people's dreams is actually a great relief; any obligation that I may have felt to be precisely (and perhaps stiflingly) loyal to my own dream images has been lifted, and I am free to interpret the set of images that has been presented to me. In this context, writing a poem from someone else's dream is not unlike writing modern revisions of folktales or other familiar works, a popular feminist and post-colonialist

> practice. The dreamer relays the narrative and details of the dream-story to the poet, who then re-interprets the dream on the page. If all has gone well, the dreamer discovers something both about the dream and the process of telling a story. The poet, of course, is rewarded by the dream's fresh scenario. Writers are notorious for spending a lot of time in their own heads, so the opportunity to spend some time writing about the contents of another person's head is to be welcomed (personal note, 1998).

I, too, have found it enlivening to get inside other people's heads through their dreams. I have permission to include examples that have been personally communicated to me in conversations, by letters, and through e-mail. Among those who were generous in sharing their dreams and comments are my friends Morgana Graham (Winnipeg), Kira Van Deusen (Vancouver), and Gail Beck (Sautee, Georgia). I also draw on material from two other students in the honours class, Gerri Cooper and Richard Pound, whose essays were eloquent testimonies to dreaming as art.

This is a subjective, poetic quest and not a rhetorical exploration of the psychology of dreams and dreaming. My guiding thought throughout is that the dreamer is an artist. There are countless studies of dreams as psychological expressions, and such works have brought dreams the serious attention they deserve. However, other than pointing out the inescapable connections between ordinary life and extraordinary dreams, I do not highlight psychological content here. Instead I want to underscore the inventiveness of both dreaming and living. Obviously the psychology of dreaming is important, since we cannot separate what we dream from who we are. This would be true of any other artistic creation as well, as evidenced by ample psychoanalytic explorations of art and literature and their makers.

Like exotic plants, dreams rise from the ordinary soil of our mundane lives; some are perennial, some annual, some occasional volunteers that drop in unexpectedly and disappear. And quite a few of them are just plain weeds, but even weeds have their value. Dreams grow more luxurious with some mindful care, and can produce astounding blooms in glorious shapes and colours and scents. To keep this garden growing, I draw on my academic training as a professional folklorist, my sporadic efforts as an amateur artist, and my ongoing experiences as a performing storyteller. Because I am intrigued with the imaginative dance from life to art to dream and back again, I begin with autobiographic memories and related dreams in order to set the stage for the stories that follow. Folktales are my speciality as both folklorist and storyteller, so I use examples of particular stories to show how art, dreams, and life interweave. Folktales are followed by their type numbers in the Aarne-Thompson Type Index (Aarne-Thompson 1973).

The material is arranged in three sections; after an invitation to enter and enjoy: the first explores biographical stories, mine and others, as they relate to dreams and folktales; the second centres on folktales as dream-like literature, and dreams as stories; the last explores dreams themselves as an expressive art, a way of appreciating our talents in nocturnal rehearsals and carrying them into waking life.

I also use my sketchy artistic training to create a dream mandala (sacred circle) that brings together several key dreams. One very special dream, "The Golden Woman," is at its centre. In fact, this dream was the initial inspiration for my work here. I was still struggling with an earlier book on contemporary storytelling (Stone 1998) when "The Golden Woman" appeared. I had told the dream casually to a friend, Christel Kraft, who has worked intensively and extensively with dreams in her Focusing workshops. She listened carefully and then said, simply but firmly, "This must be in your book." Unfortunately, the woman of gold could not find a fitting place in the storytelling book, so I had to write another one with her at the heart of it.

This has been joyful work, exploring dreams, folktales and personal adventures. I already knew that dreams were significant creations, but had this underlined for me by a comic strip, "Raising Duncan," in which a man and his dog are flying across a clear night sky over a bucolic shoreline with a crescent moon lighting the water. The man says, "I know this is only a dream, but I love it!" The dog is thinking, "What? This is a dream?!" Only a dream? Read on and decide for yourself.

Miss Kitty Sings the Blues: Introducing the Art of Dreaming

When I was four or five I met a talking rat, menacingly large and dull grey. This is the first dream I can remember, and its colours and textures and emotional content are still vivid sixty years later. Sadly, I have forgotten what that rat was trying to tell me. As an adolescent I faced a huge buffalo with shining black hooves and sombre dark eyes. It stood right in the middle of the intersection of Seventh Avenue and 101 Street in Miami, where I grew up. This buffalo, possibly having learned silence from the rat, said nothing, but I was still impressed enough to recall the dream with complete clarity for decades.

These two dreams were still so alive in my imagination that I had no trouble describing them in detail when I began to record dreams some time in the 1970s. I do not remember why I decided to do this, but for several years I wrote dreams down on scraps of paper, as part of journal entries, and in letters I wrote to family and friends. And of course I told them to anyone who would listen. Perhaps I was inspired by the dream-like folktales with their archetypal characters and events that I was reading as part of my doctoral dissertation in folklore at that time. Talking animals, beasts and beauties, crones and wise women, deep waters and dark forests, good and bad sisters, magical objects and miraculous transformations, were all familiar from my dreams.

I was puzzled but not dismayed that many of those who happily listened to my dreams, and even described their own, still seemed to think that both dreams and folktales were trivial expressions, escapist fantasies at best and amusing nonsense at worst. I understood from my own experiences that they were not escapes from reality at all but deeper voyages into the heart of life. Paradoxically, dreams and folktales pointed me towards waking up rather than staying asleep. I understood this intuitively, but had no sure reason to believe I was right. So I kept on writing dreams down, and finally in the 1990s took the trouble—and it was trouble—to find all the scraps of paper and old letters and journal entries with dreams, and to type them into a computer file. This meant I got to review several decades of wild dreaming as child and adult. I was amazed at the variety of dream figures and situations, and how some of them did indeed reach the literary heights and depths of folktale archetypes. I even met a frog who turned into a handsome young man who might have been a prince—I could not tell since he had no clothing on to identify his station in life. We will meet him again later.

As my explorations of folktales and dreams continued, I was drawn to the writings of Joseph Campbell, who led me to Carl Jung and others. Here I discovered to my delight that dreaming was much more than a nocturnal amusement. The concepts of symbol, metaphor, and archetype were valuable tools for looking at my dreams from new perspectives, since these form the language of dreams. As Jung observed, "In dreams symbols occur spontaneously, for dreams happen and are not invented" (Jung 1964, 55). The same would be true of metaphor and archetype. Each of these deepens the meaning of dreams, so that my rat and my buffalo are much more than the ordinary animals they represent, each one trying in symbolic form to tell me something. But to understand them I had to explore my own personal dream language, and then see how the notion of transpersonal archetypes might come into play.

Joseph Campbell explored archetypes as fundamental ideas, images, characters, situations, arising instinctively from the unconscious human mind. He began with the basic notion that "all over the world and at different times of human history, these archetypes, or elementary ideas, have appeared in different costumes" (Campbell 1988, 51-52). The "different costumes" depend on who we are, where and when we live, and which society we grow up in. For example, a buffalo would have much different meaning to a nineteenth-century Plains hunter than it did to urbanized, twentieth-century, pre-adolescent Kay, though they would probably agree on the archetypal buffalo as a powerful and potentially dangerous creature.

I was fascinated with these concepts, and began to record my dreams with greater care and attention. I also began to discuss them with people of like mind who led active dream lives and who, like me, found this to be delightful and enlightening. I was intrigued that my intuitive understanding was correct, that dreams arise from our creative depths. They do not simply float in from the outside, though they are certainly affected by our external lives. My buffalo presented himself unexpectedly, but only because my dream-making self called him up. And the fact that he was a very convincing buffalo revealed the artistry of the dreamer. He was no stick figure, but a flesh-and-blood creature.

I had never thought of my dreams as unusual, since much of their symbolic and archetypal content was echoed in the dreams of my five brothers and sisters. When we met at various times as adults, gathering from all parts of the continent, we regaled each other with memories of childhood adventures ("Remember when Janet hit Jolene in the head with the lead elephant bottle opener?"), and with vibrant dreams set in the house, yard, and neighbourhood of our various childhood years. All six of us had a variety of flying dreams, had met similar assortments of talking animals, and kept falling from cliffs, buildings, and other places. I assumed that everyone dreamed as vividly as we all did, and took the same pleasure in recounting the absurd humour, scary situations, and odd characters of their night-stories.

Here is an example from my younger brother, Terry, who sent me a dream about his white cat, Miss Kitty, composing and singing an entire blues song. He says:

> I've got to tell you about a dream I had the other night. Miss Kitty sang a blues song. Here's the background info that fed into the song she sang. Miss Kitty is afraid of bugs and snakes and she hates traveling in a car. Also, she likes our tile-floored house because she doesn't get yelled at for hacking up fur balls like she did at our carpeted house in Seattle. The dream locale was in our old Miami neighborhood. We were in a phone booth across the field next to our old house waiting out a thunderstorm (which Miss Kitty is also afraid of). I was wondering what was going though her little kitty mind because she was lying down with her head resting on her front paws looking unhappy. Just then she sat up and started singing her blues song, her lips moving in

sync with the words. I left out the inter-verse guitar blues riff, ba dada ba dum, but here's her lyrics:

Let me tell you a sad story
'Bout Miss Kitty's bad day.
Her owner threw 'er in his car
And he drove her away.
He drove her real fast
And he drove her real far,
Before he'd let Miss Kitty
Get outta' that car.
He took her to some place
Where she'd never been,
Said "This is where I grew up,
Way back when."

It was an awful place
Full of snakes and bugs;
No tiles on the floor,
Hadda' throw up on rugs.
The moral of this story
Goes something like this,
So listen real careful,
Or Miss Kitty will hiss:
If bad man goes to take you away,
Just look 'im in the eyes
And tell him "No way!"
Them's the Kitty Cat Blues
Yeh them's the Kitty Cat Blues.

Pretty cool, eh? I don't know how the sleeping mind can come up with these things—rhyming verse, connection to real-life events, etc. Amazing. I woke up right after the dream and was so impressed that I memorized the song before it left my mind (e-mail message, April 11, 1997).

Terry described how the elements of the dream connected with his waking world, past and present, as Miss Kitty expressed her dismay (and, of course, her owner's) at having to move by car from Seattle to Miami. Terry understood that he himself was the actual composer, not Miss Kitty, and wondered "how the sleeping mind can come up with these things."

He was inspired to create an animated video of the dream, which he sent me, with Miss Kitty dancing languidly as she sings to blues guitar accompaniment. The dream alone is art enough, but it grows in potency when taken out to the waking world, in Terry's form or any other.

Coincidentally, Tanis MacDonald was also motivated by an anxiety dream about her cat's travel adventures. Like Terry, she combines waking and sleeping worlds in her account.

> When I was preparing to move from Toronto last summer, I knew my cat would be unhappy in a (temporary) house with two pre-schoolers and two other cats, so I decided she would be happier in Winnipeg with my parents until I could join her in a month. This meant sending her on the airplane alone. The dream [I had] is much as I describe it in the poem; suffice it to say that it was an anxiety dream about being a bad "mother."

In the dream, her cat gets her own wings and flies away, without the unpleasantness of a long plane flight. Here is her poem, "Flight":

My calico cat, tired
of the tough birding
on the ground, buys a pair
of plywood wings, flaps
folded flat on her back
until she snaps them open
and coils to spring. With me
shouting *Wait, not yet,*

she leaps from the top of the garden shed,
sails a circuit around the yard.
The wooden wings sprout feathers
like fingers clutching the sky,
reaching higher. I call

head west

and stay away from the sun

even as she banks

evenly and is gone.

Tanis' flying cat, who starts with heavy wings that sprout feathers as she leaps fearlessly into the air, gives us a very fine and fluid example of how a weighty dream can glide into waking life. Her poem is enriched by the mundane life of a bird-hunting cat and the imaginative echo of the Greek myth of Icarus, that archetypal flier who soared too close to the sun with his waxed wings. In someone else's dream Icarus might not even have got off the ground, and would have lived longer, though probably not any more happily.

You might expect poets and other artists to experience dreams filled with marvelous sights and sounds and movement, but even when this happens, they sometimes deny the ingenuity of their own imagination. A painter, for example, had a vibrant dream that he was describing excitedly to a friend:

> It was one of those vivid technicolor dreams, the kind that linger on in exact detail even after waking. In his dream he found himself at an art gallery, and when he walked inside and looked around he found the walls hung with amazing paintings, paintings of passionate intensity and haunting beauty. Recounting his dream, the artist ended fervently with, "I'd give anything to be able to make paintings like that!" (Bayles & Orland 1993, 111).

His friend, of course, pointed out that as the dreamer he was the one who had indeed made "paintings like that"! Because such dreams seem to arise so spontaneously, it is all too easy to forget who the artist is, to assume a dream is coming from somewhere else instead of from one's own wild mind.

In a similar situation I dreamed I was circling a pillar with another woman and two men, chanting an extraordinarily beautiful sacred song. When we finished I said, "Oh, I wish I had my tape recorder!" The other singers looked at me knowingly and then smiled. I drifted back to the waking world, annoyed by a feeling of having interrupted the dream. By the time I recognized whose song it was and why they were smiling at my ignorance, I had already forgotten the words—but not the experience of having been there. From previous encounters with dream-ignorance (my childhood talking rat, for example), I also trusted future dreams to give me another chance to remember what I was doing as the dream-maker.

I am delighted that my dream characters often know before I do how dreams arise, and may have to remind me of the obvious—that we are all the authors, architects, and artists of our own dreams. We take dreaming so much for granted that we often do not recognize our sleeping selves as imaginative and original, like the artist who did not recognize his own dream paintings. That is one reason that we might fail to remember them at all. Also, dreams are not always so fully formed as these examples. More often they are frayed at both ends, leaving only remnants of what had been a fine tapestry. These remnants are worth calling back; if even a single thread of connection remains, it might lead us back into the dream, in much the same way that the Greek hero, Theseus, found his way through the labyrinth by following the thread his beloved Ariadne spun for him. Yes, sometimes we meet frightful Minotaurs, but other times there are unicorns.

When people ask how they can recall their dreams more fully, I suggest a simple exercise in imagination that can evoke a small detail or fragment of dream. Even a single image can call up connecting details that lead to other images, like stringing beads on a necklace. For example, to recapture the vibrant chanting dream above, I call to mind the white pillar and focus on what it looked like: how tall it was (about 10 feet), how thick (perhaps six feet across, wide enough for four people to encircle it), and where it was located (in a dim underground parking garage with a low ceiling). With this in mind I can call back the other three chanters (two large men and a dark-haired woman), feel their hands gripping mine as we circle clockwise, hear the sound (though not the words) of the chanting, and then begin to follow the dream story back to discover how we all came together in that place. As it turned out, we met in a school classroom where I was just starting to tell a story.

Imagine a detail from a specific dream, something as simple as a red ball rolling across a green meadow on a sunny June day. Colours, sounds, and emotional feelings can slowly develop and details become clearer as the dream comes to life. It does not matter if an entire dream reveals itself, because even seemingly insignificant features can uncover the artistry of the dreamer. Whatever is seen, heard, or felt, is the full creation of the one who experienced the dream—you. The full drama of action and movement are your own innovations; it is you who gave life to the characters (including your dreamself), composed conversations, chose the settings, indoors and out.

In this respect, dreams can be like movies or plays in which you are simultaneously actor, director, script writer; you are in charge of props, lighting, sound, make-up, and costumes, and of everything else that would make it a work of art. And of course you are critic and audience as well, both inside the dream and recalling it later in the waking world. The only thing you do not have to worry about is publicity and box office, unless of course your dream becomes a publicly performed piece.

Other dreams are less narrative, more like moving paintings. One writer suggested that a dreamer can be even more skilled an artist than a landscape painter, because a dreamer "makes his trees bend in the wind and his clouds to fleet across the sky" (Blacker 1973, ix). Our landscape "paintings" come to life, we can walk right into them and enjoy the colours and textures as we are in the very midst of creating them.

Some dreams are pure poetry, though I, unlike Tanis, find it almost impossible to reconstruct their poetic artistry. Joseph Campbell wryly observed that on waking we may be able to "render only prose" (Campbell 1990, 6), and that is exactly my problem. I have experienced a number of brief, illusive dreams just before waking that I call "Haiku dreams" because they have no storyline at all, usually only a quick clear image, sometimes repeated several times until I "get" it well enough to bring the image back to the waking world. But I am rarely able to render them in anything other than prose. For example, I dreamed of a young woman with dark hair who was sitting on a beach of white sand, a gentle green ocean behind her and a clear blue sky above her. She was wearing bold red sunglasses. That is it. No story but a lucid image, a kind of living, breathing dream postcard. I sent this to Tanis MacDonald to see if she found any poetic potential. She effortlessly composed a haiku-like creation that faithfully evoked my miniature dream in her "Red Sunglasses":

> Red sunglasses dare
> to protect my eyes,
> against green water, white sand.
> Beached.

Where do dreams come from? From inner impulses or external stimulants? Eating before bedtime? Divine inspiration? The sunglass dream is a good one for exploring this riddle, for which there is, in fact, no final answer despite endless attempts by serious dream researchers. When I woke up, I heard the sound of gentle tapping and saw that the red glass suncatcher in our bedroom window was being gently knocked against the glass pane by morning wind. The immediate stimulus was external, but look what the dream manages to create from this utterly mundane sound in only a few seconds, using the tapping rhythm to create gently rolling ocean waves and playing on the red glass suncatcher to form the fanciful red sunglasses. And the young woman with dark hair? Tanis noted her resemblance to the dark-haired younger Kay whose mirror image enticed me in "The Golden Woman," a likely prospect since our dreams are all connected in a complex web of unconscious imagination. I also note the dream's connection to aspects in my own life, like red sunglasses which cause the wearer to see red, an apt metaphor for my short and explosive temper. A dream rolls out in all directions, taking energy from our waking lives and giving it back transformed.

Intuition certainly plays a central role in dreaming, as it does in all forms of artistic expression. The more we trust ourselves to dream, remember, and understand, the stronger our intuition becomes. The more we practice our art, the better we become at bringing it to life. Recurring dreams are good places to practice, since they present similar situations over and over again, variations on a theme. These kinds of dreams can be particularly valuable in revealing how nightly visions arise and evolve. They reveal the creative problems we are caught up in.

Here is a colourful example of a recurring dream from Kira Van Deusen, a friend who is a professional musician, storyteller, and dedicated dreamer. She is also a scholar who has worked extensively and intensively with dreams and folktales among Siberian shamans and narrators, and has edited several collections of folktales (Van Deusen 1996, 1998, 1999, 2001, 2003).

> I have had dreams for years in which I go into a shop that has racks and racks of fabulous clothes, beautiful fabrics and colours. But I search and search and can't find any one thing that I want—taken separately they all look cheap. In waking life I feel this while cruising the sari shops in our Indian neighbourhoods. Perhaps these inspire the dreams. In a recent dream I finally bought a lovely fabric, and maybe this was some sort of resolution of this dream (e-mail message, 1997).

Dreams like this uncover creative anxieties, and often show ways of facing the challenges. Kira can see how she undercuts her artistry by cheapening the clothing that at first seems so splendid. She also notices how the dream affects her view of, and is eventually affected by, the elegant fabrics she sees in the store window in waking life. Her dream response is to buy one of the fine fabrics at last, instead of rejecting them as cheap. She might consider the suggestion of one dream researcher who advises us to literally clothe ourselves with dreams in waking life:

> One might attempt to wear clothing designed on the basis of personal dream imagery or jewellery which reminds one of a significant object from a dream. Such efforts to capture and affirm the positive energy associated with a strong dream image can serve to empower the dreamer and keep him or her in touch with this important source of unconscious inspiration (Van de Castle 1994, 171).

The writer goes on to say that "by externalizing the dream image in some graphic or plastic way, it also becomes possible to examine its gradual metamorphosis over time" (ibid. 171). This is especially the case with recurring dreams, some of which may come again and again throughout an entire lifetime, but evolving as the dreamer becomes freer of anxiety and more conscious of a dream's creative potential.

For example, I have had recurring dreams of being in a store surrounded by objects that I want to buy, just as Kira was. The earliest ones I can recall go back to childhood, when I had a tiny allowance to spend in the five-and-dime store a few blocks from home. Throughout the years the dream store expanded with my age, experience, and income—but no matter how much money I had, it was never enough to buy what I really wanted, from the cheap toys of childhood to the expensive clothing of adulthood. After five decades in these dream department stores, I finally had a dream in which I realized that I did not actually want anything at all in the store, that materialism could not satisfy a soulful dream-desire for something I could not name. By realizing and admitting that inside the dream, I was rewarded with an escalator ride up to the next level, into another resolution that involved meeting a talking bear. In this dream I went up, in other dreams—like "The Golden Woman" dream that inspired this book—I went down, always to another world of possibility.

Obviously we draw on all aspects of our past and present experiences when we dream, when we tell stories about our lives, and when we make art in any form. The interplay between these is constant, subtle, and often fascinating. Here is a quick example from an 11-year-old boy. I told a folktale in an elementary school class in Winnipeg about a boy whose dreams come to life. We spontaneously began talking about dreaming as an art, and how art comes into dreams, and I told them Kira's dream of colourful saris. One of the boys sat forward and excitedly described how a fire engine screamed by his house as he was sleeping, and how his dream suddenly filled with bright colours that moved and flowed, as if they were fabrics from Kira's dream. He was "painting" abstract art in his sleep in response to outside sounds, in much the same way my haiku dream poem of the woman on the beach was stimulated by the red sun catcher tapping against the window. He understood that his dream was significant, but was not sure how this was so until he told it to the class and heard our responses. As he recounted the story of his sound-colour dream, it became part of his conscious life, and he could have brought it further into the waking world by trying to paint the moving colours he saw.

Dreams like this highlight dreaming as art, more ephemeral but no less real and challenging than any other form of artistic expression. We only have to remember and accept that when we dream, we are the source of all those colours, sounds, movement and choreography, the full range of graphic, dramatic and literary arts. Our landscapes come fully to life, we can travel anywhere in the world, by any means we dream up. Like any of the arts, dreaming can be improved and practiced with conscious energy for anyone who wishes to do so. It seems to me that an interest in our dreams as creative inventions might inspire us to see ordinary life in a different light as well, since we are the authors and editors of our own life stories.

Obviously I do not have simple answers to how and why we dream, and sometimes no answers at all, only further artistic questions for dreams, folktales, and personal anecdotes: Are they effective as stories? How do the people in them keep on going despite all obstacles? What resources do they use to survive? A colleague, Per Brask, wondered if we remember dreams because they are already well-formed stories, or if we unconsciously re-form scattered pieces into a coherent story when we wake up. Good question, and short of sending in a dream team to investigate, I would not know how to find out whether we are artists primarily as we are dreaming, or when we wake up. I only know that we are the ones who remember our dreams as intact creations, and bring them whole into the waking world. And as they pass into this conscious world they can often suggest other possibilities. As fellow dreamer Kira Van Deusen put it, "I'm giving myself more permission to continue the dream story while I'm awake, no longer a slave to what comes from the unconscious" (e-mail, June 2000).

Another way of re-forming the unconscious mind is through lucid dreaming, bringing the conscious mind deliberately into the enigmatic world of dreams. Many people I have shared dreams with describe such dreams, the ones in which you suddenly say, "Oh! This is a dream." Practice in lucid dreaming improves your sleep artistry, and can help in waking creativity as well. Because our dreams are so spontaneous, even when lucid, we can observe our creative processes in the midst of their very arising.

Carl Jung employed another intriguing concept in his work, that of synchronicity, what we call coincidence or accident but what he felt was much more. One Jungian writer characterizes it as meaningful coincidence:

> It [synchronicity] is based on the assumption of an inner unconscious knowledge that links a physical event with a psychic condition, so that a certain event that appears "accidental" or "coincidental" can in fact be psychically meaningful (Jolande Jacobi in Jung 1964, 291).

In other words, coincidence has more to offer than meets the eye. Or the mind. Dreams, of course, are rich in synchronicity, with surprising things happening at every turn, but the waking world can be equally astonishing. For example, at the very moment I was struggling to find words to confirm that dreams lead us deeper into reality rather than escape from it, the phone rang. It was my daughter Rachel, calling to tell me that Jungian therapist and author Marion Woodman was being interviewed on CBC television, talking about her successful struggle with an eating disorder. I took a break from writing to listen to Woodman describing our psychic situation as an iceberg with only the tip showing and the conscious ego standing conspicuously on top trying to control the enormous invisible mass beneath the sea, the unconscious mind. It was a powerful image, and I added to it by immediately picturing the ego planting a flag claiming the entire unconscious territory and yelling "mine, mine, mine!" But ego alone cannot claim such realms.

Woodman eloquently asserted that "The soul is pushing through," that is, challenging the belligerent ego, and stressed that we ignore this push at our own peril. "The soul is in exile most of the time," she said, unseen like the hidden mass of the iceberg, but expressing itself metaphorically in dreams and in the arts. "Life is movement, so for me dance was my way back from addiction." She concluded by asserting, "The soul speaks in metaphors, and always has" (CBC television broadcast, March 1997). I thought of my dream of the pail falling and rising in the well, bringing up metaphorical water from the soulful depths.

I happily pondered these various ideas as I worked on this book, and realized that in the end it does not matter how or even why dreams arise; no matter how we view dreams, they are a source of vibrant imaginings in which we are dreamer and dream at the same time. We can focus on reporting the dream as accurately as possible, or we can move on from there into conscious active imagination, as Kira does; dreams are available to us in whatever way we wish them to be. They can stand alone, or they can inspire further creativity. The most valuable dreams lead us more deeply into the stories of our waking lives, our own free-flowing water of life, waiting to be released from beneath the frozen sea-ice.

The Golden Woman and the Water of Life

A rare dream and an unusual folktale illuminate much of what I want to say here about the artistry of dreams and the transformative quality of stories. The dream is unique because it is a complete story from beginning to end, instead of the usual fragment with incomplete openings and closings. The dream led me deeper into an exceptional folktale I already knew, or thought I did, about a sister who climbs a mountain and faces a dragon in order to gain the water of life. These two together reveal the intricate interweaving of biography, dream-life and story-life as artistic visions.

In a dark period when my writing was not going well, I had a surprising dream that filled my gloomy emptiness with unexpected radiance. The subtle colours, sharp images, the smell of earth and water, and the feeling of movement as graceful as a slow dance, are as immediate as they were when I experienced them several years ago. Jung might have called this a "great dream," one that goes beyond personal biography and into archetypal consciousness. That is, it is not just my personal dream, it is a dream for anyone who senses the pull of movement and the immediacy of imagery in "The Golden Woman." The dream begins with a familiar folktale motif, a mirror that reveals the truth when requested.

My daughter Rachel and I were standing together in the hall of our Winnipeg house, looking into the round, blue-framed mirror we saw every day. I did not recognize this as a dream because there was nothing dream-like about its setting or situation. Except for the mirror, which was larger than usual and on the opposite wall, everything was exactly as it was in the waking world: the dark blue of the frame, the off-white walls reflecting light from the front door, the dimly lit basement stairs to our right, the open kitchen door just beyond that. Also, I could see and hold my reflected image as clearly as if I were awake. In dreams my image faded if I looked too closely, so again I had no clue that I was not awake. I could see 18-year-old Rachel with her smooth face and her long, honey-brown hair, and saw that my mirrored image was also young, about 25, with long, wavy brown hair. I felt a surge of joy, a strong feeling that somehow I had another chance at youth. It was a very convincing feeling, but almost immediately, for no reason I could identify, there was a warning twinge that something was not quite right. The image I saw was so deeply satisfying that I did not want to let it go, but I needed to know why the glimmer of doubt arose.

Because I did not shut out this vague feeling of unease, the dream could open to its lucid potential. I began to understand that I was not actually in the front hall seeing my true face. I turned to Rachel's mirror image and said, "This must be a dream," and she smiled at me enigmatically. I turned back to my own image and said in a firm voice that seemed to come from outside of the dream, "I want to see what I look like right now." Immediately my image began to shift and I saw myself as I was in waking life, older and rounder, my face fuller and square-jawed like my father's, my hair short, straight, and silvery white.

As I studied this face and accepted the image as true, I felt a shift in the dream. I had a conscious body sensation of subtle change, and I actually shifted to the right, taking a side step into the kitchen. Still aware that I was in a dream, I saw that our oak floor was now covered in old black linoleum with random white spots, an echo of the kitchen floor from my early Miami childhood. I knew from a previous dream that the spots in the floor might be passages into another reality, and allowed myself to sink slowly through one of them right through the floor. I did not resist the movement as I descended slowly and steadily downward through the air in a crawlspace and then into damp, dark earth. I could (and still can) smell the richness of the moist living soil pressed against my nose. This seemed to go on for a long time, but I felt no anxiety. All at once I fell gently out of the earth and into a deep green underground sea. In many of my dreams water has been a frightening element, but here I had no fear. Flashes of light revealed colour and motion in the darkness. This moving sea was warm, dense, alive, my welcoming birthwater, and I was a natural part of its languorous movement.

As I sank, I became encrusted with the kind of growth that covers objects that settle to the sea bottom—barnacles, coral, other kinds of sea life. Soon I was completely enclosed in a solid cylinder that was a protection but not a confining shell, giving me firm weight in the heavy water. Inside, I was fully alert and could still sense the world around me, could experience the shifting light and the warmth of the water, and the slow movement down and down as I continued to sink.

Eventually I settled to the bottom of the sea into soft sand, where I could feel myself rolling gently back and forth with the natural surge of the water. I perceived four beings of some primal sort, more or less human, moving through the water and positioning themselves around my cylinder, two on each side. They used the motion of the sea to gradually roll the cylinder toward the shore, out of the water, and onto an island.

On the shore, a semicircle of people stood waiting around a large bonfire. The cylinder was slowly rolled right into the centre of the fire while everyone watched quietly and calmly, waiting for what was going to happen. I understood that this was a sacred ritual of some sort, and did not resist the flames.

Inside the cylinder I could feel the heat of the fire as it began to penetrate through the hard exterior, growing hotter and hotter. This was a strong physical feeling, not a vaguely dreamy warmth but real heat. I understood calmly that this heat would eventually become unbearable, knew intuitively but without apprehension that something would have to happen soon, that my situation would inevitably change profoundly. I waited. The others waited. When the heat inside the cylinder was at the point of becoming unbearable, my dreaming mind suddenly split: "I" was both inside the cylinder directly experiencing what was happening, and outside with the others observing it vicariously. At the very instant of that split in consciousness, at the peak of pain, the cylinder itself split into two perfect halves. I felt myself lying there in the full heat of the fire, glowing hot, molten gold, transformed. At the same moment, the other aspect of me as the outside witness looked into the divided cylinder and saw the living gold in the shape of a woman, free from her mold.

As the Golden Woman, I sat up and observed the semi-circle of people. As the woman in that circle, I witnessed the rising, and simultaneously saw and felt what the Golden Woman saw and felt. We became a single consciousness again as the Golden Woman began to move. I awoke rising.

When I woke, I kept my eyes closed and lay without moving for a few moments, allowing for a less abrupt passage from fragile dream consciousness back into the waking world of morning traffic and the neighbour's dog barking and dishes clinking downstairs in the kitchen as my husband made coffee. These small moments between sleeping and waking invite a dream to present at least a fragment of itself, and sometimes I can trace that fragment further and further back into the dream. But this time I had the entire dream, intact from my first gaze into the mirror to the rising of the Golden Woman. I was amazed, since I usually only manage to call back the last fading bits of a dream and have learned to appreciate even this much. Even if I had retained only that final image of the woman rising from the fire-encircled cylinder, it would have been enough to inspire imagination. But to have the full composition was a great gift.

In the bright light of that ordinary morning I allowed the dream to play and replay in my mind until I was certain I would not forget it. As I began to write it down, I could see how artfully my present and past experiences in the waking world had provided the rich soil for the rising of the Golden Woman. It was significant that the dream began in our actual home and not in one of the countless more appealing dream houses I have passed through over the years. I felt I was rooted in my mundane waking life, with all its mental and physical associations. I was delighted that Rachel was with me initially, acting as a silent witness in much the same way as my dream-self later witnessed the golden transformation.

The mirror, too, was from the waking world, but subtly changed in size and position, another hint that this was a dream. I catch this hint and do not reject it, I provide the conscious mind with a small place to enter. In this brief lucid state I know that I am dreaming, and say the words instead of just thinking them. I give up my enticing youthful image, allowing the dream to free itself and move on.

Biography influences the dream in other ways as well. There is a brief flash of my childhood kitchen linoleum not seen for more than 50 years, with white spots offering passage into another world. The underground sea, unusually benevolent in this dream, evoked childhood memories of swimming in the Atlantic waters of Baker's Haulover in North Miami, and also, I believe, the body's memory of birth waters.

Since this single dream arises from the dream-treasury of my whole lifetime, I also looked for previous dreams that spoke a similar language, revealing variations on a theme. In one from some years earlier I also passed through a linoleum floor, guided by voices to a lake where I was told I would "see the face of god." When I looked into the dark water I saw a faintly glowing face that seemed to resemble my father but one that I knew was divine, beyond the personal. A friend who read my description challenged my interpretation: "Think about it. Whose face would you expect to see reflected in water?" With the mirror in "The Golden Woman" in mind, and the realization that my face resembled my father's, the answer was clearer. The dark lake water reflected my own glowing face, that is, the face beyond my face. I see this early dream as preparation for the later one, a fine variation on the theme of our innate sacred selves.

Everything that I have said to describe this single dream of "The Golden Woman" points to its elegance and eloquence as an artistic creation. It is my strongest evidence that dreaming is an art. Let me then show what art lessons I learned, first from classes and then in the dream. When I was an art major at the University of Miami in the late 1950s, the instructor of my first class taught an effective means of going beyond what is merely pleasing to the eye. We worked for a few weeks on pencil drawings, and when we were satisfied with whatever we had drawn we were instructed to erase it. Some people were annoyed by this task, which seemed to echo that of Sisyphus in Greek myth continually pushing the boulder up the mountain and having it roll down on him time and again. But for me it was an intriguing exercise that moved me beyond "drawing pretty," of being too attached to artistic results. I learned to value and enjoy the process of creation and to worry less about its outcome and its permanence.

Years later I witnessed the creation and dissolution of two different Tibetan sand mandalas (sacred circles) in Manitoba, and remembered my art lessons. In the dream I let go of my own pretty image and was rewarded by being carried deeper into the imaginative process. Because I rejected the surface image, my dream-self could evolve, transformed by air, earth, water, and fire into the Golden Woman. I became my own artistic creation and was fully aware of the process, even witnessing it at the same time as I experienced it. This is one of the fine gifts of dreaming, being in two places at once without being disconcerted or disjointed by the experience.

This dream is a poem of the soul, rich in archetypal symbolism that carries it beyond the personal. The reflected image, the passage through the four elements of air, earth, water, and fire, the protective cylinder that acts as a transforming mold, the primal figures who roll me out of the water, and the phoenix-flames that bring about the alchemical change from base flesh to molten gold, each of these echo motifs in mythology and folktales. Tanis MacDonald captures the earthy, archetypal nature of the dream in her poetic recasting of the dream in "Golden Woman":

The mirror lied, flattered me
with plum-smooth skin and a dewy
mouth—what I thought I wanted until
I saw it, too late and false beside
my daughter. No queen born of venom
and cowl wants the truth, but I
stared the mirror down, stared
hard enough to grind it to sand
and it gave up my real face like
a hostage.

Drawn down like water, the earth
thirsted for me, pulled me
through the linoleum, past
crawlspace, foundation, worm-scented
soil pressing my nose flat,
drawn down through the earth's tap
into a dark sea and sky. I lay
as white and calm as the moon
beneath the water. Barnacles sang
my praises, their small mouths
firm against my flesh, linking
lip and leg into a breathing armour.
Waves rolled me along the sea floor,

past coral and ray, into the arms of
four gaunt figures, gilled giants
beneath the waves. They bear me
on a watery bier in my sarcophagus of
salt and sea creature

to the night shore, where flames
crackle, a crucible to burn away
my dross, split my shell, pour me
honey-limbed, incandescent, golden.

Tanis' artistry in moving from my vision to her own poetry brings this dream out into the full light of day, available to anyone. I learn things about my own dream that I had not noticed before. Tanis' conscious composition extends the power of the dream so that it frees itself from my limited unconscious mind and reaches out to touch other imaginations through her poem. To paraphrase Kira Van Deusen's comment I quoted in the previous chapter, we can break out, free ourselves from being slaves to the unconscious, build on what our dreams suggest.

This is how Tanis and I worked: I told her a dream, she let it brew in her imagination for a while, and gradually a poem began to suggest itself. This one, like the others I include here, stays true to the dream and yet takes it further, adding another perspective by weaving new details into the pattern—the worm-scented earth, barnacles that sing, and the awesome gilled giants. The poem also wisely observes the intimate affinity of birth and death, using the images of bier and sarcophagus that contain both dross and pure gold. And of course there is the truth-speaking mirror that calls up that "queen born of venom," the archetypal wicked mother/stepmother of the Grimm tale, "Snow White." Here the motif is reversed: the queen in the tale wants only her own beautiful image and cruelly rejects that of her daughter, while my dream-self celebrates the reality of my daughter's image and finally insists on seeing my actual face, for better or for worse.

That mirror, mirror on the wall, reveals who is fairest of them all, and cannot lie once this information is commanded. Even the venomous queen cannot make the mirror speak falsely, and thus she learns that Snow White is still alive and vulnerable. To carry the metaphor further, the dream itself is a magic mirror for the creative psyche, and will show us what we most deeply wish to see, take us as far as we wish to go. That is to say, this mirror responds to what the heart asks rather than what the thinking mind asks. When heart and thinking mind, unconscious and conscious, both request the same thing, dross becomes gold.

Folktales, particularly those popularized by the Grimms (not to mention Disney productions), often present young and old women in opposition, but older women also function as guides. The fact that I chose my older over my younger self in the dream allowed my dream-self to break free of the mirror image. I became my own cronish wise woman. This time, unlike the earlier passage-through-linoleum dream, it is my own voice and not others that speaks of a divine image.

The otherworld journey is so familiar in folktales (and of course in dreams) that it hints at shamanic influences. There is a wealth of work on shamanic dreaming and practices, but these rarely focus on folktale connections. Kira Van Deusen is an exception, having explored living Siberian narratives in terms of shamanic motifs (Van Deusen 1999, 2001, 2003). In both folktales and shamanic journeys, one travels to another world through a passage of some sort: One might cross over or fall into water, wander through dark forests or wastelands, climb a mountain or a tree, or be carried off by an enormous bird or a powerful wind. On the other side of the archetypal passage is another world where one can experience transformation. In the Grimm tale of "Frau Holle," for example, a girl falls down a well to into the magical world of a crone, Frau Holle. She returns home covered in gold, a golden woman. Gold is a common folktale element. We think of it in terms of wealth, but as an archetype it denotes absolute purity, often of the inner sort. Archetypally, gold is often a symbol of inner purity. Kira Van Deusen told me that in Tuvan folktales, for example, the Golden Princess is a paragon of womanhood who shines with the light of both sun and moon (this story appears in Van Deusen, 1996).

Compliance, which on the surface looks more like passive surrender than willing participation, is another central motif in folktales. Cinderella does not openly challenge her sisters, for example, nor does she resist her magical helpers. While she seems to do nothing much, in fact she willingly participates in her transformation from ash-girl to queen. She knows what she wants, and she accomplishes it without being as opportunistic as her sisters. (I am speaking here of the more traditional oral tales rather than the seventeenth-century literary version of Charles

Perrault, popularized by Disney and many other Cinderella revisionists. More resourceful heroines need no fairy godmother nor glass slipper.)

Like many "Cinderella" figures, the girl who falls down the well in "Frau Holle" also accepts the movement of her life adventures, which include obeying both her mean stepmother and the intimidating Frau Holle. The message of many folktales, and of many dreams as well, is to allow things to reveal themselves instead of always trying to control the outcome or, conversely, to avoid what is unpleasant. If I had rejected my aging face or resisted the sinking movement and the painful fire in "The Golden Woman," I would not have been transformed.

The triple challenge in "The Golden Woman" is to see the true face in the mirror, pass through the four elements, and survive a fiery transformation. Let us now see how a folktale sets up and meets its own creative challenges. In an old Spanish tale, "The Water of Life," the heroine has more perilous tasks than my dream-self in "The Golden Woman." She has to find her way up a mountain, walking over a path of speaking stones who try to stop her and turn her to stone, in order to obtain the magical water of life for a dying tree. This is challenge enough, but her task is not yet completed. After she passes safely over the stones and reaches the top of the mountain, she must face a frightening creature who demands her touch in order for the transformative water to be released (see Stone 1998, 2000). Here is my full text of "The Water of Life," where our journey begins in a land of stones.

There was once a land so dry and barren that only stones seemed to grow there—except for one tree growing in front of a plain little house. This tree was tended by a sister and three brothers. They called it the tree of joy, because every year it produced one perfect fruit, which they divided equally among themselves. After they had eaten, they felt a great joy that stayed with them the whole year. But one day things changed. The tree did not bloom, and did not produce its fruit. They stood around the base of the tree looking up at the branches because they did not know what to do. Suddenly a strange bird flew down and sat on the highest branch of the tree, and began to sing. The sister understood that the bird was singing that the tree had stopped blooming because they had not shared the fruit with anyone else, and that it would not bloom again unless they found one cup of the water of life. The eldest brother demanded to know where to find this water, and the bird sang in response that it was in a well on top of a mountain beyond the great forest. The brothers all decided they would go off together to find the water of life, and directed the sister to stay home and care for the tree. She didn't argue, but she did look carefully to see what direction they took when they left.

The three brothers walked on until they came to the great forest. When they reached the edge of the woods, they saw a red fox crouched beside the path, gnawing on a white bone. The fox looked up and asked them politely where they were going, and the oldest brother answered brusquely that they were looking for the water of life. The fox told them they were on the right road, but that the mountain path up to the water of life was dangerous. When they demanded to know why, the fox explained that each stone on the path would call out to them with insults, challenges, flattery, and desperate wailing. If they stopped to answer the stones, they would become stones themselves. They didn't really believe the fox because the bird had not said anything about talking stones, but they thanked the fox curtly and set off into the great dark forest. They heard all kinds of startling noises as they went on, and when the forest ended at last they were relieved to step out into bright sunlight. Ahead of them they saw a mountain covered with evergreen trees, with a narrow path of stones winding up almost to the top.

They all ran to the mountain and began to climb the path. The first stone each one stepped on cried out "Stop!" but they went boldly on. Then the stones began to insult them, and as the abuse became more and more personal the older brother grew so angry that he forgot all about the fox. He stopped to answer them, and was immediately turned to stone. The other two brothers went on, and each one got a little further than the last, but in the end they both suffered the same fate as their brother; the second gave in to the voices that challenged and frightened him, and the third listened to those that flattered him.

The sister waited at home until she was sure that her brothers were not coming back, and then set off on the path she had seen them take. She too met the fox, and learned about the stones on the mountain path. She was more polite to the fox and more careful than her brothers, but she still had to go through the dark forest by herself, and she was afraid. But she went on.

When she finally passed out of the forest and saw the mountain and its stony path, she too ran to it and started up, and she too heard the first stone yell "stop!" Like her brothers, she went on, and when she didn't stop the stones began to insult her, and then to challenge her, and at last to flatter her. Each time she heard her brothers' voices among the stones, but she went on, coming at last to the desperate stones who wailed in pitiful voices,

"Stop! Please! Stop! Stop! Don't leave us here like this. We've been lying here alone for so long. Please help us."

Then she really wanted to stop, but she remembered the fox's words. If she stopped now she would become a stone, then what could she do? So she went on, in sympathetic tears, until the path finally ended and she found herself at the top of the mountain, with the world spread out below her. It was an amazing sight, so beautiful that for a moment she forgot why she had come. She looked down at her feet and saw an old stone well, and remembered the water of life. On the edge of the well was a small silver cup. She reached down to pick up the cup, but as soon as her fingers touched it she heard a deep hissing sound. The earth under her feet started to shake, and then the well was filled with a deep roaring like the sound of a fierce storm approaching. As she stood there in terror, the head and neck of a great golden dragon rose up slowly from the well until it towered above her. It spoke to her in a voice like rolling thunder:

"Why are you here, and what do you seek?"

She explained in a trembling voice that she had come for one cup of the water of life, for the dying tree. The dragon agreed to allow her to take one cup if she agreed to polish the golden scales on the top of his head, until each scale glowed like the sun. She was frightened to touch the dragon, but had to agree. The dragon bent down his great golden head and she began to polish the scales, each one carefully. When she finished, the dragon lifted his great head and hissed slowly,

"One cup is more than you think. Take care how you use it."

As the golden dragon sank slowly back down into the well, the water surged up. She seized the silver cup and filled it, turned quickly, and started back down the mountain.

When she came to the first stone she tripped, but held firmly to the cup. One drop of water fell from the cup onto the stone. She watched in amazement as that stone began to change shape and slowly turned into a human being. They looked at each other in wonder, then she looked at the water in the cup. She put her finger into the water and touched the next stone with one drop, and watched as this stone, too, became a human being. And the next... And the next... And the next.

She noticed that the water in the cup did not diminish, and then she understood the dragon's words. One cup was much more than she thought, and she used it carefully. She moved down the path touching each of the stones with one drop of precious water, and watched as each stone took its own human shape again. When each of her brothers was freed from immobility they greeted her with gratitude and humility. Together, followed by all the people who had been stones, the sister and her brothers carried the cup back to the tree.

The people gathered in a great circle and watched as the four poured out the precious water at the base of the tree, and as it sank slowly into the earth the tree began to put out new leaves, then blossoms. As they watched, each blossom turned into perfect fruit, exactly enough for all who were there. The sister and brothers divided all the fruit and shared it with every person there. Each who tasted it found that their new year was filled with joy, which didn't mean they had no sorrows, only that their troubles did not overwhelm them. Trees began to grow in that stony land again, but only one tree bore the fruit of joy.

So it was, and ever will be, even now to this very day.

Just as "The Golden Woman" opened out as I continued to tell it and to hear other responses to it, so "The Water of Life" has evolved after several years of telling and listening. Some elements of the story have become more explicit after listeners' reactions, like the bird's unusual song, the fact that the stones offer flattery as well as insults, challenges, and supplications, and that the dragon now calmly says, "What have you come here for," instead of belligerently accusing the woman of coming to steal his water.

Some of the most insightful responses have come from the classes of troubled students I have met over the years. For instance, I learned from 12-year-old girls in the "difficult" class, who insisted on acting out the story and speaking in the voices of the angry stones, that the verbal assaults were specifically personal and not generic: "You're ugly, you're stupid, you'll never make it!" The boys in that class added, "What? A girl! Forget it!" These were familiar insults, heard in the schoolyard every day.

I learned the most from the small groups of troubled 11-year-olds in a suburban Winnipeg school where I worked with the guidance counsellor and social worker for three years. Let me describe one of these occasions to show how a story opens out in the same way a dream does. On a Thursday morning in April (it was still snowing outside), about a dozen students sat in a rough circle on couches and chairs in the guidance counsellor's office. As storyteller I sat in the circle, but the other two adults sat just outside where they could both observe and take part. The basic rule at every session was that the story was not to be interrupted once it began, no small feat for children who could not sit still for the 20 minutes it took to tell most stories. On this particular day, the four most disruptive attention-deficit-disorder boys sat together on the sofa, playfully kicking and punching each other and grumbling about school. The other two boys sat across from them, fidgeting a bit but remaining silent and attentive. The only two girls in the group sat utterly quiet and immobile in chairs next to each other, looking straight ahead and pretending not to be part of the "gang." In this unpromising but familiar atmosphere I began the story. Attention gradually shifted until everyone was listening, not without occasional small shoves and kicks, but with no interruptions.

It was our practice to retell a story as a group as soon as it was finished, with each person, adults included, contributing a sentence or two of the story. After the usual grumbling one of the boys on my left began hesitantly, and the story was off and running. The two girls, who had almost never taken part in previous group stories, were completely active this time, perhaps because the protagonist was a courageous young woman. The group's attention to detail was impressive, and their involvement with the story was enthusiastic enough to arouse their questions: "Why did they trust a talking fox?" "How did they know he wasn't lying to them?" "How did the first stone get on the path?" "Could some of the stones be animals instead of people?" One of the quieter boys who loved mythology asked if the bird was related to a roc or a phoenix.

The ensuing conversation on these topics cast new light on this familiar story. I pondered each query carefully, discussed them in a casual conversational way that kept our dialogue open. I thought it was interesting that some stones might be animals, and asked what animals might be on such a quest. I suggested that the fox might be our own trusting voice that we need to hear above all the other negative voices that try to turn us to stone. They, even more than I, were all too familiar with such voices inside and out. I wondered about how they might be able to identify their own "fox" voice that could be trusted, and how failing to hear it could make you the first stone on the mountain path. We agreed that the first stone must have stopped itself with its own voice and then decided it wanted company. We played with the image of the singing bird as a small cousin of phoenix and roc, and I noted that sky creatures like these mythical birds were often associated with earth-based serpents and dragons.

It was interesting for me to see how they took the story into their own lives. I told them their questions would keep me thinking about "The Water of Life." I know that all of these collective reflections will inform future tellings of "The Water of Life," though the fundamental story itself will not change.

Because I already know that this story—and all others—will go on evolving in depth and meaning over the years, I see as I write it down here how it has taken on increased familiarity from my mundane life. The tree of joy now echoes the old grapefruit tree in my childhood Miami backyard that grew from a sapling with a few fruit to a magnificent tree with fruit too high to reach (except by birds). The modest house of the sister and her brothers has become the white frame house my siblings and I grew up in, and I can see the sister looking out the back window to see where her brothers are going. The silver cup that will carry the water of life has taken the shape of the engraved baby cup of our son, Nathaniel. The brothers, of course, speak in the voices of my brothers, Allen and Terry, and perhaps—now that I think of it—my deceased brother, Kenneth. These changes have evolved slowly and spontaneously, not by conscious design on my part, and while they do not alter the basic shape of the folktale, they certainly transform my understanding of it.

My understanding of dreams and life memories evolve as I age, much as the folktales I tell deepen with experience. I find that the dream of "The Golden Woman" and the story of "The Water of Life" bring a transformational touch to all others parts of this book of dreaming as an art. Just as a drop of water contains the ocean, each dream contains the whole of all your dreams and a single folktale echoes every other story. And everything begins when we do, and grows with us as we live our life stories.

section I–Biography

Okay, Kay: Life and Dreams

Several years ago I dreamed that I was sitting on the front porch of the white frame house of my childhood in Miami. It was entirely familiar until I looked out into the long side yard and saw our old swing set, no longer rusted and losing its last flakes of paint, but pure glowing silver. I was intrigued, so I went out the front door and sat down on my favourite seat on the left side, and immediately a thick silver rope of pure silk dropped down from the sky. I stood up and started to climb, like Jack on his beanstalk, but my situation in space and time was my own mundane life and not a fairy tale, still rooted firmly in the home and yard that I grew up in.

This dream came to me decades after I had left Miami in 1962, long after that rusting swing set had disappeared from the yard. Yet the geography of that place was still as clear as if I had actually been there in waking life—the colour and feel of the grass, a summer sky with towering white cumulus clouds, the croton and hibiscus bushes my mother pampered through the years. If I had been able to listen in this dream I probably could have heard her call, "Kay, stop daydreaming and come in for lunch." When I talk about dreams with my five siblings, they all report that they, too, still find that many of their dreams are situated in that small house and the large yard that surrounded it on three sides (the east side was a narrow strip only a few feet away from the house next door). Other people have also reported that much of their dream geography is inspired by actual places they have lived, and of course, the family, friends and enemies, and others who were part of their lives. Our very real lives, past and present, inspire the settings and characters for many of our dreams, even the most fantastic. Our dreaming artist skilfully interweaves mundane and fantastic as we sleep.

Since our biographies so often provide dreams with familiar places in our nightworld adventures, a survey of sites and events can provide a rough map of the dreamworlds we pass through. When I tried to put my life together as an illustration of what I mean here, I found that thinking chronologically was not helpful. Our various former selves do not come back to life in any sort of neat order, chronological or otherwise, as you might know from having read tediously reconstructed memoirs. Our recollections are more naturally triggered by seeing an old photograph, getting a letter from a long-lost childhood friend, touching an object that evokes instant tactile memories, or smelling and tasting certain foods. The remembered smell of Juicy Fruit gum in its yellow paper wrapper instantly calls up my grandmother and her black leather Sunday purse that held a package of gum, one piece for each of us every Sunday after church.

While I did succeed in stimulating remembered experiences by looking at old pictures and picking up a few things that go back to my childhood, the fragmented stories these called up did not find a connecting thread for some time. I needed another form of expression that would prime the pump and get the water flowing. This stimulus finally came serendipitously, when I was no longer searching for it.

Some time ago I was standing in line somewhere filling out a form with name, birthdate and age, birthplace, education, marital status, current address, and all the other bits of information I have filled out hundreds of times on countless forms. As I grumbled silently to myself, it suddenly occurred to me that every single one of those small bits of information evoked stories. I even startled the people nearest me by laughing out loud as I was filling out "marital status" and thinking of how I lost my one-of-a-kind gold wedding ring on our honeymoon while struggling up Mt. Washington. "Place of Birth" brought back Detroit of the early 1940s, and the memory of my sister Janet and me destroying brother Allen's mean-faced snowman. "Date of birth" called up my mother's description of the doctor coming too late to take part in my speedy arrival in the upstairs room at my Aunt Carrie's house in Detroit, and also my father's amusement at telling me again and again, at every birthday, how he yelled with joy, "Damn if it ain't a girl!" And that sent me off into a reverie about a dream I had just after my own daughter, Rachel, was born in 1976. This dream, like many others, ingeniously combines the geography of my birth at home in Detroit, a beach I loved as a child in Miami, and the lake our cabin is near in a community north of Winnipeg. More amazingly, the dream recreates the body's physical memory of my own actual birth.

In the dream I was standing alone on my favourite beach in Miami, Matheson Hammock. I cautiously put my right foot in the water to test the temperature and tried to pull it back because the water was cold, as it is in Lake Winnipeg. But it was too late. I was immediately pulled in to the water and propelled just below the surface by an overwhelming force from behind. I was moving headfirst and face down, my nose pressed shut by the strength of the movement. Suddenly I was pushed out onto an island, and lay half in and half out of the water, utterly exhausted and unable to move. I sensed that someone was coming, and managed to turn my head just enough to see three human forms walking across the white sand to greet me. I had no idea who they were but I trusted them entirely.

Here are the relevant facts from my waking life that inform this dream. I was born at home in my Aunt Carrie's house, my mother's oldest sister, who we lived with briefly in Detroit. There were no bright hospital lights, no anesthetic to deaden the experience, and no harsh noises, just the natural light and sounds of the bedroom. These are echoed in the dream's pleasant setting and the easy passage from beach to water to island. There were three people present other than my mother: my father, the nurse-midwife, and eventually the doctor. It was an easy birth for my mother, no complications. In the dream I actually felt the physical force of birthing as I was propelled just below the surface of the water with my nose pressed flat by the pressure, but there was no anxiety.

The dream uses the birth experience to move me to a calm beach in Miami, where I am not expecting anything to happen, though I am still hesitant to enter the water. Something in my dreaming mind recalls two separate ordeals when I was almost carried out to sea by powerful undertows, both times at Baker's Haulover, my other childhood beach, but there is no time for fear in this dream. The force of the undertow is used, but transformed into a powerful pushing motion in the calm waters of Matheson Hammock. As in "The Golden Woman," where I was drawn downward through earth and then through an underground sea, I passed through the birth water without resistance or fear. When I emerged, I was welcomed into my family, the symbolic island of the dream.

My guess is that this dream was triggered by my daughter's birth in 1976. Like me, she was born so quickly that the doctor did not arrive in time. Though it was not a home birth it was calm, free of the usual hospital routine since neither the anesthetist nor the doctor was there. Rachel was efficiently and quietly delivered by two nurses, with no bright lights or any invasive noises other than my own. A bodily memory of her easy birth might well have sparked a flashback of my own. More important for my purposes in this book, actual physical events are the inspiration for an imaginative dream.

This dream, like most others, is not bound by time and space. It draws on these as it artistically interweaves details of biography and geography from three different periods and places in my life. Archetypal wisdom is also at work here to create the aesthetic depth: dreaming of being born or giving birth highlights a profound level of creativity. Since I have twice dreamed of giving birth as a man, I can only guess that this archetypal experience is not limited to women.

Carl Jung, who devoted much of his professional life to developing an understanding of archetypal forces, stressed the universal nature of its imagery in all times and places and for all peoples. Water in particular was interpreted as "a metaphor for the collective unconscious," an ocean from which our unique inventiveness ebbs and flows in dreams and in waking life (Jung 1984, 198).

This single dream, then, evokes my own and my daughter's physical births by using the familiar geography and history of waking life, and does so with archetypal ingenuity that reveals artistry as well as biography. These elements are common to our most creative dreams: our own sense of time and place and our veiled and enigmatic archetypal unconscious. But I am getting far ahead of my biographical goals here.

Let me return briefly to the line I was standing in and the form I was filling out. My experience there has stayed with me, allowing me to smile every time I fill out a form because stories arise with every item, spinning out in every direction. There are artful possibilities in every form. Here is my brief biographical report with information organized specifically for this book.

NAME: Kay Frances (Mitchell) Stone

BIRTHDATE: June 14, 1939, Flag Day in the United States.

PLACE OF BIRTH: Detroit, Michigan, upstairs in my Aunt Carrie's house.

SIBLINGS: Three sisters (Janet, Jolene, Lois) and two brothers (Allen and Terry). Two brothers (Kenneth and Keith) died before I was born.

CHILDHOOD RESIDENCE: Pinewood Park, Florida, an old and unincorporated working class neighbourhood north of Miami. No sidewalks or streetlights, no city water, gravel-and-tar roads.

PRESENT AGE: Somewhere in my seventh decade.

SPIRITUAL AFFILIATION: Christian by birth, Jewish by marriage, Buddhist by commitment, curious by nature.

EDUCATIONAL BACKGROUND: Pinewood Park Elementary School (not actually a school but a group of portable classrooms); Horace Mann Junior High and Miami Edison Senior High (the low years of my life); The University of Miami, Florida State University, and Indiana University (the high years). Life as teacher, ongoing.

MARITAL STATUS: Married to Daniel Stone on April 23, 1967, in Manhattan, his island. Still married, after graduate school at Indiana University, two challenging years in Warsaw, Poland, and a very long residence in Winnipeg, Canada where our two children were born (Nathaniel in 1970, Rachel in 1976).

OCCUPATIONS: Babysitter, waitress, cartographer, writer, wife and mother, university professor, professional storyteller, writer, workshop leader and consultant, craftsperson/artist, struggling human being.

I could begin anywhere on this list and stories and dreams would arise on their own, but I choose to begin with two stories related to my name. I grew up being told that I was named after Kay Francis, an actress of the 1930s and 1940s admired by both my parents for different reasons. My father thought she was beautiful, my mother liked her because she played the roles of independent women. On my fifteenth birthday my parents took me to see her in Somerset Maugham's "Theatre," an adult comedy that went way over my still-innocent head. I still have the play bill with my father's scrawled note to my mother across the back: "This OK for Kay?" It was not OK for Kay but we stayed anyway, and I was taken backstage to meet her. No doubt she had met hundreds of girls named after her, but she was gracious. She did not autograph my program, she kissed it, and the faint pink imprint is still there to show me that we were in the same place at the same time, alive and well.

The second story about my name, the unofficial explanation, is more subjective and elusive because it takes place in a dream. I am second oldest, nine years younger than my brother Allen because there were two boys who died between us, Keith at six weeks and Kenneth at three years. I knew Kenneth only from photographs, Keith not at all. I used to sneak into my parents' bedroom to look at the large hand-tinted portrait of sharp-eyed Allen and curly haired Kenneth, hidden on an upper shelf in their closet. I do not recall how I discovered it, but once I had, I could not keep myself from studying Kenneth's young face, already starting to echo my father's eyes and smile, and trying to imagine what he would look like if he had lived. Years later, as an adult, I dreamed that Kenneth appeared to me as a young man, an adult version of that childhood portrait. He smiled at me warmly, put his right hand on my left shoulder, and said, "It's okay, Kay." I drifted back to the waking state pondering these enigmatic words, silently asking the dream to reveal itself. And suddenly I saw the name connection: Kenneth, Keith, Kay. When I went home for Christmas holidays that year, I asked my mother about these names, hoping that my question would not reopen the wounds of old grieving. We were in the living room watching the Orange Bowl parade, she at one end of the sofa and I at the other. My father was relaxed in his big brown recliner across the room half listening. When I told her the dream she was silently thoughtful for a moment, then smiled. "I never thought of it before. Guess I just liked the sound of "K," she admitted. That left "Frances" a mystery until, looking through old photographs of Detroit, I found my father's last and most beloved dog, Fanny, a shortened form of Frances. I was never able to get him to admit that I was named after his dog, but I am amused by the prospect. I am fond of an old black and white photo of Fanny sitting next to me (age three) on the Coke machine at my father's Sunoco gas station in Detroit.

I spent my first five years of life in Detroit, the big city my mother's family had come up to from the rural south and my father's father had come down to from rural Canada. My parents met at a Halloween party at my mother's church, in costume, I suppose—I never thought to ask—and were married barely a year later when my mother was not quite 18. She looks even younger in her honeymoon photographs. Allen was born the next year as the Depression hit with full strength.

I appeared a decade later in happier and more prosperous times on June 14, Flag Day, in honour of the supposed creation of the United States flag by Betsy Ross. For the first few years I thought everyone in the neighbourhood was putting up their flags for my birthday, and was disappointed to learn this was not so. This early disillusionment was offset later, when I learned that some of the earlier American flags had coiled rattlesnakes on them with the motto, "Don't Tread on Me," my silent motto in a rapidly enlarging family and a foreshadowing of my future invisible friend, Snakey the Rattlesnake.

I was the first girl after three boys, hence my father's joyful cry at my birth, "Damn if it ain't a girl!" with which he greeted me on every birthday for years. I would eventually be joined by three sisters and another brother, but for a short period of life I was a princess. I was also a tomboy as soon as I could walk, judging by early photographs. My favourite one shows me standing a bit unsteady on my feet but with a determined look, a holster and six-gun weighing down my diaper.

Janet, born 18 months later, replaced me as princess. She was the archetypal good girl of the fairy tales, or so I thought for the eighteen years we shared a bedroom. I fell easily into the role of mean elder sister and I have photographs to prove it. In one, taken in the backyard of our last house in Detroit, I hold Janet's wrist in a vise-like grip as I smile sweetly and innocently. Despite our imagined enmity, Janet has always appeared in my dreams as a positive figure.

Brief images rise up from those first five years in Detroit: one perfect crystal icicle hanging outside my upstairs bedroom window alive with morning sunlight; white curtains lifting in a summer breeze as I sit in the dining room listening to "Superman" on the radio and waiting for my father to come home from work; a folded newspaper sailing through the air and landing perfectly as I balance precariously on the back of Allen's bicycle while he delivers newspapers (did my mother know about this?); a tiny snowman, real snow, that my mother made and placed in the window where Janet and I were quarantined with scarlet fever. And there was also that tall metal swing set with two seats, "monkey bars" across the top, and a small slide. Janet and I spent hours in trance states, flying on those swings and swaying upside down from the monkey bars. It is no wonder that this same swing set figures in my dreams well into adulthood.

I was almost six when we moved to Florida. On this trying journey I acquired an imaginary friend, Snakey the Rattlesnake. I entertained my father by telling him rambling and repetitious stories about the adventures of Kay and Snakey. Years later, my mother told me how she listened with amazement at the stories I was spinning out. While I have no conscious memories of these stories, Snakey is surely related to the interesting serpents that turn up in some of my dreams, not to mention folktales in which the archetypal beast is a giant snake. I understand the Freudian implications of phallic imagery, but the deeper archetype of the snake as guardian of deep wisdom resonates more fully for me. I remember being perplexed in Sunday school when I first heard the story of the wicked serpent who tricked Eve. Snakey was not at all an evil figure, but he surely belonged in the Tree of Knowledge. Only when I began to study folklore decades later did I find that I was right about snakes and wisdom—and their associations with women.

One of the first things I remembered learning in Miami was to watch out for deadly little coral snakes. I never saw one, but I secretly searched for them in the coral rock fence in my grandparents' backyard, where we stayed for the first few weeks until my parents found a house. I can still hear my grandparents' soft North Carolina voices, and smell the wonderfully combined scent of leather and Juicy Fruit chewing gum from her black purse. I remember being sent to nap in their front bedroom and watching white curtains lifting in the breeze; I recall sitting on a high stool in her homey kitchen while she baked. For years after their deaths I still had dreams of that house. It was a safe haven, one where monsters never threatened.

The small house my parents found became even more central to my dreams. It was a small frame house with only two bedrooms plus front and back porches that were used as bedrooms at various times. The large living room and kitchen were the gathering places for the family, and the bedrooms were for escapes into solitude when the family got to be too much. Years later, as an adult visiting home from Chicago, I asked my mother how eight people had managed to live in that little house, and she admitted that it was supposed to have been a temporary place. To me as a child, it had never seemed too small, but then children often do not question their surroundings in the same way adults do. For me it was the centre of the universe, that house and the yard around it, a double lot in an unincorporated neighbourhood of old Miami.

I will lay out the geography in more detail from childhood memories, since it was in that state that it most often appeared in my dreams for many years. Our area was misleadingly called "Pinewood Park," not because it was the least bit parklike but because it had a lot of old pine trees. It was, as my mother said, "Out in the sticks." Perhaps it was some developer's dream that never came to be. This was old Florida, southern and working class, a neighbourhood of simple wood frame houses with no basements or second floors, not at all like the solid two-story brick houses of Detroit. There were no sidewalks, no street lights, no municipal water supply. Water came from an electric pump in a little shed outside the front bedroom window that Janet and I shared. Whenever anyone took a shower, it came on with a distressing thump and roar that might have accounted for a few of my early nightmares.

Because this was not yet a part of urban Miami, the lots were larger. When we moved there in 1945, our double-lot yard was bleak and bare, except for a huge loblolly pine in the front yard and a young grapefruit tree in the back. There was plenty of room for my mother's clothesline, and for the swing set we brought from Detroit. This became a magical entity for me and Janet. We could spend hours swinging, climbing, daydreaming. My first flying dreams took place over the backyard, where I invariably tangled myself in my mother's clothesline or in the higher electrical lines, until I finally learned how to fly safely.

The yard was eventually filled with bushes and trees of all sorts, but that took years. My mother loved to grow things, and got many of her citrus trees and other greenery from Mrs. H. across the street. Because she seemed odd to us, Janet and I imagined Mrs. H. as a witch, and her tree-filled yard as an enchanted forest. We never went there, even on Halloween. Especially not on Halloween.

In my waking world, unclaimed areas covered with pine trees and fierce palmettos were the "jungles" that Janet and I played in. I learned later that my mother had not been comfortable in our strange new home, but for me and Janet it was wonderfully wild. We explored, climbed trees, and pretended that the dead palm fronds we pulled off the coconut tree were horses that we rode around the yard. And of course there was that magical swing set, brought in pieces from Detroit and reassembled in the backyard, and eventually moved to the side yard when the trees crowded it out. The neighbourhood, too, gradually became more "civilized," with more houses and people, but in my dreams it stayed wild for a very long time.

Two more children, Terry and Lois, were born in Miami, making a total of two adults and six children surviving together in a small two-bedroom frame house with one bathroom, and two porches that doubled as sleeping rooms. All of these details figure in my dreams for several decades. I still have very vivid memories of our up and down times in that house with its wide wild yard full of trees and bushes and tenacious crabgrass, and the old swing set we brought all the way from Detroit. This setting, complete with the swing set, figured in dreams well into my adulthood. I remember, too, the night sky in full glory; it was deep black then, not the pallid grey of today, and stars and moon shone with full brilliance. This sky exists now only in my dreams. In one from several years ago I was standing in the front yard looking up at the brilliant stars alive in the night sky. I watched in amazement as a huge silver moon began to rise, and with it a glowing pathway sliding down into our side yard. I ran inside the house to get my mother and my daughter Rachel, and we began to walk up the moonpath. We were still walking when I woke up, with a strong sense of having actually been there in that radiant moonlight.

When Janet and I began elementary school several blocks away from our house, a 20-minute walk on streets covered by tar and gravel, Allen gave us new names. Janet became "Tenaj" because she wrote her name backwards, and in honour of this I became "Yak," a name I still use for special occasions. Pinewood Park Elementary was not really a school at all but a collection of portables. I loved it because each class had its own separate building. For years I dreamed of that semicircle of portables raised up on cement blocks and connected by dirt paths, with a wide playing field just beyond it to the south. Once an odd little travelling sideshow was set up there, and I had nightmares for weeks after visiting several times what they claimed was an unwrapped Egyptian mummy. I was as fascinated with the rough brown mummy as I had been with the portrait of my dead and living brothers.

In my northern ears the language I heard at school seemed exotic. I came home from school the first day and asked my mother what "ovayanda" meant and she laughed. Because she had been born in North Carolina, she was able to translate this as "over yonder." I had a best friend, Betsy Bonner from Virginia, who shared secrets, adventures, and plenty of fights, one of them involving rolling around in a nest of red ants.

We walked to school together every day, and were often late as we talked and played along the way down Sixth Avenue. My first successful flying dreams were inspired when Betsy's family left Miami suddenly in the middle of the sixth grade, and I tried to try to find her in dreams by flying north to Virginia. I never found Betsy but I did learn to dream-fly at last.

My junior high school years were notable for two things: the first is a recurring dream of being lost in a hallway, a dream that continues to find new ways to express itself even now that I have retired from all hallways. Many others I have since talked to report similar recurring dreams. For example, here is a dream from a student in the honours class in which this book began:

> I had a dream in which I arrived at the University of Winnipeg, prepared to write my exam. The room in which I was to write had changed so I went looking for the posted exam schedules in order to find the right room. I couldn't find the place where the schedule was supposed to be posted so I got directions that took me into a part of the campus that I had never seen before. Of course I became hopelessly lost, and I kept running into people who wanted to talk to me and ask me questions. I went looking for the exam room, and again got lost, wandering through unfamiliar areas of the university (that don't really exist), begging for someone to tell me where to go. When I finally got to the exam room, I didn't recognize anyone from my class, and everyone had already started to write the exam. I got my paper and started to try to answer the questions, but the harder I thought about the questions the less I knew how to answer them. I realized that I was writing an exam for the wrong subject (Cooper 1996).

The student sees her dream experience as a failure, but consider this: only in our dreams can we write exams in the wrong subject and come up with something creative. She did not stay in the dream long enough to find out, or she might have been surprised.

These kinds of dreams, mine and others, echo the labyrinth motif, best known from the Greek narratives of Theseus and the Minotaur, who waits for the lost souls to stumble into his lair so he can devour them. Theseus had the advantage of gaining the aid of the king's daughter, Ariadne, who provided him with a long cord for finding his way in and out, but we have to provide our own. In my adolescent dreams and in my waking world as well, I often felt that I had no guiding cord for passing through dream labyrinths and school corridors, and some teachers I had over the years came close to filling the Minotaur's role. In the realm of archetypes, those elemental images that arise in dreams as well as in folktales, mythology, and in waking life, our labyrinths can take the form of ordinary hallways in familiar places. All these decades later I am still getting lost in school corridors, though the lurking monster is no longer a threat.

Adolescence is a fertile age for expressions of anxiety. Being late and lost was my general state of mind in this period. In addition to the general angst of leaving childhood, I was burdened by losing my best friend, and by the fact that my mother was busy with her eighth and last child (Lois); my older brother Allen, my hero, had dropped out of school to join the army and was now in the bloody centre of the Korean War at the age of 20; and I was becoming a girl in ways that my tomboy self was not ready for. I felt overwhelmed by everything. In response I dreamed of a large dark buffalo, a nightmare Minotaur who surprised me by obeying when I somehow managed to command the beast to walk out of my dream. This single dream temporarily eased my feelings of being overpowered by life, but what really got me through this difficult period was horses.

My parents' attempts to encourage me to be more ladylike by enrolling me in ballroom dancing and then in piano lessons were a failure. All I learned was how to subvert the best efforts of dedicated teachers. In desperation, I suppose, my father got my mother to agree to a summer of riding lessons for my twelfth birthday. This was a turning point in my life. I loved horses and everything about them, including the very mundane and smelly task of cleaning stables. I got through my adolescent traumas by riding horses, and through senior high by drawing them. In fact, the only clearly pleasant memory I have of high school is my art class. When I entered university as an art major I was still drawing horses. But by the end of that year I had expanded to still lifes, landscapes, and, most difficult of all, people. I had found something else as well—anthropology, a developing field of study that fed my hungry curiosity about how and why people were so different, and why these differences were a delight and not an affliction.

Sometime in high school a friend had given me a copy of an odd book entitled *Autobiography of a Yogi*, that I read intently. By that time my parents had left their church, and I was curious. This new book, while it was often distressing (was I ready for reincarnation, not to mention various peculiar yogic practices?), it also opened my mind to eastern religions. A few years later my brother Allen, who was immersed in karate and Zen, had me reading all the Alan Watts books he could find and pass on. I read more and more widely in various Buddhist sources, and knew just enough to be utterly confused but still curious. This would, eventually, lead into Buddhism as a spiritual practice, but first I became a Jew. I carried my curiosity about people into full practice.

Daniel Stone and I married in New York, and I agreed with the rabbi that my future children should have two Jewish parents. When I insisted that he know I was an atheist so that I would not be dishonest, he said that was my problem, not his. Standing before the sacred Torah scroll and reciting the most sacred of the blessings, the "shema," I was spiritually moved. But I was still a bit hungry for a something, and kept heart and mind open to other expressions of religious belief. And I was still reading Alan Watts.

One December day in 1969, the second year of our marriage, I was standing on the wide staircase at Grand Central Station. Dan had left me there (I was going to visit my sister Lois on Block Island) while he went on to Penn Station, headed for a conference in Philadelphia. I was terrified at being alone in an enormous station in this huge metropolis, and as often happens when I am frightened, I used anger as a defence. I boiled up a good rage, and actually hoped someone would bump into me so I could scream at them. Hundreds of people were milling on the platform below me, and I told myself they looked like insects. As I took my first step downward, that roiling rage suddenly transformed itself. I was astonished by a feeling of profound unity, as if I were so intimately connected to this mass of strangers that there was no difference between us. At the same time we were each entirely ourselves. I looked around the cavernous station, and nothing I could see, animate or inanimate, seemed removed from me. In Zen terms this was a small satori, a touch of enlightenment, but so brief that it probably did not last for more than a few seconds. I had no one who could teach me how to go any further, but I kept it in mind and memory. I even spent a summer at

Georgetown University studying Japanese, hoping to visit Japan one day. I have not yet made it to Japan, but in 1998 I finally did become a practicing Buddhist.

The curiosity about people that had led into studying both anthropology and geography eventually drew me to folklore. To make quite a long story very short, I spent the next three decades studying, writing about, and eventually performing folktales as a professional storyteller.

Dan, a historian with a specialty in Polish history, had taken me on lengthy stays to Poland that gave me new sources of dream geography. It was a challenge to learn how to survive in a country where I had the vocabulary of a two-year-old, no friends of my own except my husband, and nothing at all to do except grocery shopping. I learned the value of humour in desperation. My sense of losing my footing began to appear in dreams at this time, as I fell off cliffs or into the ocean or down bottomless pits. I also began to have recurring dreams of losing my suitcase, or finding it impossible to pack, or too heavy to carry if I managed to fill it. The archetypal dream suitcase has been with me since this time.

Three decades later I am still married to the same man and living very far away from Miami, in the middle of Canada. As a child in Miami I used to dream of living in snow deep enough to tunnel through, but I never imagined that this would actually happen to me. Here I had two children, began to perform as a storyteller, and taught classes in folklore and storytelling in the English department for three decades. That is where this very book began, in an English class, bringing us full circle on this biographical path.

This summary sounds much more coherent and connected than life as I have actually lived it, with all the peaks and pits, all the self-doubt and ambivalence, and my strong urge to take long naps instead of writing. The bare warp of biographical particulars—name, birthplace, education, marital status, current residence—supports the living tapestries unfolding as dreams in further chapters.

Our lives are the fertile ground that dreams arise from. The stories we tell about ourselves and the dreams we dream, good and bad, reflect back to us in the stories we experience vicariously when we hear and read about other people, factual and fictional. Our personal patterns, then, are expressed in our lives, our dreams, and the stories we prefer in books, television, movies, and on the daily news. All this enriches our blossoming dreams.

In all of this movement from waking to dreaming and to fictional lives, we are the artists. Our own lives and dreams are constantly evolving as we go on, and we continue to create ourselves right in the midst of living and dreaming.

Finding words

If I had been walking up a mountain path of talking stones like the young woman in "The Water of Life," I would not have made it to the dragon. I would have been stopped by the stones that insulted or worried me into an angry fear of failure. I keep these stones in mind as I explore a continuing struggle with what I call the good girl/bad girl syndrome: the good girl has to pass through her own fear, like Snow White racing through the frightening forest; the bad girl is fuelled by the anger and spite she needs to overcome. I was always anxious about being too much like the elder sisters in so many of the folktales, but I did not want to be the passive younger sister either. What lies between them? I can now look at my "good girl/bad girl" dynamic as an expression of an artistic enigma as much as a psychological predicament, and I search for the energies that arise from the friction. Finding these, I can imagine arriving at the dragon's mountaintop domain and being willing to touch the beast, no matter how timidly, to obtain healing water. It seems to me that I would have to have crossed such an imaginary threshold to be able to dream of being transformed by fire into a golden woman.

The Golden Woman is silent, but that is deceptive. That is, she is not encouraged to be quiet as I was, but simply has no reason to speak. She chooses silent transformation. But it took me a long time to meet her in my dreams. Patience and silence, and being seen but not heard, were the goodgirl qualities of my growing up. I chose too, but in negative ways.

I always thought that my "good" sister Janet had these qualities naturally, while I was fiercely ambivalent. Sometimes I thought I was too quiet, other times I was sure I made too much noise. I cannot remember at what age I began to say to myself, "Shut up, Kay!" These voices were contradicted by the other voice that nagged, "Why didn't you say something?" I remember being surprised when a male friend complimented me on what a good listener I was. I could imagine my mother laughing and saying something like, "Oh, you should hear her at home," but now I am not sure I was right about her. No matter. What is certain is that I had some problem with speaking and not speaking.

When I was in my first year of university I went to a party with my brother Allen, and came home scolding myself silently: "Kay, you did it again. Why do you talk so much?" I was stunned when one of Allen's friends asked him the next day if I was always so quiet: "She didn't say a word the whole night." Are we talking about the same person?

I know I am not the only one with this problem of silence and noise, judging by all the women (and some men as well) whose voices I have heard over the years. Author Brenda Ueland, active and outspoken well into her cronish 90s, suggested that we begin life "full of light and the clearest vision" but are silenced by external and internal voices all too soon:

> Then comes on the great army of school teachers with their critical pencils, and parents and older brothers (greatest sneerers of all) and cantankerous friends, and finally that Great Murderer of the Imagination—a world of unceasing, unkind, dinky, prissy Criticalness (Ueland 1987, xi).

Challenging our internalized "prissy Criticalness" is a lifetime endeavour, raising our voices above the noises inside and outside. I am fond of the still, quiet voice of the fox in "The Water of Life," who speaks the truth about those stony voices of despair, but does not prattle.

There was certainly an abundance of noise around me growing up, with the large Mitchell family bustling around in a small house, and there were many opportunities to add to it, especially at chaotic mealtimes. But the unspoken ideal (how did I learn it?) was that boys could be boys but girls were supposed to be quiet—at least in public. My grandmother was so quiet that I can hardly remember her mild North Carolina drawl, though her soft laugh is still with me. I remember my mother as quiet, too, but then I can clearly hear her annoyed voice trying to rouse several children for school in the morning, or shouting "That's enough!" when Janet and I engaged in constant guerilla warfare in our bedroom. She was also the power behind the throne, speaking from the kitchen when she disagreed with my very vocal father.

She raised her voice more often after the birth of "Terrible Terry," whose escapades began as soon as he could walk. On the many days when he failed to appear at supper time, she would stand on the back step and call his name across the neighbourhood. This stopped one day when she was embarrassed by the parrot in the house behind us screaming, in exact imitation of her voice, "Terreee! You git home right now!" I also recall being shocked when she yelled "God damn it!" to me and Janet on a particularly bad day in her last pregnancy with Lois when we were behaving even worse than usual. We stopped fighting and got back to cleaning.

I see how I have inherited my mother's conflicts about speaking and holding one's tongue. One way I could see my own ambivalence was in dreams. For example, several years ago I dreamed that I was shocked into utter silence at the very moment of potential artistic fulfilment and recognition. The dream cleverly used my muteness to release a quiet voice that broke through into a story, giving me the exhilarating experience of being part of language at the very moment it was being created.

In the dream, I was on the way to hear a famous storyteller I had been waiting years to meet, but I could not find the room, a recurring situation that went all the way back to junior high school anxiety dreams of finding the right classroom. I was sure I was late as I wandered down a long empty corridor, looking for room #36. I finally found it, a large room with a little glass window in the door through which I could see everyone sitting there waiting. There was only one vacant seat right in front. I slipped in as unobtrusively as I could, but of course everyone, including the famous storyteller, could see me as I sat down. I was surprised that no one seemed to be annoyed. I was even more surprised when the storyteller immediately stood up an announced, "And now, just what we've been waiting for. We're going to hear a story…from Kay Stone." There were murmurs of anticipation from behind me. I sat forward in shock, realizing that I had to do something because everyone was watching me expectantly. I stood up with the intention of saying that I really was not prepared to tell a story, but found that I could not speak. At that moment I could actually feel every story I ever knew disappearing from mind, and then all my words began to disappear as well, slipping away like pebbles dropping into water. I could not even say "no!" My head was utterly empty of thoughts and words, and at that point, even of fear. I was just there, standing. It was a Zen moment that I did not appreciate.

Because I had already opened my mouth to say "no," a sound came out on its own. I was amused by the experience, and opened my mouth to see if it would happen again. Another sound floated out effortlessly, and then another. As I listened in curiosity, I realized idly that these sounds seemed to be connected in some way, like musical notes in a score, and to have some meaning. I slowly recognized that they were called "words" in some language that I knew, but I was not "making" them, they were making themselves. As the words continued to unfold slowly, one at a time, I perceived that they were forming phrases, sentences, and paragraphs. I was fascinated. All at once I realized that I was telling a story—or rather, the story was literally telling itself. I listened as eagerly as the audience, since I had no idea what would happen next.

The dream might have ended there, since I had finally got the message that I did have a story to tell after all. By luck it went on for long enough to provide a coherent plot. The mute Kay did actually manage to begin telling a story that made sense. Here are the words, written as I heard them in the dream, as well as I can put them in writing to communicate the halting oral experience that finally breaks into story:

Once

there

was

a

girl

named

Molly.

One day Molly went out to the green meadow to pick a red apple. "I want one good apple."

Molly climbed the tree. When she got to the top she saw a cloud of dust on the road. It was large and far away, and Molly said to herself,

"It must be the king and his servants because there's a lot of dust. I'll wait for them. When they come by I'll throw them an apple."

Unfortunately I woke up before the mysterious dust cloud revealed its secret, so I never found out what happened next. I spent the next year trying out various stories to see if I could discover who or what it might have been. I was delighted by the suggestion offered by some storytelling friends who listened to the dream. They told me it sounded like a story they had heard me tell several times, combining three variants from the British Isles and Kentucky (see Briggs 1970, 155-58; Roberts 1955, 60-63, and 1969, 86-90). This folktale is very widespread in Europe and North America, and has antecedents throughout the world. In some stories the beast appears on the road in a great cloud of dust as in my dream, so for the next few years I told my recomposed story with the dream as its introduction. Here is a summary of the story, which is told more fully in chapter 6 as "The Three Walnuts."

The story begins when one of three sisters carelessly wishes to marry the ugliest one in the world, and gets her wish when a huge dark bull appears to carry her away. She learns that he is a bull for half the day and a man for the other half and chooses to have him as a man by night. Eventually she loses her husband because she speaks when she is supposed to remain silent, but in the end she succeeds in saving him by chanting to him as he sleeps, telling her own story. Perhaps he was dreaming of apple trees and a girl named Molly.

The dreams and stories I struggle most with have silence and obedience in them somewhere, and because so many folktales build around these goodgirl assets I understand that it is not just my problem. One well-known story-type, with variants as far as India (where it most likely arose), features the good sister and the bad stepsister, a story so well-known that an entire folklore study is devoted to it (Roberts 1958). Kira Van Deusen found many variants in parts of Siberia as well (Van Deusen 1999, 2001). In each country the details of the story vary, but the basic plot is all too stable: the obedient, quiet sister is rewarded for doing what she is told, while the rebellious and sassy one is punished or even destroyed. The Grimm tale of "Frau Holle" is a typical example, featuring the all-too-familiar cruel stepmother (Zipes 1988, 104-107).

A stepmother angrily commanded her unwanted stepchild, the youngest and most obliging daughter, to retrieve a spindle accidentally dropped in a well. The girl had to leap into the well to accomplish this. She fainted from fear as she fell, and was surprised to wake up in a wide green meadow. As she followed a path across it she met an oven that begged her to take out its baked bread and an apple tree that implored her to shake down its ripe apples, which she did. She went on until she came to a house of a strange woman with long teeth who said, "Don't be afraid, I'm Frau Holle, and if you work well for me here you will be rewarded." The girl did everything she was told and was well treated, but got homesick for her father and asked to be allowed to return to her family, cruel as they were, asking nothing for all her work. Frau Holle accompanied her to a doorway back to the world above, returned her lost spindle, and watched as the good girl was covered with gold when she passed through, a reward for her obedience and industriousness.

When the girl returned home covered with gold, the greedy mother sent out her own lazy daughter. This girl impatiently threw her spindle into the well, jumped boldly into it, and found herself in the same strange land. She refused to help the oven and the apple tree, and was too lazy to work properly for Frau Holle. The crone soon dismissed her from work and told her to go home, which made her happy since she now expected to receive her own gold. Instead, when she passed through the doorway she was covered with sticky black pitch, which remained on her for the rest of her life.

In some variants of the story she is also given a sack in which she expects to find treasure, but instead ugly toads and snakes climb out to bedevil her. In a Russian variant I summarize in the next chapter, she fares even worse. As a child I hated this story but could not keep from reading and rereading it. When I have such a strong negative reaction to a dream or story, I try to imagine myself back in the middle and see if alternative solutions arise. For example, in a similar story from African tradition, the good girl is rewarded with a necklace while the disobedient one is swallowed by an ogre. I regularly used this variant in my folklore classes, where I had my students play with other possible endings. While they did suggest other solutions, none envisaged the one I loved: inspired, I suppose, from living the role of the elder sister, I had the "bad" girl travel like Jonah in the belly of the ogre until he cannot stand it any more and spits her out, sending her off on her own adventures. While I do not change traditional tales simply because I find them unsatisfactory, I do keep my imagination open.

I am fond of a story from India retold by a friend and colleague, Margaret Mills, at a meeting of the American Folklore Society in 1988. In the story, a woman lacking in imagination had a story and a song but did not recognize this, and failed to tell her story or sing her song. Because she did not use her gifts, they found other ways to come to life: the story appeared as a beautiful cloak and the song as a pair of embroidered slippers. The woman still did not notice them and remained silent when her husband tried to describe them. When she refused to listen there was a fierce argument, and the husband left for the night. From magical candle flames he learned about his wife's song and story, but even when he begged her to tell the story and sing the song, she remained silent.

Because this story seems so unresolved, it is another one I play with, not to make it come out rosy and happy, but to see if it wants to go anywhere else. Stories and dreams cannot be pushed into shape, but they can be invited to lead. In fact, I have found that unresolved stories and dreams are often more memorable precisely because their incompleteness is a challenge. I often use stories like these in workshops to encourage participants to use their imaginations. I ask them, as I have asked myself, to describe the cloak and the slippers, and in this way "speak" for the woman in the story, reminding them that the cloak is her story and the slippers her song. In this way they see that even when we ignore our natural creativity, the beauty will find some way of breaking through the silence. Some listeners carry this further and have the cloak tell the woman her own story, or have the woman put the cloak on and go off on her own adventures as a teller of tales. They give her a voice.

I learned more about the dangers of being too good in *Dream Symbol Work*, a book that centres on an extraordinarily complex dream, "The Child in the Golden Mask" (Berne/Savary 1991). The book was lent to me by two dream-masters, Gordon and Mary Toombs, who were helpful in guiding me in dream explorations after hearing some of my "good girl" dreams. In "The Child in the Golden Mask," the dreamer hears a baby crying, goes upstairs to look, and finds a beautiful baby girl quietly sleeping in her crib. The wailing continues, and when she discovers another door in the nursery and passes through, she finds another baby girl, this one emaciated. Her head is encased in an exquisite golden mask that has slits for eyes and nose, but no mouth. After trying in vain to remove the mask, the dreamer calls a goldsmith, who promises that he can do it easily and will come immediately. She awakens with mixed feelings of rage, guilt, sorrow, and also relief that help is on the way. She understood that she had locked herself in a beautiful golden mask by being a silent "good girl," and in waking life explored ways of releasing herself without destroying the radiance of the golden mask.

The book in which her dream is described uses it as an excellent example of how to try various ways of creating a dialogue with our significant dream symbols, in order to discover what they are trying to tell us. I, of course, used "The Golden Woman" to explore how these suggestions might open the dream out further. The contrast between "The Child in the Golden Mask" and "The Golden Woman" was profound, and helped me to see more clearly how my dream reveals the evolution of my own good girl/bad girl struggles. To begin with, gold as a symbolic metal is pure, untarnished, malleable, and very strong. It can entrap, as it does the emaciated child, or it can be a free-flowing element, as it is in "The Golden Woman." In fact, as I reconsidered my dream in light of the entrapped child, I could see even more effectively all the points at which I might have felt imprisoned in this dream but did not: when I am being pressed firmly as I pass through the earth, when I am encased in the shell-like cylinder in the underground sea, and when I am firmly held by it in the fire. In each of these situations I am free to move, my senses are not blocked in any way, and the experience is utterly liberating rather than constricting.

The authors of the dream-symbol study make suggestions on how to bring a dream out into the world, including recreating it as an artistic work. Because this is so central to what I am trying to say in this book, let me quote them in full:

> The purpose of this technique is to give the symbol physical presence in your life. The simplest way is to draw the symbol on a piece of paper.
>
> Others have represented their symbol in sculpture using wood, clay, metal, or paper. Still others have written poems or songs about their symbol. Some have created a dance about their symbol and danced it. Others have turned their dream into a story, skit, mime, fairy tale, or drama. Many have created a mandala, collage, or a painting to express it (Berne/Savary 1991, 38).

They go on to say that it is not important if you do not feel qualified "to draw or paint or sing or dance," because this activity is not "a test of your artistic abilities" (38). This is a significant point, since many of us are stopped by those inner voices of "prissy Criticalness." The woman who dreamed "The Child in the Golden Mask" began her own work by composing a continuing story of the dream in which the child is finally freed and the golden mask placed on her mantelpiece. In the waking world she took part in a mask workshop where she actually made a gold-painted mask with tears running down its cheeks, and hung this on a wall where she could see it every day. It "spoke" to her in its golden silence.

In waking life as well as in dreams and stories, our voices can surprise us. I am certainly not the only one to have had the experience of hearing words come out that were not intended, as if someone else were speaking. Often these are embarrassing occasions, but sometimes the words are exactly what needs to be spoken. I recall two such incidents with great clarity. The more innocent one happened to me when I was only ten years old and still very short, skinny, and quiet in public. It was in the schoolyard of Pinewood Park Elementary. I remember that I was standing outside the lunch room waiting for something or someone when I suddenly found myself surrounded by other children sensing blood. They were following Mary Lou, one of the tough girls of the school, as she stormed over to accuse me of something. I had no idea what she was talking about—and I do not recall it now—but her rage was unmistakable, and I knew I was in trouble. She had not been taught, as I had, that girls were not supposed to brawl, and she did not stop at hair-pulling and scratching. Though she was my age and size, she seemed seven feet tall. As in my "Molly" dream that would come years later, I was unaccountably in the middle of it all, front row centre, with everyone watching to see what I would to do. Mary Lou told she was going to beat me up, and I was speechless with terror. I wanted to run but my feet would not move, just as in many dreams with threatening figures. As panic took hold of me, I was stunned to hear a calm voice that turned out to be my own say firmly, "My mother doesn't allow me to fight." Then I turned my back on her and walked boldly away as if I knew exactly what I was doing, still shaking with fear. Luckily for me, she was too surprised to follow. Whose voice was that? The same voice that would sometimes speak out in both waking life and dreams, startling me out of fear. What seemed like the wrong thing to say was just right.

A year later I had another opportunity to be surprised by my own voice. Janet and I were coming back from the local grocery story, pulling the groceries in the red wagon my father had made for little Terry. A man stopped us and asked where a certain street was, tried to get me into the car to show him. When I refused, he tossed open his coat and exposed himself, saying, "Have you ever seen one of these?" "Yes," I promptly answered, "My father has one." He slammed the door and roared off, but not before I got his license number, which, by the way, is still my secret. It sounds like I knew exactly what I was doing, but I certainly did not. I was terrified, and I have no idea where those perfect words came from, but they still make me smile.

Unexpected words with strong consequences turn up in folktales as well. There is an oral tale that Shakespeare transformed into the tragic play, *King Lear*. This complex tale has elements of two basic types: the first is the familiar story of Cinderella and the second is a tale called "Love Like Salt." In the tale, as in the play, the youngest daughter speaks the wrong words—she honestly says that she loves her father like meat loves salt—and as a result she is treated like the "bad" girl in other tales. Abandoned by her family, she makes her own way in the world, marries well, and invites her now-impoverished father to the wedding feast where she serves him meat without salt. He recognizes his daughter and now understands the truth of her words. Unlike King Lear, she does indeed live happily ever after, and so does he.

I had not seen the "bad girl" potential of this Cinderella-like heroine until I listened to friend and fellow storyteller Gwenda LedBetter read me her poem, "Like Meat Loves Salt," as we sat in a café in Asheville, North Carolina in 2000. I reprint it here with her kind permission.

> Once upon a time…not this one…a man, so rich
> he was like a king, had daughters, three,
> two, one, and rich-man-like, one day, he asked,
> "How much do you love me, my dears?"
> Not "Do you?" or "Will you?" "How much?"
>
> Rubbing the cloth of their affection between
> thumb and forefinger, chomping down on
> that kind of coin with a rich man's gold-capped
> dentures, for this is a tale with a bite…and
> forgiveness…but not yet.

The eldest, hand to her heart, replied "More…
than life itself." The next one, sweeping the air
with her hands, said "More…than all the world." The third and
youngest (some say his pet) gave it serious
thought, and said, "Hummmm… Like meat…loves salt."

What! Too practical. Too out-of-the-kitchen,
face to face with who we really are. The rich man,
with face screwed tight like a corporate executive
in the old black-and-whites, yelled, "You love me not.
Get out!" That's what he did with bad value.

She stumbled, blinded by life gone wrong, through
muck, morass, jagged stone and other metaphors
for pain. No honcho hired by a wicked queen planning
to cut out her heart. Just grave-cold killing rejection,

and all for the wrong words. She did not, could not understand.
Her sisters' purred platitudes had earned them ease.
Telling the truth had bought her an empty belly,
and no place to sleep on a night colder than life itself.

Ashamed and afraid of thieves she made
a cape of cattails she found there in the fen.
(For those who do not know old stories, a fen is
a bog, a quagmire, and she was in one. She
didn't know herself.)

She went to work in an eatery, a medieval Waffle
House where life became a degreasing of the grill,
and washing pots and pans. Her cattails molted,
(as cattails will), leaving her cloaked in thorn-thick
vines, sharp-ended sticks,
and a gut-strong desire to beat the system and live.

Enter…the prince. He's always in these tales
but somehow out of fashion. By what name shall he
be called? Earth-walker? Cool dude? Handsome
harbinger of fate? Or some name you might
care to relate, remembering
all of this started using the wrong word.

There was to be a party, otherwise known as "The Ball."
This was a twirl on your toes, wear out your soles, leave the floor
lying contra dance. Who knows what spark inside
made her throw off that trash pile she was wearing
and come dancing in…as her Self.

What's-His-Name was a wonderful dancer. They spun,
glided, left the floor. She raised his heart, his hopes
(and more), but left him in the middle of a four-hand star
and went back to washing pots.

He grieved. Pined himself sick over losing his dancing
lady. She heard of his illness and remembered
the stop-the-heart-cold of having your love rejected so…
she made him some soup.

(The tale calls it gruel but that's for small starving
boys. This was potato. French. Creamy, smooth,
cool on the throat and flavoured slightly with onion.)
She dropped in the ring he'd slipped on her finger.
She'd planned on selling it if things got worse.

The soup was good. He found the ring. Sent for
the one who made it. The next part I leave out. In this
time of over-exposure, some things should remain
unseen and certainly unheard…
When it came time of the wedding, she had
the feast prepared without one grain of salt.
Here we are back at the start, for her father
came to eat tasteless turkey,
meaningless mashed potatoes,
and would have spewed it all out
but looked into his daughter's eyes
and she offered him…salt.

And finally he knew. No longer a rich man,
or a king. As just plain kin, he knew
there aren't enough words in the world, not
even in this poem, to hold all the heart can feel.
It's like…meat…loving…salt.

The heroine in both folktale and poem strikes me now as a transitional figure between good girl and bad. She does not faint like the heroine in "Frau Holle," but accepts the consequences of answering her father with bold words. She responds with action rather than silence, facing her fears of abandonment creatively, thus triumphing in the end. Through her actions she proves that her wrong words were right after all, but she holds no grudges. She compassionately takes her father in and treats him with generosity. Like meat loving salt.

One of my English students, Gerri Cooper, inspired by the heroine in "The Water of Life," who also responds with action, was intrigued with the way problems can function as creative stimulants (Cooper 1996). In her essay for an English class, she described a dream she had before beginning music lessons:

> Recently I started to take flute lessons at the Manitoba Conservatory of Music and Arts. Part of the procedure of beginning lessons at the Conservatory is that each new student has a consultation with their teacher so the teacher can place their skill level and recommend music, etc. Before my consultation I had a terrible dream. I was in a room standing by a piano. My flute case was open on the top of the piano and I started to put my flute together. My teacher was sitting at the piano on the bench smiling at me and her teacher (of piano) was leaning on the other end of the piano also looking very friendly and encouraging. My flute would not go together. Its pieces were curved rather than straight and wouldn't fit together. I couldn't find the ends that fit together. Every time I put two pieces together they would sort of melt and flow away from each other as though the pieces repelled each other (like magnets with two negative poles put together). I saw, sitting on the floor in a circle around me, a number of small children, five or six years old, all with their flutes assembled in their laps. After trying for what seemed like an endless time to fit this instrument together, I realized that the pieces were wooden not silver and that this was not my instrument. I found my flute and put it together with no trouble at all.

Gerri's essay described how fear leading to silence was a central issue in her dreams and in many life experiences, as well as in the favourite stories she read again and again. She could see that her task was to transform these problems into challenges instead of viewing them as obstacles to be feared. She used "The Water of Life" as an example, retelling it as she remembered it from a workshop I had presented at her church. In Gerri's story the characters were woman and man instead of sister and brothers:

> I first heard the folk tale "The Water of Life," my favourite folktale, at a workshop, and have heard it twice more. The outline of the story is that a tree is growing in the yard of a man and woman. Every year it grows a special fruit and when the fruit is eaten by the man and the woman, it guarantees them a fortunate year. One year the fruit does not grow and the tree is sickly so the man sets out to find a way to cure the tree. He meets magical helpers and is advised to get the water of life from a well at the top of a mountain and how to avoid the traps and pitfalls on the journey. The stones of the path to the top of the mountain speak to him and when they insult him, he is unable to resist responding and is also turned to stone. The woman sets out to find the man and the cure and finds herself on the same path. She can resist the temptation to stay and have fun with the rocks and the temptation to respond to their insults, but has trouble not responding to cries for help. The man and the woman in the story face my worst nightmares, represented by the various stones in the path, and although the man is caught, there is a happy ending to the story. The woman reaches the top, faces a dragon, and gains the precious water for the tree.

I include Gerri's summary here to emphasize her personal associations for this story. Comparing her summary with my earlier story text underlines Gerri's interpretations: she emphasizes the woman's interaction with the rocks but underplays the encounter with the dragon, and omits the woman's startling discovery that the water of life has the power to return the stones to their human form. These last aspects of the story were not as central to Gerri as the woman's determination not to give in to the stony voices on the mountain path:

> For me, the focal moment is when the woman is on the path up to get the water of life and she recognizes the man's voice calling to her for help and though she wants to, she doesn't stop.

She knows how to resist the temptation to stop and the temptation to help when no help is possible. She makes the difficult choices all the way through the story. She braves the path and then the dragon in order to get the water, and then is ready to risk what she has gained in order to help others.

The heroine in this story gets beyond the voices of doubt and fear, highlighting Gerri's challenges in facing her own fears without falling into silence. She concluded her essay by noting that "Many creators can say the same: facing fear that binds us in muteness and paralysis, holding skilfully to the tension between action and inaction, allows us to recognize ourselves as natural artists, one way or another."

Gerri is certainly not the only person who has found dreams and folktales to be powerful sources of practical knowledge. But there are also many others who insist, "That's only a story," or, "That's only a dream," or ignore them altogether like the woman in the Indian tale who did not tell her story or sing her song. No doubt she did not recall her dreams, either. Unlike her, we might find artistic balance by learning how to put a flute together in a dream, as Gerri did, or by vicariously experiencing the passage up a folktale mountain with its stony critical voices trying to stop us. Or we can experience our own voice surprising us in the waking world when we, like the fox in "The Water of Life," speak the words that need to be said.

In the dream of the Golden Woman I spoke only twice, once to Rachel and once to the mirror. This balance of silence and speech was the catalyst needed to move the dream further into artistic expression, to bring about the transformation of the woman. What if that Golden Woman were to meet the Golden Dragon who guards the water of life? I am imagining a conversation between them, wondering what words they might speak. Or perhaps they might respectfully regard one another in silent wonder.

There was a Little Girl who Had a Little Curl

While I am still ambivalent about silence and noise, I have no ambivalence at all about anger. I have never been patient, from my first year of life, when I wailed for nine months, until now, when I scream at my vexatious computer. Perhaps it is no coincidence that snakes are symbolic of anger in Buddhism, a path that had attracted me from adolescence and which I now follow. This gives me another perspective on my imaginary friend Snakey the Rattlesnake, who was my conscience rather than my enemy; what he often punished me for was anger. The bad press snakes have unjustly earned in the West should have made his authority entirely negative, but I intuitively trusted this archetypal force. I am aware of Snakey's Freudian potential, but I feel that he was as much an ethical guide as an erotic symbol. I also sense his positive kinship with his mythical reptilian cousin the dragon in "The Water of Life."

More in anecdotes my parents told me over the years than in my own memory, I was at the height of my wicked behaviour between ages four and five—the period of my talking rat dream and of Snakey. Janet, eighteen months younger than me, was my convenient target in this brief time span. I cut up her precious "blankie" to make a doll dress, cut off half of her hair just before we were to have family portraits made, and threw her Raggedy Ann doll into the fireplace. The doll survived, singed but intact, and went into family legendry. (On Janet's fortieth birthday I presented her with a new, hand-made Raggedy Ann doll, and she was amused.) Janet was not my only motivation for naughtiness. On my sixth birthday, I was annoyed when my Aunt Lois sent me a frilly pink girlish slip instead of something more adventurous, so I stuffed it into the kitchen garbage can when my mother was not watching. She found it, of course, and though I do not recall the consequences, they could not have been pleasant.

This golden age of open rebellion was brief. By the time I started school I had learned to be more furtive, and Janet had learned to fight back. We now amuse each other with battle stories, and compare our tiny crescent-shaped scars gained after all those nail-scratching and hair-pulling years of sharing a bedroom. Our classic fights were on Saturday mornings when we were supposed to be cleaning our room and were, instead, engaged in territorial warfare. Janet kept her side clean while mine, in my mother's words, "looked like the aftermath of a hurricane." One Saturday she was so mad she drew a chalk line across the room, thinking that would keep our sides separate. The door was on my side.

Our mother was opposed to physical punishment. She preferred to make us stand in the short hallway between our bedroom and the living room with our faces to the wall, for varied lengths of time appropriate to our misdeeds. She never seemed to notice that we spent much of the time making faces at each other and giggling quietly, entirely unrepentant.

As I have already admitted, I had a low tolerance for frustration and a short temper, in contrast to Janet's calmer nature. My father often joked me out of anger that arose when I tried in vain to connect the elastic band that held a doll's arms and legs together or reattach a broken leg on a horse statue. He was fond of reciting the old nursery rhyme about the horrid little girl with a curl whenever I got heated up:

> There was a little girl who had a little curl,
> right in the middle of her forehead.
> When she was good, she was very very good,
> And when she was bad, she was horrid.

(I prefer the Mae West version that ends: "When she was good, she was very, very good, and when she was bad, she was better.") This chant used to make me even angrier than I already was, but now I can see that this was as much an accolade as censure. I think I knew at an early age that my father was at least a little pleased to have a child who was a bit horrid, stubborn, independent, and impatient, that damn-if-it-ain't-a-girl Kay.

I was never sure about my mother, though. For years I was convinced that she preferred good Janet to horrid Kay, and I interpreted her stories about me in this light. I hated it when she told me how I began life by wailing for nine full months and would not stop no matter what she did. One day, she said, she looked out the window while I was in full voice and saw the neighbour's dog lying in the yard with his paws over his ears. She laughed. Only many years later, when I had my own wailing babies, could I understand that this was actually a story of survival humour, a mother listening helplessly to a screaming child and just that once rescued from despair by a dog. I wonder now, thinking of my infant screams and my mother's stories about them, if these did not contribute to my eventual struggles over silence and noise.

I was disappointed to discover that I was not such a horrid girl after all, especially compared to "baddies" I have shared anecdotes with in adult life. My brothers were certainly more adept at disobedience than I ever dreamed of being: Allen stole hubcaps from the school buses in junior high school, began to drink alcohol in adolescence (a huge taboo in my teetotal family), and dropped out of vocational school to join the army by faking his birth certificate (and these are the milder of his exploits). My younger brother Terry set fire to our empty lot when he was barely three, and later perfected the art of shoplifting. Even Lois, my youngest sister, showed more overt potential than I did when she punched the bratty boy down the street hard enough to make him cry, and came to be known as the terror of the neighbourhood.

In contrast, I had become silently sullen by the end of elementary school, except for muffled outbursts of frustration behind my closed bedroom door, when I would sometimes express frustration by throwing my white Bible across the bedroom. Because the Bible was a gift from my gentle grandmother, it felt like a truly wicked act that I always regretted.

I secretly admired girls who did what they wanted without seeming to care what anyone thought of them, girls like Mary Lou who wanted to beat me up. I cannot imagine her bothering to throw a Bible across the room when she could throw me. A friend of mine, hearing my attempts at maliciousness, could not believe I was such a goody-goody, and regaled me with her own adventures as a good Lutheran girl in a small midwestern town. One in particular made me envious. She and a friend were in a public place and saw a woman's coat hanging unguarded on a peg. They went through the pockets and took all the loose change, and also found the address of someone in another state. They stole it and wrote an insulting letter to the person, using all the nasty words that two sheltered young girls could come up with in the more innocent 1940s. She said she sometimes wonders, with more curiosity than guilt, how the letter was received and if it was ever answered.

Though I never achieved such open mischievousness, my covert naughtiness would have earned me nips from Snakey if he had still been around. I regret a small but rankling incident from my pre-adolescent horse-loving days. My father came back from a business trip with small gifts for each of us. I could see by the shape of the rough wrapping that mine was a horse, but when I opened it eagerly I found that I was wrong. It was a crudely painted mule, squatting on its brown haunches with its wide red mouth open, showing long white buck teeth—a joke bottle opener. I was deeply hurt and insulted that my father, who had introduced me to horses, would give me such an ugly thing. Remembering the pink frilly slip incident, I did not say or do anything until I was sure I could do it without being caught. That night I crept out the back door, found my mother's gardening trowel, and managed to break through stubborn crab grass and dig a small hole and bury the offensive mule. I felt smug for a while, but by the next morning I was ashamed of myself and slipped out to the backyard after breakfast to rescue the mule when no one was watching. I dug and dug but never found it, and never told anyone why it was not displayed proudly with my horse statues on top of the piano, nor did anyone ever ask. Somewhere in the backyard of the house at Northwest 101 Street in Miami, there is a small pile of rust with flecks of brown, red, and white paint.

Something happened the following year that brought me closer to the mean sisters in the folktales I read, though I discovered that I was not, in fact, that kind of sister. Janet and I had gone to the gas station to take my father his lunch, and because he was too busy to pay attention to us I enticed Janet to come with me to the nearby canal, strictly off-limits because neither of us had learned to swim despite all attempts to teach us. As we played on the banks, Janet slipped, slid down the moderate slope, and fell in. I was horrified, and tried to reach out and grab one of her flailing hands, and ended up in the water right beside her. The canal was relatively shallow, so after our initial panic we managed to stand up sheepishly and pull ourselves out, wet and mortified, and went home without telling a soul about our misadventure. Years later when I was retelling the story, Janet began to laugh. "I didn't fall in," she insisted, "you pushed me in!" While I honestly do not remember it happening that way it does make more sense, given our fractiousness, and it does take me closer to being that mean older sister. But I still do not believe that I pushed Janet in. Such disagreements are not uncommon when siblings retell family stories.

Earlier I outlined "Frau Holle," in which both sisters end up in water as we did, with much less happy results for the older sister. Here is a Russian variant of the kind and unkind girls, featuring the archetypal witch Baba Yaga, who, like Frau Holle in the previous chapter, tests both girls. (For a full text see Afanas'ev 1973, 194-95.) It begins with the familiar theme of a father with poor taste in second wives.

A merchant remarried after his wife died, taking a woman with a daughter of her own. She immediately began to mistreat the merchant's daughter, and eventually compelled the father to take this girl to the witch Baba Yaga as a servant, in hopes that she would be destroyed. Instead the girl listened to helpful mice, and did everything so well that she was well rewarded with fine clothing, and came home looking like a princess. The angry stepmother then sent her own daughter so she could be similarly rewarded, but of course this girl complained about the work, chased away the mice, and did nothing she was told to do. When the father came to retrieve her only her bones were left, so he brought them home in a basket.

If I had read this story as a child I would have been horrified, but reading it as an adult made me curious about what might happen with a basket of bones. In folktales, after all, death is reversible and a basket of bones might be transformed into someone with interesting experiences. Poetic license is most certainly granted to a concerned older sister like me. I want those bones to walk again.

It took a lot of reading to reach this detached response to the kinds of stories that had bothered me so much, and much of my objectivity was inspired by people I talked to about stories over the years. I was curious about what other people remembered about folktales they read or heard as children, so when I began working on a doctoral dissertation on traditional tales, I interviewed people of all ages, my own family among them, to discover what their reactions were to women in folktales. I was particularly curious to learn what Janet and Jolene remembered. Their full comments are in my doctoral dissertation (Stone 1975, 262-3 and 299-300). Both claimed not to recall much at all, but then gave examples that still seem to carry emotional echoes. Janet, for example, recalled "Snow White" and "Hansel and Gretel," and commented that "there was always somebody old and vicious." I was pleased that she did not single out the mean older sister as the "vicious" one, and wondered if she, like me, had Mrs. H. across the street in mind for "old."

Jolene, the middle child who always felt left out, fondly recalled "Cinderella," saying that she remembered it because of the two stepsisters: "This part of the story was realistic, I thought, because of the jealousy of the sisters to Cinderella." Fortunately for me, she seemed unaware that one of the real-life villains in the story was sitting across from her at the kitchen table, and I did not point it out. Later, though, when I reported the conversation to Janet, we shared a guilty laugh as we remembered how we conspired together to aggravate Jolene, who was as pretty and blonde and patient as the stereotypical Cinderella. We were relieved that we could not recall any examples of overt cruelty, only minor pranks. The worst thing I ever did to hurt Jolene was entirely accidental, and I suffered as much as she did. This is a story I did not even tell to my family for years, and I have never written it down until now.

On her eighth birthday Jolene was given a plain grey-blue parakeet, the only indoor pet other than goldfish my mother could abide since she was allergic to furry creatures. The bird was smart and unusually affectionate, much loved by the whole family. It was a gifted speaker and possibly also an oracle, since one of its favourite expressions was "Kay's got B I G feet," shrieked out with great clarity and enthusiasm. Its vocabulary came from twenty-one-year-old Allen, just back from the Korean War. He taught it to say, "Terry is a dope," "Shut up, stupid!" and my personal favourite, "Birds don't talk!"

The bird was free to fly around the house, and was especially fond of the kitchen and bathroom because it loved the sound of running water. One night I was taking a shower in preparation for my first babysitting job. I was nervous, and did not even hear the bird talking away at the bathroom mirror, which it always did, nor did I notice that it was on the floor when I stepped out of the shower.

While it was a bloodless death, I was devastated. I could not manage to tell Jolene what happened. In fact, it took me 25 years to tell Jolene, and another year or so to tell the rest of the family. Lois, only two years old at the time and raised on legends of The Bird, was the only one who could laugh. She did a perfect imitation of the bird's voice saying, "Kay's got BIG BIG BIG feet!"

Violent as it was, this act was not premeditated murder, any more than my part in the canal incident with Janet. The fact that I failed as a deliberately cruel elder sister gave me distance from this character, and freedom to imagine older sisters in the stories leading more adventurously unrepentant lives away from their families, perhaps living in rooms that looked like the aftermath of a hurricane.

Kira Van Deusen wondered about this same theme in some of the Siberian tales she studied, suggesting that both sisters experience transformations, not only the good one:

> In these stories, that lazy and not-too-smart older sister turns into some kind of monster and actually winds up transformed and shaman-like. The smart younger sister is more likely to marry, say, an animal, and later give birth to someone remarkable (personal correspondence, July 2000).

True, becoming "some kind of monster" may not sound like a very positive change, but Kira notes the "shaman-like" potential of such transformations. The good sister follows a more traditional pattern of female behaviour and does not actually gain the power to shape-change. The "bad" girl has creative potential, perhaps because she does not listen to the admonishing voices of "prissy Criticalness" described earlier by Brenda Ueland.

Since my waking life did not reveal enough of the bad sister in me, I searched through my recorded dreams hoping to find a more malevolent character with transformative possibilities. Even in my own imagination I was barely more than troublesome. In one I managed to be disruptive and spiteful, but only as an invisible ghost with no substance.

In the dream I was a poltergeist trying to haunt my own house and annoy the people who lived there, who for some reason had named me "Christina." I caused things to fall off shelves, pulled covers off sleeping people, made terrible noises at night, and in general revelled in my invisible disruptiveness. The people became as frightened as I had hoped they would but I found that I did not enjoy terrifying them after all, and flew away to leave them in peace.

By leaving, I was unconsciously asking for a new stage set, another act in this dream-play. In response, the scene shifted immediately. As I flew, I saw a man waving up at me from a rowboat, inviting me down to an island. When I landed we walked uphill to a large old house with many rooms, where I was shown to a small room and left alone. I decided to explore the house, still invisible, I thought, and wandered down elegant hallways and peeked into luxurious rooms. As I roamed, I heard two women talking about "Christina" and remembered that I was now called by that name. They said something about looking in a mirror, so I stopped to look in a hall mirror with an ornate gilded frame. There I saw my own face overlaid by another, a double image worthy of a Gemini. I touched my Kay-Christina face with both hands and discovered that I was no longer a ghost. I had no idea who this mischievous Christina was, but accepted her odd presence. I was possessed.

As if this were a signal for another change of scene, the man from the rowboat reappeared, walking toward me. He was saying something nonsensical, so absurd I actually laughed in the dream, and remembered it verbatim as I awoke:

"I named this place Christina after you so it's your place now. I guess if Mr. Wurst can name his sausage 'Liverwurst' I can name this place after you." I was delighted to learn that the mansion was my own place, and awoke with a strong feeling of satisfaction. Somehow the poltergeist had been rewarded.

I enjoyed being the pesky poltergeist Christina and the doubled Kay-Christina, and liked having a place named for me. The twin names were intriguing, as was the verbal artistry of that silly last line, a delightful play on words that repeats in miniature the dream message: Liverwurst—live her worst. It took me several days to see how the dreaming artist had managed this bit of lyrical creativity. When I told the dream to a friend, Gail Beck, some years later, she reported a similarly inane concluding line that left her perplexed at first. She was calling for her mother-in-law, whose name is Gussie in waking life but was "Helen" in the dream. Gail drifted back to awakening with her own voice calling out, "Helen Beck! Helen Beck!" and caught the word play on hell and back, which she thought was appropriate for the previous bad day in her waking world.

Anger and transformation were central motifs in a dream I had sometime after the poltergeist dream, perhaps fuelled by my acceptance of the live-her-worst aspect of the dream. I was in our recognizable basement with an electrician who had come to rewire our house. He was rude and impatient, and refused to help after I touched a light bulb and was paralyzed by a surge of electrical energy. He just stood there watching, which suddenly filled me with helpless rage. The energy of righteous indignation broke me out of paralysis, and I was able to pull my hand off the lightbulb. At this point I realized I had been transformed into a powerful monster. I ran up the basement steps to get away because, like Christina, I did not really want to harm this man—but he foolishly followed me up, laughing. I caught a quick glimpse of myself reflected in the back door window; I was huge and ferocious, with the enormous head of the Chinese lion dancer complete with elaborate red and gold decorations. As the man came out the door after me, I picked him up and tossed him across Queenston Street, jumped up on the neighbour's roof and karate-chopped her brick chimney to pieces, and let out a King Kong roar that stopped traffic and silenced the entire neighbourhood. It felt wonderfully liberating and deeply satisfying.

Obviously this transformation has deep psychic meaning, but, again, it is the artistry of the dream that stays with me now; the cartoon-like zap of the electricity passing through and immobilizing me, the reflected head of the Chinese lion figure in vibrant reds and golds, and the panorama of my neighbourhood from the rooftop, complete with suburban streets lined with old elms. If I were a professional animator I could turn it into a vivid comic strip or video.

Part of my search for "bad" Kay is an attempt to see and accept perceived negative qualities—my shadow selves, in Jungian terms. Instead of denying or repressing them and becoming the good quiet girl, I want to fly free, released into fuller imagination and creativity. I knew exactly what I wanted when I heard Tanis MacDonald read her poem, "Classic Beauty," where humour functions as a powerful medicine in a transformation of a classical Greek myth (MacDonald 2000, 92-93).

When Perseus snuck up on Medusa,
sandals not as stealthy as he thought,
her snakes woke first and
flicked warning tongues in her ear;

a quick glance over her shoulder
petrified him in mid-step.

He revived the next morning
after she was long gone, and said,
"Man, last night I was so stoned…"

Finding a skull-white boulder,
he flung on a heap of seaweed,
held it aloft and shouted,
"I have slain the beast!
Look on me, Atlas,
and quaver!"

On another continent,
wrinkles slither onto Medusa's face —
world's oldest surviving Gorgon.
She invests well, retires early.

She combs her green curls back,
moves to the coast,
opens a bookstore,
sells copies of *The Beauty Myth*
and keeps a section on reptiles
by the cash register for impulse buys.

A sign on her shop door reads,
Here lives the beast.
Look on me, world,
and discover.

Her green curls carry her well beyond the horrid little girl with the curl in the middle of her forehead. This monstrous woman opts not to do permanent damage, as did my repentant poltergeist "Christina-Kay." Instead, Medusa uses her Gorgon powers to temporarily immobilize ego-maniacal Perseus, and escapes to run a bookstore in Canada. Over her door is the sign that reveals the true power of the beast—look and discover. We might guess that a modern Perseus might still be shaking his head in confusion and then pretending that he has succeeded, missing a chance at deeper transformation because he is stuck in his heroic image.

Letting go of self images, and accepting apparent darkness, figure in a dream I had some time ago. It began with the familiar theme of walking down a corridor trying to find something, but this time I recognized the pattern of the dream and thought, "If it's a dream I can ask someone where I'm going." Where could you do that except in a dream? Immediately I saw three beautiful dark-haired women in splendid, vibrantly coloured saris, talking together animatedly. I approached them to ask my question, but before I could speak they all turned to me with glowing faces and said excitedly, "We've just discovered a new kind of meditation. When you are completely relaxed you will hear a voice telling you a story." They asked if I wanted to hear one of the stories and I nodded eagerly and speechlessly. Here is their dream story:

There was once a woman who was possessed by a demon. She wanted to be free, so she went to someone who could get rid demons, but it didn't work. Then she tried to hold it down, but it would break out at unexpected times. So she tried to ignore it but it was still there, and it would cause her a lot of trouble. One day she realized that there was only one thing left to do, so she did it. She possessed the demon.

I woke up with those exact words from the dream story still clearly in mind. The possession of the demon in the dream turns things around, like Medusa outwitting Perseus. The dream woman accepts her negative self, and thus transforms a destructive demon into a daemon, a source of inspiration. In dream life I made the first steps in "Kay-Christina," and was ready for further possessions with the unconscious knowledge that to possess such power is a gift and not a curse. I sense Snakey coiled invisibly in the darkness of these dreams, now more muse than ethical guardian, having waited all those years for me to wake up.

My growing-up myth was a long dream, a discomforting dance between the good girl I thought I was supposed to be and the bad girl I thought I was. That woman possessed by a demon/daemon took a long time to free herself into the artistry of storytelling and of writing. This book is my Medusa statement, snakes and all. Look and discover. Inspired by this poem, I wanted to discover what happened to the bad sisters in the folktales, after they were given snakes and toads or had themselves covered in black pitch. I also wanted to know how the punishing witch got to be a witch in the first place. This was an artistic challenge to me as a storyteller. I decided to answer the challenge with a story that would grow as this book grew.

These ideas floated around in my mind for some time before a thread of a story began to emerge from all the folktales I had read about the adventures of "good" and "bad" sisters, most particularly the German tale of "Frau Holle," the Russian story of "Vasilisa the Beautiful," and the English folktale of "Kate Crackernuts." This last story is a rare one because clever Kate, the eldest, not only rescues her stepsister instead of opposing her, but even finds her a husband (Jacobs 1967, 198).

Since this book is about dreaming as an art, and how dream experiences can inspire further creativity, let me demonstrate how I have woven an original story from the thread of an idea spun out of dreams, folktales and touches of lived experiences. This thread leads us along an imaginative path where sister and stepsister meet a magic apple tree and a challenging crone. There are hints of Janet and Kay and the mother who seemed to prefer one over the other, of Mrs. H. and her overgrown garden, and of course all those cranky old crones from my dreams. This is the first part of "Dark Kate and Light Kate." The story continues in the ninth chapter ("Some Day Your Witch Might Come"), and will of course go on transforming orally after this book is completed.

Here it begins, in a time that never was and always is. There was a man who had a daughter named Kate, and he married a woman who had a daughter with the same name. Since the man's daughter was fair and fine he called her "Light Kate," and called his brown-haired stepdaughter "Dark Kate." Now, Dark Kate's own mother did not like this, and decided to punish the fair one by making her life more difficult. Light Kate did whatever she was told and did it well, and never complained a word to her father. Dark Kate paid no attention because she was too busy with her own things. She preferred black nights to sunny days, and loved to walk in the darkest part of the woods where she could catch the odd creatures who lived there, toads and snakes and strange beetles. While Light Kate's room was always spotless, Dark Kate had bags and boxes and dusty jars filled with all sorts of things that she gathered in the woods. Her stepfather complained, but her mother said, "She's just being creative."

One day the mother gave Light Kate a bucket and said, "Go fetch me some water from the well at the world's end. We need it for cooking our supper." Light Kate asked politely, "But where is the well at the world's end?" Her stepmother growled, "If I knew that I'd get it myself, you silly girl. Out with you." So Light Kate obediently picked up the bucket and went out the door of their small hut. She wanted to ask her sister where the end of the world might be because she was sure Dark Kate would know, but her stepsister was nowhere to be seen, and might not have told her anyway even if she did know.

Light Kate carried the pail for a long way, growing more and more tired and hungry and frightened with every step, but she went on. Soon she came to a fast moving stream, and saw that she could cross safely by stepping on the rocks that made a path through the water. When she came to the other side she saw a small apple tree growing beside the road. Its branches drooped with the weight of the ripe apples, but they were too high to reach so she sat down to rest in its shade. The tree called down to her, "My branches are too heavy from all these apples. Shake me until they all fall, then take as many as you like." Light Kate said that she wasn't strong enough, but the apple tree encouraged her, so she began to push and shake the tree as well as she could. Apples fell all around her, and when the last one had fallen, she picked it up and ate it. It was a very sour crab apple, but Light Kate didn't complain, she simply thanked the tree. "And thank you as well," it said. "Now, can I help you as much as you've helped me?" "Oh yes, do you know where I can find the well at the world's end?" she asked courteously. "Of course, just go back to the stream."

Light Kate went back to the stream, and thinking that this must be the well itself she dipped her bucket into it. Instantly the water pulled the bucket out of her hands and swept it way. Poor Kate. She ran along the bank trying to grab the bucket back but the stream was much too fast. As she ran, she tripped on a rock and the next thing she knew, she was in the stream herself, being pulled down and down. She fainted in terror, and when she awoke she found herself in a strange land. In the distance she saw an odd little house, and in at an even odder old woman who invited her in. "Are you a hard worker?" the woman asked? "Oh yes," said Light Kate.

She was fed and given a bed to rest in, but in the morning the crone commanded her to clean the house, cook the meals, and feed any animals she met. She did exactly as she was told, and the old woman smiled and invited her to choose her reward. There were two small chests equal in size and shape, but one was made of battered tin and the other was of dark wood with elaborate carvings of peculiar creatures. She chose the modest tin chest and was told to open it only after she had crossed the stream again. "It's so heavy. How will I carry it home?" she sighed. The old woman told her to close her eyes and spin around and around until she fell down in a faint. She obeyed, and when she woke up, found herself beside the stream. The crabapple tree she'd helped pointed the way home. When she crossed the stream again she obediently stopped and opened the tin chest. Inside she found a fine silken sack full of gold. Her bucket was nowhere to be seen, and she was sure she would be punished for losing it. When she came safely home with a fine silk sack full of gold but no bucket, she told her stepmother how she fallen in the stream and found another land, where she'd worked for a strange old woman who rewarded her with gold.

The stepmother, entranced by the treasure, called her own daughter, intending to send her off to find more gold. Kate was far off in the woods collecting toadstools and didn't hear her mother until an owl, awakened by the yelling, hooted in surprise. Kate looked up, listened carefully, and heard her mother's angry voice. She put the toadstools in her pocket and went home. "Now listen to me," her mother said, "I want you to take this bucket and get water from the well at the world's end, and come back with a sack of gold like your sister did." Kate grumbled, but when she saw the gold she thought she could certainly do as well as her silly sister. She set off dragging the heavy bucket along. She came to the same stream and splashed through it, and saw the small apple tree, once again covered with ripe apples since it was no ordinary tree. "Good. I'm hungry." She set the pail down and climbed right up into the little tree, paying no heed to its shouts to shake its branches free of apples. At the top she found the biggest and ripest of the apples, and sat up there eating it. "Oh, too sour," she said, but she was hungry. When she finished she jumped down, her movement knocking off all the apples.

"And now off to the well," she said as she stood up.

"This is not how I like it," the tree grumbled, "but I guess I'll tell you anyway that you'll find the well at the world's end if you go back to the stream." Without a word Kate picked up the bucket and went back to the stream, thinking, as her sister had, that it must be the right place. She tossed the bucket in and dove in after it, felt herself pulled down into the water that grew darker and colder as she sank. When she touched bottom she went right on sinking down into the earth, until at last she found herself in another land. She, too, saw the odd little hut and met the same strange old woman who asked if she was a hard worker. "Sometimes," Dark Kate answered honestly. She was fed and given a bed to rest in, and in the morning told to clean the house, cook the meals, and feed any animals she met. She began to work, but didn't do anything very thoroughly because she was too busy looking out the windows of the hut and wondering what animals might come to be fed. She didn't care much about the hens and geese and chickens and pigs, but when a bear came she fed it well, and even found food for an old warty toad, just in case.

"Not quite what I expected," the old woman said, "But your work will be properly rewarded." She led her to two chests and said she could choose what she deserved. Dark Kate did not hesitate to choose the fine wooden chest with its elaborate carving of peculiar creatures. "To each her own," said the old woman, and sent the girl on her way, telling her not to open the chest until she'd crossed the stream.

With no delay Dark Kate set off. She could hardly wait to open the box and find her reward. She hadn't even got as far as the crabapple tree when she stopped, sat down beside the path, and threw back the lid expectantly. Inside was a rough woolen sack that seemed to move when she lifted it out. She didn't mind that it wasn't fine silk. She pulled the sack open and jumped back in surprise when snakes slithered out and ugly toads leapt away in all directions. The largest of the toads headed back down the path in the direction of the old woman's hut. Kate yelled, "Hey, come back here! You belong to me!" And off they went together, with the toad in the lead and Kate running after. And what happened next you will soon know.

Dark Kate's new adventures begin here, and spin out further in the chapter 9. I am imagining the dreams of toads and crones Kate might have as her life becomes increasingly challenging. In our dreams and in our life stories, we are speaking directly to ourselves, artist to artist, so fictional Kate can do the same. After all, her mother said she was creative.

Like Kate, I want to take my chances, choose the box with the unusual contents and see where it leads me. As I dream up this continuing story I allow my voice to play freely with many possibilities. Anyone from past and present life, from dreams, or from stories I have read or movies I have seen, can come to life and interact. Frau Holle and Baba Yaga compare gardening methods with Mrs. H., the good girls learn a few tricks from their bad stepsisters, and maybe the Chinese lion in one dream can ask the demon/daemon in the other a few questions about anger.

In My Mother's Garden

As I child I sometimes dreamed that my mother was a witch who was chasing me, and I escaped her by flying off the roof of our house in Miami. I grew up certain that my mother the witch preferred Janet, the good girl whose half of our shared room did not look like hurricane damage. This misconception coloured my relationship with her well into my adult life. I was surprised, then, to learn, late in our up-and-down relationship, that she had warm memories of my early stories of "Snakey" and that she was proud and delighted that I had become a public storyteller. She herself was not at all a public person, choosing to hide behind the scenes, usually in the kitchen, where she could watch what others were doing and attempt stage directing, especially of my father.

Her interest in my stories gave us a long overdue channel for communication. I learned to appreciate her understated cronish wisdom and humour as we talked about folktales, dreams, and life, and she heard many of my stories over those last few years we had together. Her favourite, especially in her final months of cancer, was "Jumping Mouse," about a curious desert mouse who is determined to find the sacred Blue Mountain (Storm 1972, 68+). While the collector of the story has been criticized by anthropologists as well as by the Cheyenne people, the story is still compelling. I told it to my mother whenever she asked. This is a considerably abbreviated version, with a gender change to suit my mother.

A desert mouse disobeyed her elders and kept jumping too high, risking being caught by eagles. One day her joyful leaps took her up so far that she saw a blue mountain far off in the distance and yearned to find it. She was guided by other creatures who knew the way: a frog who repeated the warnings about eagles but told her how to cross the desert; a buffalo who protected her and accompanied her to the base of the mountain in exchange for her right eye; a wolf who carried her almost to the top, but at the cost of her left eye. "How will I know I'm there if I can't see?" Mouse asked. Wolf explained that she would feel the winds blowing from all four directions at the top of the mountain, and that she should leap up as high as she could and let the winds carry her. Jumping Mouse reached the top, felt the winds swirl around her, and leapt into them. As she was carried down on the wind, expecting to die, she began to regain her sight, seeing more clearly than she had ever seen before. As she floated over her helpers she called down to each of them in turn, "Hello, Brother Wolf! Hello, Brother Buffalo! Hello, Brother Frog!" Each looked up, and called out, "Hello, Sister Eagle!"

My practical mother, the gardener, said that she usually did not enjoy "stories that couldn't happen." She liked this one because of "the stubborn little mouse who didn't do what she was supposed to." She was intrigued by the enigmatic conclusion: "What's happening?" she asked. "Did the eagle eat the mouse or did she turn into an eagle?" Since she was facing death herself, this mystery was very real, more than "just a story." I told her it was up to her. She smiled, and chose transformation.

Dreams, too, often leave us wondering "what's happening?" My mother understood that "Jumping Mouse" was a very human story, and that the ending is not about death but about rebirth. She found that message moving, comforting, and all her own; I had declined to interpret the story, wanting it to remain open, though of course that's exactly how I saw it myself. And I did truly see it. In a different way it is the story of anyone who has struggled to find their own creative path without being turned aside by discouraging voices, that "petty Criticalness." Flying in this sense is not an escape from adventure at all, it's a joyful leap deeper into it.

My mother said that this little protagonist reminded her of me as a girl. "Her name could be Kay Frances," she suggested once with a smile. I thought the mouse was also like that fun-loving girl who was my mother, who met her husband-to-be at a church Halloween party.

She was fond of all the stories I told with resourceful protagonists, but she probably never heard the one I most wanted to tell her. It came too late, when she was in the final stages of cancer and lost on pain killers, though a friend assured me that she might be able to hear it even in this state. I will try to recreate the sequence of events that brought the story to a new shape, but this is difficult because it is not, in fact, a simple sequence of events. I struggled with this in a preliminary article about my mother and her garden, "Inside Out: Folktale and Personal Story" (Stone 1997, 13-23), and am still trying to piece it all together from faulty memory aided by responses from my sisters. While the story was coming into being in relation to my mother and her garden I was a daughter and storyteller, not a folklorist, so I was not studying its gradual development. Let me begin my exploration with a dream I had that showed me how important that garden had been, after some explanation.

Late in her life my mother became a gardener. Wearing a battered hat to protect herself from the Miami sun, she began to plant a modest vegetable plot to supplement their diet, since they were living on my father's small pension and occasional contributions from the family. That was her practical reason, but in fact she had always loved working outside, trading plants with Mrs. H. across the street. I just never paid much attention when I lived at home. She began the garden after we had all left home, and after all of her grandchildren had grown beyond babysitting age. As far as my sisters and I can figure, this was some time in the late 1970s and early 1980s. Theoretically Florida has a year-round growing season, but she still did much of her gardening in winter (in Miami, the season of brown grass) because summer was too hot for her, even in her gardening hat, and for many of the vegetables as well. I am sorry that I paid so little attention to her garden. I had married and moved to Canada by that time, and we visited only once a year, usually in the Christmas season when we had time off from teaching. I remember that our children, Nathaniel and Rachel, were excited at being able to go out to her backyard and pull up vegetables for their supper, the only time I could get them to eat carrots and peas willingly.

For about four or five years the garden was larger every time we returned. It had begun as a small patch between the clothesline and an old grapefruit tree, and ended up covering half of the backyard. She even had my father move the clothesline to another part of the yard to accommodate the garden, and considered cutting back the grapefruit tree to provide more light. In the end she let the tree grow, because it had been "a friend" from our first difficult days in Miami in the 1940s. My mother was modestly proud of her very ordinary vegetables—carrots, beans, peas, two kinds of peppers (the hot ones to discourage bugs), green onions, and of course tomatoes. But she was especially happy with her old southern favourites that none of us would eat as children because they were "hillbilly" food—things like collard and mustard greens, and others I couldn't even identify. She remembered them from her childhood in Melvin Hill, North Carolina, which she left at age eight when her family moved north to Windsor and then to Detroit. She even tried to grow a small cotton plant once, as a joke, in memory of her hard work picking cotton as a girl. "We all had to work when we weren't in school," she told me, as she showed me the souvenir cotton bole she'd brought back from a family visit in the 1960s.

We all took that garden for granted. It seemed like a perfectly natural thing for her to be doing, since she'd always loved growing things indoors and out. I learned to appreciate her green thumb when I left a spindly house plant with her once and found that it had become a tree when I returned to get it. Because I took her green thumb for granted, I don't remember now when the garden began its decline nor how long that took, perhaps only a year or two. I only remember, sadly, that one year when I went home it was gone. Only a bare patch of grey South Florida sand was left, not yet reclaimed by crabgrass. Even then, I did not understand just how important that garden was to her—or to me—until I had a remarkable dream a few years later.

In the dream I was visiting Miami, walking up the familiar cement driveway to the front porch of the house I grew up in. When I entered the porch my mother came out to greet me. She gave me the usual hug and then said, "Go out back and see what I've done with the garden." I dropped my suitcase on the porch and walked directly through the living room, kitchen, and back porch, and opened the rear door. I stepped down onto the green cement steps my father had built and painted in my mother's favourite colour. I was stunned at what I saw. The garden began right at the base of the green steps and went on and on and on, right to the horizon. I woke up in surprise, amazed, feeling as if I had actually been there. My mother's garden covered the earth.

Obviously the garden was much more than a practical vegetable patch. When I visited my parents later that year, I told my mother the dream and said, "I had no idea how important that garden was to you." She just smiled and nodded. But I still did not fully understand how much of her creativity and her love had gone into the garden, where she could justify such "indulgence" (she was having fun) by growing everyday food. Flowers would have been too much of a luxury, I think. But in the dream garden there were both flowers and vegetables together. The memory of this dream and the actual garden it evoked was in my mind when I heard one of my university students tell a folktale about a grouchy old man who fools death and the devil. It took a hard blow to bring garden, dream, and story all together. In the late 1980s my mother was told she had cancer. My visits became more frequent, two or three times a year instead of once at Christmas, and during my visits she asked me to repeat some of the stories she had heard me tell in the past.

The one story I wish I had told her was an odd one I had just heard from a student in my folklore class. At first I didn't connect it with my mother or her garden, because this was not implicit in the folktale as it was told. I was slow to see the possibilities, but as I understood them the story began to bloom.

The folktale is popularly known as "Wicked John and the Devil" (AT Type 330). There are hundreds of similar stories collected in Europe and Euro-America. One index lists titles of 24 collections with variant texts, from England and Ireland, France, Italy, Norway, Iceland, the southern United States, and Maritime Canada (Ashliman 1987, 72). Two southern variants follow the usual pattern of the story (Chase 1943, 172; Chase 1948, 29). In these a crotchety old man uses wishes granted by St. Peter to outwit both death and the devil, but as a result he is not permitted to enter either heaven or hell and must wander the earth forever, carrying a coal from hell.

The story told casually by my folklore student, Chris Barsanti, was unusual. He identified it as "a gypsy story," but did not list his source, so I have been unable to identify the exact text. It does not match any of those I have explored, so I assume that it was his original interpretation—and I so credit him. His story is atypical because the protagonist is a more pleasant character, and also because he manages to trick his way into heaven by using a fourth wish, one more than what we expect in folktales.

This intrigued me, as did the nature of the wish: The man says, "Where my old hat is, there I will be."

There are some folktales that reach beyond the entertaining qualities of the story, and we may be unaware of why a particular tale is so instantly absorbing. This was just such a story for me, and I began to tell it soon after I heard Chris Barsanti's version. It took many months of performance for the story to begin to reveal its connections with my own life, and even longer to find its connections to my mother and her garden. Since I was telling the story rather than studying it, I cannot remember quite how and when my mother and her garden began to influence it. The old hat offered me a clue, since it is in both the story and in my mother's life, and probably in the dream too if I had looked at the peg it hung on before stepping out the back door.

By the time I sent my mother a tape of the story in 1990, the old man had been firmly replaced by an old woman, less crotchety but no less wily. I put her in to amuse my mother, but that woman has refused to leave, being entirely comfortable with her place in the story as I tell it. She is not my mother, but for me she is a kind of memorial to my mother. Here is my text, "Old Woman and Her Hat," as it has evolved over several years of telling.

An old woman sat under her old apple tree, enjoying a bright fall day. She was remembering the vegetable garden she once kept before age and infirmity caused her to abandon it. She thought about all the things she had grown. "Ah, those ripe red tomatoes and the crisp green lettuce—I can almost taste them right now. Oh well, I still have my crisp juicy apples, and I'm sure this old tree will live well beyond me."

Suddenly a voice broke into her thoughts: "Kind woman, may I have one of your apples? I'm so hungry and weary, even an old dry one would nourish me." She looked up and saw an old man, a beggar, leaning on a gnarled walking stick. Now, no one had ever called her "kind" in her entire life, and indeed she was not. In fact, she was known to be a bit sharp-tongued and short-tempered. His voice, and the memories of her garden, made her feel warm and generous. She said to the ragged man, "Take what you want. I have more than enough for myself." She even stood up and picked three of the ripest apples that hung just within reach.

The man took the smallest of the apples and ate it slowly. As he swallowed the last bite, a strange thing happened. She watched in amazement as the old beggar began to transform. His bent back straightened and he grew taller, his shabby clothing began to fill with light, his face glowed like the full moon. He smiled down at the woman as he spoke: "As you can see, I am St. Peter, the guardian of heaven's gates. I walk this earth looking for acts of kindness and generosity, and when I find them I am delighted. Old woman, I offer you three wishes, one for each of these apples."

Being a practical woman, she began to look around her small yard and inside her small house. She chose her wishes from what she saw. Her first wish was that anyone who picked an apple from her tree would be stuck fast until she released them. Her second was that anyone who sat in her favourite rocking chair would be unable to rise until she permitted them to do so. Her last wish was that anyone who looked into her rain barrel would be pulled in and held there until she let them out.

St. Peter, exasperated that she hadn't wished herself into heaven, cried out, "I've never done this before, but I'm going to give you one more wish. Use it well!" Again she looked around her, and when she saw her old gardening hat hanging on a peg beside her door, she said, "Ah, there's my fourth wish—wherever my hat is, I will be." The glow left St. Peter's face. He frowned down at her. He grumblingly acknowledged her wishes with a gruff "So be it." He stalked off without a backward glance, muttering to himself as he went, "Silly old fool. She'll get what she deserves."

More years passed, and the old woman went about her life from one day to the next, as she had always done. One bright morning a knock came at her door. She slowly opened the door, and there stood the Angel of Death. She was surprised to see that the Angel of Death was a young woman, who said to her in a calm voice, "I've been sent to claim you now. Please come." The old woman, thinking quickly, said, "I'll be right with you. I just have to find my old gardening hat. But you must be tired after such a long journey. Why don't you refresh yourself with an apple from my old tree." Death, who was rarely greeted so politely, was happy to oblige—and was soon stuck fast to the tree. "Let me go!" she demanded. "I have many more people to visit today." "Oh yes, I can do that," said the old woman, "but only if you grant me seven more years." Death had to agree. When she was freed she went away, grumbling like St. Peter, and vowing to return.

Indeed she did return, exactly seven years later. When the old woman opened her door she saw that Death was now older and wiser. "I won't touch that tree," she snapped. "You'd better come with me straight away." "But of course I will," the old woman answered. "I've been waiting for you—I just have to get my old hat. I'll be only a moment, so why don't you rest in my rocking chair while you wait." Death sat down, and rested much longer than she wanted to. She only won her freedom by promising the old woman seven more years.

Time passed as it always does. The old woman was too busy to notice, except for her growing aches and pains. At the end of seven years the apple tree still bloomed, the rocking chair still rocked, and her rain barrel was full of fresh water. This time when the knock came she opened her door expecting to see Death even older and warier, but it was not the Angel of Death who stood there. It was the Devil himself. "Death has given you up, so now you belong to me. Come along now, and no tricks! I know all about the apple tree and the rocking chair." "Oh, I wouldn't think of it," she said. "But if you know about the apple tree and the chair, then you must also know that I never go anywhere without my old hat. While I get it, why don't you take a nice cool drink from my rain barrel? You must be thirsty after such a long journey from such a very hot place." The Devil, who was rarely offered anything so pleasant, was happy to accept. And when he lifted the wooden lid and reached in for a sip of fresh water, into the barrel he went. "You crafty old woman! Let me out immediately. I have important souls to claim—politicians, for example, and others more important than a silly old woman!" And so she won another seven years.

"Perhaps I could start another garden, just a small one," she said to herself. But she forgot, too busy enjoying the days and weeks and months of those seven years. The apple tree went on bearing fruit, losing leaves, blooming again, and putting out more fine apples, for seven more years.

At the end of this time no one appeared. She waited for that last knock at the door, but it did not come. She was weary of life, having lived far beyond her years, and found herself actually wishing to see the Angel of Death again, or even the Devil himself. But finally she understood that neither Death nor the Devil would come to her now. "Oh dear, she said, I'll have to find my own way to the other world." And being a practical woman she set off right away, taking only her old gardening hat with her, and one fine ripe apple to eat along the way. She walked farther than she had ever walked in her entire life, and at last came to a crossroad. She set off on the road to the right, and gradually it began to descend. After some time she found herself at the gates of hell, and knocked loudly. The Devil himself answered and saw who was there. "I forbid you to enter here, old woman. You don't belong here. Go away—go up to the other place."

She retraced her steps and eventually found herself back at the crossroad. This time she took the road to the left, which led her up and up to the very gates of heaven. St. Peter answered her knock, but when he saw her he called out, "Old woman, you had four chances to wish yourself into heaven and you refused. I cannot let you in." He began to close the great gates of heaven. They moved slowly together, and just as they were about to swing shut the old woman remembered the hat on her head, whisked it off and tossed it inside. It rolled and rolled until it came to a stop at the base of an ancient tree. And that is where she found herself, standing in heaven looking up at that towering tree that seemed to have been there forever. Slowly she sat down under the tree, reached over and placed her old hat on her head, and leaned back against the warm bark of the tree, enjoying the beauty all around her. She felt the seeds of the apple in her pocket and remembered the tree in her front yard.

"Well now," she said, smiling to herself, "this looks like a fine place to start a new garden." And she was surely right.

I am not at all certain that my mother ever felt that she was surely right. I think of her now as always wavering firmly between decisions. Perhaps six children would bring that out in a person. She told me, when I visited her last a few months before she died, that she had been agonizing over heaven and hell. She said, with an embarrassed smile, "I haven't thought about that since Sunday school. Now isn't that silly, to be worried about that old Sunday school story?" Her words stayed with me when I returned home. Soon after this visit, as I was telling the story of the stubborn old man, I saw how it addressed the issue of finding one's place in the afterworld. Other connections with my mother began to fall into place.

Several aspects of the story as I had heard it opened to new possibilities. There was the unusual granting of a fourth wish, which gave the protagonist another chance to save himself, and with an ordinary and familiar object—an old hat. His tenacity evoked my mother's determination to go on under adverse conditions: past illnesses, the early deaths of two of her eight children, constant economic hardships, the suicide of her nephew, and now a fatal disease that she had long feared. She had lived her own hell and could still hold up her head. I could imagine her confronting St. Peter with wishes that seemed foolish to him but very down to earth for her: Don't climb my tree, don't sit in my rocking chair, stay out of my rain barrel. And of course, the hat used to gain entry to heaven conjured up a battered cloth hat that hung near the back porch long after my mother no longer used it. But she herself was not yet "in" the story for me.

It was when I returned home after that last visit I decided to send her the story on tape, thinking she would appreciate the cleverness of the old man at tricking himself into heaven. When I began to tape the story I found myself changing the protagonist from male to female, just to try it out. I suppose I had the unconscious hope that she might find herself in the story and perhaps gain a bit of peace. While I never found out whether or not she actually heard the tape, telling the story with her in mind permanently altered it for me. It became a living story instead of an interesting folktale. I must emphasize that it is a story inspired by my mother, not about my mother.

As I have already said, folktales and other metaphorical expressions do not share a one-to-one relationship with ordinary reality. Yet they still can, like dreams, speak deep truths about lived experiences. People have been exploring the deeper meanings of folktales for more than a century and from many different points of view—artistic, historical, social, psychological. I suggest that no final interpretation is possible because every response is unique and personal. Even a single tale type like "The Smith Outwits the Devil" has as many possibilities as there are people who have heard and told it. Mine is only one of countless interpretations, and it evolves as I continue to tell the story. And, of course, this is exactly how new variants and versions arise throughout human history.

I did not consciously rework this story with the intention of transforming it into a story about my mother. I am aware, however, of the changes that have arisen through the actual telling. The apple tree, incidental in the story as I heard it, takes a more central role, echoing the grapefruit tree that grew for 40 years in the backyard. The old woman's memories of her garden shifted my view of the protagonist's character; I thought of the unending care and patience that a garden requires, and realized that a gardener would be practical and down-to-earth rather than as mean or greedy, as the hero (often a blacksmith) is typically depicted in this tale. Story characters become real to a teller as a story becomes familiar. This does not mean they take on the personas of known people, which could in fact limit a story, but rather that they take on their own life. When this happens, in oral and written literature, it is a gradual and often unconscious evolution. It was only after many tellings that I could see, through the story, my mother's actual cronish qualities in a positive light. Crones know what they want and they aren't worried about their feminine image. They know how to work with earth and plants, and they are not overawed by supernatural forces. Why not capture the Angel of Death in an apple tree and the devil in a rain barrel? In the end of this story it is the woman's choice to seek out her fate rather than having it forced upon her. I can imagine my mother smiling when she heard how the old woman was banned from hell, when she herself was worried about ending up there, in "that old Sunday school story."

For me this story of wishes, gardens and trees, helpful and threatening figures, and the old woman who succeeds in finding a path into paradise, is a living story. It reveals my mother's struggles with adversity, in growing her garden and in facing death; it is exactly this reality, this actuality, that allows me to continue telling it with a sense of integrity, not as lived history but as living metaphor.

I do not have a sentimental image of my mother sitting under an ancient tree in paradise, planning her new garden. That is not the point of the story, and would narrow its meaning rather than broadening it. For me the story echoes her difficult life, her garden, and her love and respect for stories as well. All of these factors continue to provide living energy for an old tale that is entirely relevant today, not because it is a consciously re-formed "modern" folktale, but rather a traditional story that continues to speak in a new voice. This is how folktales express truths that both encompass and transcend personal history.

Here is another example of how archetypes challenge our too-narrow perceptions. I dreamed that I am walking down a long hall with a friend and say to her, "Oh, this is another one of my hall dreams." She looks at me and smiles in recognition, as my daughter Rachel smiled in "The Golden Woman." I notice her smile, and try to explain the situation to her.

"Listen! I know this is a dream and we can ask for something we really want." I think about it carefully and realize my mother has not appeared in any dreams lately, so I say with resolve, "I know—I want to see my mother."

Instantly the scene shifts and I am looking into a dimly lit space that seems to be a small domed room or a cave. I can see the figure of a robed woman, her face covered by a cowl, seated in a chair right in the centre. It is too dark to see who this is but I am sure it is not her. I reject the image, saying in a disappointed voice with a touch of anger, "That's not my mother." As the scene fades and I move toward the waking world, I vaguely notice that this robed woman is somehow connected with a crescent moon and, I think, stars. I suppose if I had been raised as a Catholic I would immediately identify her as Mary, but that does not feel right to me, somehow. This is a darker archetype, deeply earth-connected in spite of the moon and stars she seems to be associated with. Her feet are firmly on the ground. I feel the same dual sense of elation and frustration as in other disturbing dreams that I was not ready to accept. The frustration arises when I send away a powerful figure, as I sent away my buffalo in adolescence, and lose whatever they might have to offer. The elation comes from knowing that such figures do not give up easily, and will eventually return in an altered form. We will meet her in the guise of various crones later in this book.

I have waited for another chance for the seed that wants to be planted, and perhaps that is how I finally experienced "The Golden Woman," who passes through all four elements and rises transformed. With this in mind, I can see how my mother's garden covers the earth.

Tanis' poem, "Horizon," based on my dream, is a fruitful way to conclude (MacDonald 2000, 69-70). Her words transform the dream in ways that I resisted at first, since they were not "correct" in terms of my dream details. I reminded myself that artistic re-creation is what I am exploring here, and let the dream go free:

I'm not over the swept threshold
of my mother's house when she says
come see what I've done with the garden.
Treading through the cool dark rooms,
I am a needle steadied for darning,
the fuss-and-fix-it that made me,

that chafed me. But by the back door,
on that single step that passes as a porch,
I stop, rooted, because

my mother has finally done it.
She's gardened the surface of the earth entire,
hoed and watered the world into neat rows,
tinkered the planet into good working order.
She's planted all the way to the horizon,
its calm line drawn perpendicular to
sixty staked rows of stringbeans,
pulling the sun down each night,
yanking it up each morning. Raspberry canes
swarm in the middle distance, snarling
their fruit forward. Rhubarb begs
for pies, heliotrope dogs the sun,
the spider-spread of portulaca
webs the soil at my toes.

My mother walks the rows,
bends to turn a tomato and show
me the blush, how the sun ripens
one side first.

The Creature in the Kitchen: Helpful Animals

From my mother I learned to appreciate what grows from the earth, while my father inspired my curiosity about the creatures that move on, under, and over it. He could sit on the back steps for hours watching the activities of the anoles, small lizards who lived in our coral rock fence. He could name all the birds that came regularly to my mother's garden, and was especially fond of the bright cardinals. In our early days in Florida, he took the family on Sunday "buffalo hunts" after church, out to rural areas to see cattle that we pretended were wild buffaloes. And he was the one who introduced me to horses.

My father's respect for his fellow creatures came from an unhappy experience with a gun, a story that he told me more than once. As a boy he went squirrel hunting with his first gun, and was proud when he managed to hit his target. But when he saw the result, he swore never to deliberately kill any creature again, if he could help it, and developed a great interest in animals of all sorts. My mother, in contrast, had serious allergies to anything that had fur, which meant that his favourite dog Fanny (who, I believe, inspired my middle name of Frances), had to stay at his Detroit Sunoco station, and all the succession of cats we had over the years were strictly outside pets. We were allowed goldfish, but never managed to keep them alive for more than a few weeks, and they were not very compelling creatures, unlike the talking fish who turn up in folktales.

I remember my father, claiming that we needed pets since we had none at that time, trying to talk my mother into getting a monkey. She pointed out that he already had six monkeys—us—and asked why he wanted another, and he had to agree. It was my father who took us all to zoos in Detroit and Miami, and pointed out characteristics and habits, especially of the monkeys, and observed that we, as primates, were very much a part of the animal realm, not above it. This was a surprising thought to me then, and quite the opposite of what I was learning in Sunday school. It has stayed with me resolutely in waking life and in dreams, which might be a good reason why I continue to meet so many animals, and why they are friendly more often than they are threatening. Except for bears and other large predators.

I still go to zoos, though I am much less comfortable with caged animals now, all the more so after I dreamed I myself was a caged animal. Creatures in their own habitats still intrigue me, though I am not foolhardy like those who risk bear and bison attacks in Yellowstone Park and elsewhere. Still, I have horrified a friend by stroking a harmless rat snake on a mountain walk in California, and distressed another friend by whistling (from a safe distance) to a wild lynx in the Canadian shield area of eastern Manitoba. The lynx was curious too, and stopped to stare at me with its piercing yellow eyes before bounding away. It was exciting, moving, to have this brief exchange with a creature in its own habitat. My long-standing regard for animals of all kinds, and their subsequent roles in dreams and folktales, certainly contributes to my comfort with creatures, wild and domesticated.

I wondered, then, why I had so many animal dreams that were distressing, and was relieved to read that such dreams are common in childhood as we meet our inner forces (talking rats, for example) but do not yet understand them (Van de Castle 1994, esp. chapter 12). So we run or wake up. But bears continued to follow me into adult dreaming, as we see in the following chapter, and horses were also frequent challenging dream creatures. I was dismayed to read in Van de Castle's book that animal dreams are far less common for adults than for children, and may signal immaturity. I did not like that at all, and then realized that the author did not consider the powerful aspects of dream creatures, only their frightening potential. Perhaps this bias arises from the fact that western cultures tend to view animals as "other," and definitely as inferior. Many people I know do not even like animals, other than their well-behaved pets.

I have learned more about domestic animals from my good friend Norlaine, who keeps sheep in Maryland, and who tried to teach me to milk her patient cow, Louise. She was as surprised as I was that many people are uncomfortable with animals, even with domesticated sheep and cattle. She laughed when I told her what happened several years ago when my husband and daughter and I were in Ireland. They had got well ahead of me, and when I caught up I saw them halfway up a hill gesturing wildly for me not to come closer. "There's cattle down there," my husband called. At the base of the hill stood four black yearlings, looking more curious than threatening. I approached slowly, waved my hands at them and called out firmly, "go home." They moved off nonchalantly while my husband and daughter climbed down warily, looking at me with surprise and a hint of respect. Rachel informed me that black cattle were sacred to Anya, the Celtic divinity whose hill we had just climbed.

Horses are still my favourites, now more in memory and in dreams than in actuality. My father took me riding for the first time on my sixth birthday, on a real horse and not a pony from the local pony ring, and from there I graduated to riding lessons in junior high school. But it has been a long time since I had a good fast ride. This happened several years ago when I was visiting my sister Jolene in Orlando. Her youngest daughter offered to take me riding on her horse "Lady," a name that did not describe this horse at all. She was a headstrong mare who had to be reined in with a very firm hand to prevent her from turning around and cantering back to my sister's trailer at full speed. When we got beyond the halfway point of our ride, my niece yelled back to me, "You can let her go now." But she forgot to tell me something important as I let her go and went racing down a dirt road, elated to still be able to stay in the saddle at a gallop, waving gaily to the people sitting on their porches as I swept by. What I did not know was that the last house on the road had been Lady's former home. In the middle of her gallop she came to an abrupt stop at the mailbox in front of that house while I went on, sailing over her head. I have a clear image of lying flat on my back with Lady looking down at me, wondering how I got there and why I could not breathe.

It is not surprising that the challenging horse I dreamed of a few years later was called "Lady." In this dream I was walking by a stable when I was called over by two anxious-looking stable hands. They told me that my horse, "Lady," was ready, and warned me that she had never been ridden. She was a beautiful brown mare with a mischievous gleam in her eye. As I approached her, Lady tossed her head and threw off her bridle. She stared at me boldly, daring me to put it back on. I still remembered the methods of control I learned in those long-ago riding lessons, but quickly rejected the idea of forcing the bridle back between her teeth by holding her nose forcefully. "She's not that kind of horse," I thought to myself, and Lady seemed to read my mind. Instead of trying to force her, I asked politely if I could put the bridle back on, and she nodded her head. After I managed that tricky procedure, I asked if I could get on her bare back, and she turned herself for me to mount. As we began to walk away from the stable, she silently let me know through dream telepathy that she wanted carrots, and not the store-bought sort but fresh ones that were large, orange, and twisted. She was asking for wild ones that push their way up through hard soil and around rocks and other obstacles—as wild as Lady herself. She was very specific, and I knew she would not settle for less.

I found exactly the carrots she wanted, a rich dark orange colour with the dirt still clinging to them, and brought them back to her. I was stunned to see Lady trying to climb on a bicycle, and asked her what she was doing. She spoke to me, saying that it was time to go. I responded, perplexed, "But you're a horse, you don't need a bicycle." "Oh," she said, and got off. I woke up smiling at the cartoon-like image of cantankerous Lady trying to get herself positioned on a bicycle, but when I told the dream to a friend, she distressed me by asking, "Why did you diminish that power-animal?" I recalled the dream in which I asked to see my mother and then rejected the robed archetypal woman who appeared to me, and saw that I had done the same with Lady. This leaves me with a continuing feeling of incompletion in such dreams. Lady has given me other chances, appearing in a more agreeable temper in other dreams, perhaps in recognition of my initial decision to respect her instead of challenging her forcibly. But she never asked for carrots again, nor tried to ride a bicycle.

It seems to me that this dream at its best shows the benefit of finding a balance of authority and of graciousness, of taking command of your artistic medium but not being too unyielding. To take this analogy further, I suggest that a metaphoric horse—any artistic medium—will carry us willingly if we do not force it to submit to overly stern handling. But even then it might forget that it is a horse and try to get on a bicycle, and from there on you might be on an adventure worthy of Magritte or Dali.

This message of not being excessively determined and goal-oriented is strong in both dreams and folktales, though it seems to go against much of what we learn in life. Helpful creatures who offer advice, assistance, or magical objects often do so precisely because they have not been compelled to do so. When I began to study folktales I was interested to discover what central roles animals—especially horses—play in these stories. There is hardly a tale without a helpful creature prowling in it somewhere. These need not be large animals, either, but may be humble insects like ants and bees. They often help merely because protagonists, unlike their cruel siblings, notice the small creatures and avoid doing them harm. Other helpful creatures are actually bewitched people in need of transformation; foxes who beg to have their heads cut off so they can become princes again, swans who turn into maidens, mice who can do surprising things, and of course that annoying frog in the Grimm tale who, by the way, is not kissed but thrown against a wall. In all cases, creatures respond to respect and generosity, as did Lady.

One of my favourite examples is a Polish story I heard in 1970 from Sophie Mukoid, a Polish-born student in my husband's history class. It is a variant of AT Type 313, "Wife as Helper in the Hero's Tasks," but Sophie called it "The Red String" because that was how she remembered it from childhood. The woman transformed into a white duck has echoes of a swan princess.

The hero had been unknowingly promised to a sorcerer by his parents, but because he had helped the duck-woman by not stealing her feather cape, she agreed to help him. When the sorcerer proposed three impossible tasks, she was able to magically accomplish the first two in only one night: to clear and plant wheat on untillable land and make pancakes out of the flour, and to make a lake in a wasteland, create an island in the middle, and build a bridge to the island. In the final task the hero was to ride and subdue a fierce black horse who, the woman warned him, would be the wizard himself. He succeeded and was released, rescued the duck-woman from her enchantment, and rode away.

When the sorcerer followed them, she used her own skills to protect them with magical objects she tossed behind her—a comb that became a forest, a scarf that became a fierce storm, and a mirror that became a lake in which the sorcerer was eventually drowned. Other folktale animals assume human form only at the end of the story, and few are quite so resourceful as she was, but without their help the protagonists would fail to survive to the end of the story. Imagine Cinderella—Grimm, not Disney—without the doves who provide her beautiful apparel and later warn the prince that he has the wrong women (the stepsisters, who in turn cut off pieces of their feet to fit the tiny shoe). And where would Dick Whittington or the hero of "Puss in Boots" be without their ingenious cats?

My dream animals have rarely been so obviously helpful or clever, but they are friendly from the start, or at least not so obviously threatening as are the beasts in the following chapter. For example, the assertive horse in the Russian tale of "The Little Humpback Horse" is one of many who not only give advice but command that the hero follow it, and reprimand him firmly when he fails. Lady, my dream horse, might have filled this role admirably if the dream had gone on longer. I was certainly willing to follow her advice.

Smaller creatures have come in and out of my life as well, tame and wild. There have been the various childhood pets like outside cats, short-lived goldfish, Jolene's unlucky parakeet, and a number of hamsters and rabbits, all expert jail-breakers who rarely stayed with us for long. I have had a long succession of my own cats over a 30-year period, each of them a master of living in the moment.

In dreams I have met monkeys, cats, deer, horses, birds large and small, and occasional snakes. As I said earlier, in the very first dream I remember, I was faced by a talking rat, but I was too frightened to find out if this was a helpful creature or not. In the dream my mother had sent me downstairs to a small dressing room (which did not, in fact, exist) to bring her a hairbrush. The room was lovely and comforting, with walls and curtains in a peach-toned pink shade. There was a white-topped counter backed by a large mirror. The brush lay beside a pearly white sink. As I reached for it I heard a voice, and saw the large rat sitting in the corner of the counter. He did not threaten me or even make a move, but his unexpected voice caused me to drop the brush and run, up the stairs and back into the waking world. I still regret not being able to remember his words. I am guessing that he might have said something as simple as, "Here I am," words that are open to any number of interpretations. I thought about this rat when I came across a fine Hopi legend in New Mexico in 1994, in which an ordinary mouse plays a heroic role (Kennard 1977).

Mouse lived on the edge of the pueblo, where the people called him "that dirty little field mouse." One day a hawk began killing the people's chickens and they were helpless to stop it, since it was not afraid of their weapons. People laughed when Mouse offered to help, but the chief agreed to accept his offer. Mouse dressed himself carefully as a warrior, painted himself and wore the tips of eagle feathers in his hair, and carried a tiny war club and his bow and arrows. He set up a pointed stick at the back entrance to his underground home, and taunted the hawk with his war song until the angry hawk flew down to catch him and was impaled on the stick. The people were amazed, and after that time they no longer called him "that dirty little field mouse." They called him Tusan Homichi, Warrior Mouse.

I am fond of this small champion, calm in his determination to help the people even though they revile him, like the stones on the mountain path in "The Water of Life." His modest example has helped me stay on the path of imagination. But I have not yet dreamed of mice, perhaps because I did not listen to what my enigmatic rat had to say.

In waking life I have met two memorable mice, and learned from them, as the hawk did in the story, just how fast a mouse can move. When we spent a year living with my sister Lois on Block Island, Rhode Island, I woke up early one morning to a familiar sound of our black cat chasing a mouse down the hall. I decided to rescue the mouse, and after a lot of futile dashing around, I managed to toss a dish towel over the darting creature. I carried it outside wrapped firmly, gave the towel a good shake, and sent the mouse flying to safety. No doubt it was back the next night, but that was its own decision to return to the field of battle. It would have benefitted from Tusan Homichi's example, using cleverness as much as speed.

I met an even more determined mouse in the closet of Gail Beck's house in Georgia. Somehow this adventurer had managed to get up to the highest shelf in the closet, where I had it backed into a corner with nowhere to go. It leapt straight at me, hit the floor running, and disappeared behind a large wardrobe on the other side of the room. We set traps for it and I was actually sad to hear one of them snap shut early in the morning, but when I got up to check the trap there was nothing in it. We gave up trying to catch Mighty Mouse, as he (or she) came to be called.

My favourite dream mouse appeared in one of my many performance anxiety stories, in which the half-hour I was supposed to have had been whittled down to two minutes. Since I had no time for any of the stories I had prepared, I decided to just see what would appear on its own, and was rewarded with a small gem. In it a mouse who lived in the igloo of an Inuit shaman wanted to learn how to heal, so he watched intently from the shadows as the shaman carried on his practices. When the shaman fell ill one day, shamans came from all over to help, and the mouse himself played a tiny drum and danced and sang in the shadows. When everyone had left, the shaman sat up, said, "I saw you down there. Come out and we'll learn together." And so that mouse did one day become a shaman himself. Like Tusan Homichi, he proved himself worthy of human respect.

These mice were determined survivors, but for cleverness, my dream monkeys are unrivalled. Unlike their capricious living counterparts, they have always been clearly helpful creatures in my dreams. Despite their potentially tricksterish dispositions, they have given trustworthy advice. For example, several years ago I went to sleep feeling anxious about a difficult meeting I was to chair the next day. In the dream I was walking along a path and noticed a monkey hiding behind a tree. As I approached it kept peeking out and chattering at me. At last I stopped to hear what the monkey wanted, and was surprised to hear it speak in a clear voice. It advised me to be cleverly cautious rather than confrontational: "If you don't have an army don't attack directly," it suggested. I followed the monkey's guidance, presenting a proposal tactfully and creatively and managing a tricky negotiation.

Monkey-like creatures in two other dreams were equally wise, though not of such immediate practical benefit. In one of these I am a caged cougar and a small ape shows me an evocative red symbol that releases us both from our cages. In the other, the dream figure is more enigmatic, teaching me that the line between threatening beasts and helpful animals is sometimes quite fine. This creature, like the rat in my earliest dream, seems to begin in a threatening guise but, when faced, turns out to be wise instead of menacing. Here is the dream.

I dreamed that I was visiting Miami, and, to my astonishment, was alone in the house that was always so full of people. I felt utterly at peace as I stretched out on the living room sofa enjoying my rare solitude. Suddenly I had a sense of foreboding that I was not alone after all, that something unpleasant was in the kitchen. I got up to look and saw a dark shape crouched in front of my mother's stove. Terrified, I turned and started to run for the front door. I stopped myself before I got to the threshold, saying something like, "Don't run away this time, just turn around." I willed myself to go in to the kitchen, where I knelt down and addressed a monkey-like figure politely though I was still full of fear. The only thing I could manage to say was, "Please tell me something," but this was enough. This creature turned to look at me and said slowly and calmly in a clear voice, "People are a little better than you think they are." While this might not seem like much of an answer, it was apparently just what I needed to hear, because I was instantly elated. I rushed out the front door, this time filled with joy instead of fear, and leapt up into the air to float ecstatically over the neighbourhood. The scenery below me was clear enough that I could have painted a picture of it as I floated over green palms and citrus and pine trees, house roofs and yards, and the square grid of roads spreading out from the white house sitting in its long yard on 101st Street. This time flying was not an escape but an expression of bliss, similar to what I feel when an artistic undertaking is going well.

My waking sense was as strong as my dream elation. The seemingly mundane message from the monkey-creature was like a small key unlocking a door I did not even know was there, and finding a room with a small treasure that belonged to me. This experience reminded me of "The Golden Key," a story with an enigmatic conclusion that comes toward the end of the Grimm collection (Grimm number 200 in Zipes 1988, 288-89).

In this brief story, a boy was out gathering firewood when he found a half-buried golden key and dug it out. "Where there's a key there must be a lock," he said to himself, and dug deeper until he found and unearthed an ancient iron chest, locked, of course. The golden key fitted the lock perfectly and the boy slowly began to lift the lid, but we are not told what the boy found in the old chest.

The story is deliberately left unfinished, hinting that the readers of the Grimm tales would find their own treasures in the "box" of the imagination. This is often true of dreams as well, since many end as enigmatically as the Grimm tale. The buried treasure is waiting to be discovered, and the dreamer is the one with the golden key. The challenge is that a dream is often more difficult to open to the light than a box is—and the key is invariably harder to find.

Sometimes the key might be found in the waking world, and might come from past or present incidents. For example, here is an enigmatic dream with a very different kind of treasure, an unexpected deer in my backyard, hiding in a heap of snow not unlike the one that revealed the golden key to the boy. Since the dreaming mind has a very different time sense than does the waking mind, this dream weaves together various incidents that might have inspired it years earlier. Imagination is patient, holding its treasures until the time is right, so let me explain relevant biographical details that I think influence this dream.

In the early 1980s my husband and I, with school-age Rachel and Nathaniel, spent almost a year living on tiny Block Island, Rhode Island with my youngest sister Lois and her family. The small school on the island was only a 15-minute walk from my sister's large house, so I walked them to school every morning and then continued on to the other side of the island for another 20 minutes or so down the gravel road and onto the beach. Sometimes I found deer tracks on the beach and followed these back up into the trees, wandering through wooded paths for as long as I could trace the tracks.

Deer were protected from hunters and wandered wherever they wished, including the steps of the town hall. Most islanders rightly considered them pests, but I was neutral. There was a shifting herd of about two dozen, so tracks were plentiful. I enjoyed occasional glimpses of them on my walks, admiring their grace and beauty, and their curiosity when they were bold enough to peek at me through the trees. One day I followed a promising trail well into the small forest and held to it as it grew narrower and narrower. I finally came to one of the old island stone fences, still standing firmly in the undergrowth. A deer could easily leap over but I could not, so I retraced the path back, watching for deer on the way. I imagined them watching me with amusement as I blundered my way through the underbrush.

When we returned to Winnipeg I was more alert to deer, and knew now how to identify deer paths in the walks my husband and I took in the forest preserve on the southern edge of the city. We were willing to get ourselves lost occasionally just for the fun of it, and saw occasional deer alone and in small groups as we wandered. This might be an important element in the deer dream I had several years after our Block Island adventures.

The dream was set in winter, which in Winnipeg means sub-zero temperatures and continuous snow cover. In the dream I was going out somewhere dressed very warmly, slogging through deep snow between my back door and the garage. I noticed an odd hump of snow in the centre of the backyard and went over to investigate. Suddenly the hump began to move as I watched with a hint of anxiety. It burst open before I had time to become fully fearful, and a deer stood up, shook itself off, and inspected me with a bold look worthy of Lady the mare. I looked back in surprise, wondering what would happen next. The deer began to dance gracefully in the snow, looking at me expectantly. I understood that it wanted to play, so I did. We danced and rolled around in the snow before the scene shifted back to the garage and I lost the story thread. I awoke feeling light and animated. This deer was quite unlike other dream deer I have met, openly playful rather than shy and vulnerable like other deer I have seen in dreams. If I had been the least bit hesitant it might well have turned aggressive, perhaps even threatening. It could have quickly grown sharp antlers, for example, or jumped at me with its sharp hooves. As in the dream with Lady, my willingness to see what might happen next allowed the dream to play itself out in a more satisfying way.

Also like the "Lady" dream, this dream went on to another scene that did not fit the story as it had progressed up to that point. The deer did not climb on a bicycle as Lady did, but simply faded out of the story as the dream shifted. I did not remember the rest of the dream when I woke up, which I see as an unconscious artistic decision; the dancing deer image was balanced and complete, not in need of further elaboration, so the dream-creator deleted the irrelevant scenes. This was done by the dreamer as artist, not by my judgmental waking self. I do not recall any other clear examples of dream editing, but I do know that dreams stay in mind when they are more coherent in storyline or imagery, that is, when they are more effective as artistic creations. We are already forming them artistically as we are in the middle of experiencing them. It is a delightful circle, not vicious at all, though sometimes frustrating.

I can trace other aspects of my deer experiences in the dream, and in waking life, to my interest in folktales. Story characters are often lost in the forest, as I was on Block Island, and as a result have some unexpected adventures. Also, curiosity is usually stronger than fear for story protagonists, and this is important in terms of influencing how a story or a dream will evolve. In popular belief we say that animals can "smell" fear; in dreams, where creatures are our own inventions, a feeling of fear might well call up a beast and not a beauty. For example, a tiny white alligator increased enormously when I grew frightened, his growth exactly matching my escalating fear. Surprisingly, when I willed myself to face the fear and open the door to this beast, I found a white unicorn standing there. But I am more likely to take the cowardly way out of fearful dreams by waking myself up. The dreams might have been different if I had been braver. What might my dark bison have become if I had managed to stay in the dream?

Here is a good example of this process. Once in a dream I dove into a luminous blue swimming pool, and immediately noticed that something dark was moving up through the water toward me. As in the deer dream, the movement was so quick that fear did not have time to get a grip on me. The dark shape, which could easily have been a shark, resolved itself into two white dolphins who swam straight up to me in a playful way, like the dancing deer. Because I am looking at dreaming as an artistic expression, I stress how unconscious creative decisions are constantly at work. The dream story is not planned in advance but develops as a dreamer participates in it. We are artist and actor at the same time in the unscripted adventure, improv theatre at its wildest. An apt motto would be "expect the unexpected."

Birds have always managed to surprise me with their utter unexpectedness, seeming to appear from nowhere in the midst of other dream action. A small bird tiny enough to sit in my palm rose up from my mother's periwinkles, for example. They are invariably too fast for me to really get a sense of their place in the dream. Eagles, on the other hand, have considerably more presence in their unexpected appearances, at first threatening but then helpful. In one dream from the early 1980s, a gigantic eagle appeared just as I was about to be overtaken by enemies.

In this dream there was some sort of ceremonial gathering in which two women, one young and one old, were going to be burned as a sacrifice. They were stretched out on the ground, tied down to stakes. As I watched in dismay I realized with horror that I was somehow a part of this initiation, since I saw that I was holding an axe. I decided to use the axe to rescue them. I cut the ropes and we all ran. As we dashed across a desert landscape a huge shadow passed over us and I looked up to see an enormous eagle. I screamed to the women to hide but it was too late. The eagle landed beside me and said, "Get on my back." I managed to get all three of us onto the eagle and we flew away to safety. We landed far away from pursuers and the eagle flew off, leaving a chant that was basic enough to be carried back to the waking world:

The eagle flies into the night
bearing gifts for those with sight

Not exactly great poetry, but the eagle was in a hurry. The three of us hearing this chant carried on the wind were deeply moved.

About ten years later I had two more eagle dreams, one in which an immense eagle was flying back and forth over my Winnipeg yard casting a shadow much like the earlier rescuer, but I was too afraid to stay in the dream since I was sure it was looking for me. I was annoyed when I woke myself up before the dream resolved itself. Obviously I had forgotten Eagle's heroic role in the earlier dream. Some months later Eagle came back, this time appearing too fast for me to escape. I was trying to fly but having trouble getting off the ground. Eagle swooped down, grabbed me by the shoulders, and flew up with breathtaking speed. Somehow I managed to pull myself on Eagle's back just as he began a nose-diving swoop. I was terrified, certain he was going to kill me, but instead Eagle said calmly, "Put your arms around me neck." When I obeyed, I was carried back up in an ecstatic flight. Changing my response from fear to acceptance allowed the dream to follow its rising path. Erotic? Of course. But much more. This was a stubborn Eagle, determined to get to me for a decade, and it is this generous tenacity that I have appreciated. My own change of heart allowed the recurring dream to finally resolve.

The action in folktales, too, evolves in response to how a character reacts to situations. For example, in many stories the youngest son or daughter is lost in the woods with no trail to follow. A small animal or bird indicates by its movement that there is a path, but this path only appears as the person trusts the creature and begins to walk as directed. The path then opens up before them as they move, and it closes up behind them. When they stop, the path stops. If it were an older sister or brother, the ones who do everything wrong, they would see the path closing up behind them and become overwhelmed by fear, but the younger protagonists just keep walking, looking ahead and not behind. As I learned in my experiences on Block Island and in the deer dream, trust in the adventure and willingness to take risks allowed me to follow curiosity, to be led astray into adventures. That is, to get off the expected path and to allow ecstasy to develop. And of course that is just what happens when artistic intuition leads us off in unplanned directions. Some of these paths might end in dead ends or rock fences that only a deer could clear, but others might lead into an unexpected dance of joy in the snow, or perhaps a wild flight on an eagle's back.

section II–
FOLKTALE WORLDS

The Monster Under the Bed: Beasts and Beauties

I admit that when I am alone at night, as I am just now in our cottage at Lake Winnipeg, I climb into bed very quickly. I joke with myself about it, a kind of whistling in the dark, but I get my feet off the floor fast. My mother recounted how I used to yell for her when I was three or four, insisting that there was an alligator under my bed. Alligators in Detroit? They must have come from stories my father read to Janet and me at bedtime—and they anticipated our eventual move to Florida. In any case, my mother would get down on her knees and patiently search for this beast under my bed, and report calmly that she could not find it. Sometimes it would be a bear, and I knew I could hear it growling under there even after I woke up. My mother would come in, check under the bed, and explain that what I heard was my father snoring. I was never convinced.

Thinking back on these nightly events, I am impressed with my mother's willingness to take my fears seriously instead of casting them off with those well-meant but unfortunate words, "Oh, it's only a dream. Go back to sleep." If you have ever been chased by monsters at any age of life, you know that these words are no comfort. By addressing my fears as genuine, my mother set an unconscious pattern for me that would eventually allow me to face these imaginative creatures and even to transform some of them creatively. More importantly, she verified that dreams were worthy of respect. Perhaps it was this early confirmation that allowed me to turn and face my buffalo in a much later dream.

I understand well that the dark under the bed and the dark in our imaginative minds are sources of archetypal beasts of great power. Freud and Jung were the master explorers of the unconscious mind, seeking out its dark figures and observing how they appeared abundantly in dreams and in folktales, not to mention our sleepless nights and difficult days. The beast is a ubiquitous folktale character, and as such can teach us some valuable lessons. The first lesson is not to run away, a real challenge when a beast approaches. The second is to learn how this creature might be transformed. With transformation comes whatever gift the beast has to offer.

I will summarize a composite story from the various texts I read while squatting uncomfortably in the small chairs of children's sections in libraries from Toronto to Miami, reading every collection of European and Euro-American tales I could find. This one, like others that pulled at me most persistently, is one of the many variants on the "beauty-and-the-beast" theme. These stories feature a host of creatures, everything from flop-eared hounds to dragonish serpents, not to mention bulls, bears, and lions. To give you an idea of the rich variety of individual stories in the general beauty-beast tale (AT 425), here are some of the titles I found in collections:

The Black Bull of Norroway
Bully Bornes (two variants)
The Girl That Married a Flop-eared Dog
The Glass Mountain (2 variants)
The Little Rusty Cook Stove
The Pretty Girl and Her Lost Children
The Red Bull of Norroway
Sorrow and Love
Three Feathers
White Bear Whittington
Wolf of the Greenwood
A Bunch of Laurel Blooms
Daub it with Clay
The Enchanted Cat
In the Cat-hide
The Rosy Story
The Small-tooth Dog

The story as I summarize it here took on its own life after several years of performances, inspired by texts from Appalachian and British traditions: that is, "The Black Bull of Norroway," "Bully Bornes," and "White Bear Whittington" above. It is definitely not the Disney version. Like others of its basic type, this story describes a double transformation: The Beast (usually but not always male) regains his human form while the Beauty (usually but not always female) attains resourcefulness and strength in the quest for the lost beast. To put it briefly, they both get what they ask for, though not quite what they expected.

The story begins, as these beast tales often do, with a father returning home with a gift for his daughters. In this variant he brings a wishing chair, and each daughter sits in it and wishes for a man. The youngest, perhaps not very interested in marrying, impulsively wished for "the ugliest one of all," and he soon arrived—as a huge dark bull. Since she herself called up the beast, she had to go with him. As she rode on his back he gave her the choice of having him as beast by night or by day, and she chose day, perhaps not wishing to have the monster under her bed in the dark. As a man by night he became her true husband, though of course she could not see him. Their nightly unions and daily travels continued as they visited the palaces of each of his three brothers. As they departed in the mornings, each brother in turn gave the heroine a walnut with these words of advice: "Open this only in your time of greatest need, when you feel your heart is breaking." She put the three walnuts in her pocket and forgot about them.

On the fourth day of their journey the bull told her that he now had to fight "The Old One," and that if he was victorious his enchantment would be over. He warned that the sky would turn blood red if he was defeated, brilliant blue if he succeeded. She was warned to sit without moving or speaking until she saw him again, or she would lose him. He disappeared over the hill and she heard the terrible sounds of a raging battle but sat without speaking or moving as she had been directed. At last she saw the sky begin to turn brilliantly blue, and was so relieved that she leapt to her feet. She knew instantly that she had lost him, and decided to seek him out instead of returning safely home.

As she set out she met a strange old woman in the forest, and asked politely if anyone had passed by. The crone described "a handsome man in a bloody shirt," and told her that in order to find him she would have to wear a pair of heavy iron shoes, and must walk until the shoes were worn through. She put on the iron shoes and began her long journey, walking until the shoes were finally worn through. She met a woman who was scrubbing a white shirt with three spots of blood, who told her that any woman who washed out the blood would be married to the lord of the palace. The heroine took the shirt and washed out the bloodstains easily, but it was torn from her hands by the other woman, who ran to the palace to claim her man.

The true bride remembered the three walnuts, and opened the first to discover inside it a tiny golden woman carding (combing) wool. She traded this to the false bride for one night with her husband, but could not wake him from a deep sleep brought on by the false bride's drugged wine. She traded the two remaining walnuts, containing golden women who spun and wove, and on the last night finally succeeded in awakening her husband. Completely free of his enchantment at last, he recognized and accepted her, and they were happily reunited. The fate of the false bride is another story. (My performing partner, Mary Louise Chown, and I have created a story that follows the adventures of this woman, who we have named Urtrid.)

This story follows the basic pattern of most of the beauty-beast stories I am familiar with. The beast is a powerful figure who does not come as a helper, as do the creatures in the previous chapter. It comes to challenge, and the person who can meet this challenge can eventually transform the beast as well as themselves. But of course these stories, and our own anguished dreams, do not tell us this overtly. Because we do not know, or we forget that we know, the outcome is almost always reached as much by chance as by design, and invariably more by plodding determination than by bravery. The protagonists stumble through stories as we stagger through our nightmares, trying to figure out what to do next. In the summarized tale the woman first loses her mate because she moves too soon, must find him and wash the bloody shirt, loses him again, and wins him back at last by trading her small treasures and compelling him to wake up and recognize her. Success usually comes as a result of the protagonist's willingness to track the monstrous creature instead of running, and, in the end, to express love and trust.

There are a number of tales in which a succession of women (often sisters) reject the beast and are killed by him. Often these women treat him with outright disrespect, or uncontrollable terror. They refuse to touch or be touched. The youngest sister is more willing, and succeeds in the transformation. With these narrative patterns in mind, we can look at the many variants of the murderous "Bluebeard" tale as failed beauty-beast stories, where the unredeemably beastly man is destroyed instead of being transformed.

The power of this dark figure in both negative and positive guises is sustained by villains in popular culture, notably films. Darth Vader from *Star Wars*, for example, played a role in a number of my dreams, and in the two where I managed to face the dark figure as the mask was removed, I found to my surprise that Darth Vader was a woman. In traditional tales and ballads there are, in fact, a number of beastly women. Old oral lore inspires Chaucer's "The Wife of Bath's Tale," for example, an elaborate literary retelling of traditional tales featuring a hideous woman who will not take no for an answer. In the powerful English ballad of "King Henry," a mythical king is confronted in his hunting lodge by a "fiend from hell" whose head touches the ceiling and whose teeth are like "tethering pegs." (This is Child #32. See Sargent/Kittredge 1932, 58-59.) She, for a woman it is, commands him to slay his horse, his dogs, and his hunting hawks, then devours them, skin and bones. Henry tries in vain to draw the line when she orders him into bed. When they awaken in the morning, he finds a beautiful woman beside him. Ah, but she is no genteel lady even then. She informs him that he is the only man she has met who has "given her all her fill," and, incidentally, all her will, which is the meaning of the woman-fiend's riddle in Chaucer's tale. In another ballad on the same theme, "Kemp Owyne," a beastly woman can only be disenchanted by three kisses from the hero, whom she forbids to touch her on pain of death. (Child #34, related to the Icelandic saga of "Hjalmter and Olver" in Sargent/Kittredge 1932, 59-61.)

It is important to note that the beast, for all its dark power, is really helpless to disenchant itself. In the story above, the beast (even in human form) cannot distinguish the false woman from the true until he is awakened. In both dreams and many story variants, the beast is often called up innocently by either the protagonists or by someone close to them—usually a father. Once called up, it cannot be ignored. And that brings me at last to the buffalo dream I mentioned earlier. This classic archetypal dream occurred sometime during my first year of junior high school, an unhappy and distressing time. One night I went to bed feeling heavily burdened by adolescent life, afraid that I could not bear five more years of school. I wished for a peaceful dream that would be a balm for my anxieties, not knowing at the time that I was asking for more than I thought I was. The only true balm is a cure, not an escape, but the cure is not necessarily pleasant. The dream began peacefully enough, but then it went its own way, not mine.

I was walking down 101st Street, past the houses of many of my friends, with no goal in mind, feeling completely calm. (Only after years of dreaming would I begin to understand that sublime peace in my dreams is usually a sign that trouble is on the way.) It must have been early summer, my favourite season, because the grass growing beside the sidewalk was a rich green and not the brown of late summer. I looked ahead and saw that I would soon come to the intersection of 101st Street and Seventh Avenue, the main road through our neighbourhood. Much later in life I would learn that crossroads are archetypal places of transformation, but in the dream I only saw it as a place I knew well, and continued toward it innocently. As I neared the intersection I could see a dark shape in the distance, moving slowly and steadily toward me from the west. I continued to walk, watching as the shape grew larger, and resolved itself into a buffalo, huge and dark and threatening. I saw that we were going to reach the crossroad at exactly the same moment, and tried to turn and run. Unfortunately my feet stuck to the ground—a commonplace situation in dreams—and I forgot that I knew how to fly. I had to turn back and face the buffalo, and when I did I saw that it was patiently waiting for me. I did not look at the face of this animal, only at its hooves. I was paralysed with terror but managed to stammer out, "You're spoiling my dream. Go away!" And it did, turning and going off to my right, headed north on Seventh Avenue. I still recall the feeling of exhilaration I had on waking, as if I had actually faced and overcome some overwhelming force in my life. This sense was so strong that it affected my general attitude at home and at school for the next few months. The dark beast had retreated for the moment, but would return to other dreams in altered form.

Such a powerful force, overwhelming as it is, also holds a wealth of creative energy. I saw my dream in a different light in an intriguing interpretation by Tanis MacDonald in her poem "Buffalo." Her words capture my sense of fear, sadness, and awe in the dream, and also the waking situation that inspired it, particularly the loss of my childhood friend:

My best friend, my saviour
against the daily scrape,
is moving away. She tells me
in the voice I will use later when
I am grown and must tell my mother
she is too old to drive. My friend's
voice is moving, tearing a great snarl
in the earth, a humped rift between
us. The air crowds my skin. I walk
for miles in that August purgatory,
I count sidewalk cracks or sneak looks
at the junior high squatting like
a brick toad seven blocks away.
Over and over I watch her father's car
fade into a dark dot on the horizon
and I walk far enough that the dark dot
on the horizon grows nearer, gathers
bulk, swallows the distance between
us. I lower my head but can't escape
the musk and mange, a tang ranker
than cattle. A buffalo stands before
me, rude as a push. It shifts its bulk,
its hooves sink into the road tar, we
are glued in place, stuck. The buffalo
wheezes a soft adenoidal huff, unwell
despite its mass. It wants. It dares me to
look in its watery eye, shiny and black as
a snooker ball. Endgame. I turn and let
the slump of my spine accuse her –
You're ruining everything, go away.
I shut my eyes and hear a faint suck of tar
and a steady clop of hooves, the smell
recedes to a sniff, a whiff, then nothing.
The even rows of houses, the blank
birdless sky say nothing. The tar oozes
in and erases the footprints, dulls the creaking
sway of a beast waiting my command.

Tanis' words capture the wonderful ambivalence of my dream, and hint at other beauty/beast stories as well. Buffalo left the dream because I asked, but never left my imagination. I wondered for years what the creature might have said if I had not sent it away. Did it have a message for me, or perhaps an explanation of its appearance?

Years later I had a chance to answer my own question when I was asked by a dream counsellor to retell the dream from the buffalo's point of view. I tried to refuse, still unwilling to face the darkness even after all that time, but then agreed to try. I was certain that it would be impossible for me to become that shadowy figure. I was wrong. What I experienced would not have surprised those familiar with Jungian psychology, but it certainly surprised me at that time. As soon as I closed my eyes and imagined the buffalo, I was a formless mass of energy growing and taking shape in the darkness. Something seemed to be calling me up, commanding me to evolve and to move forward. With each movement I could sense myself assuming form and power, finally understanding that I had become a large dark buffalo with enormous strength. I looked down the road ahead and saw a skinny young girl who seemed to be calling to me, and I went to her willingly, ready to respond to whatever she wanted. To my surprise, as soon as I reached her I could see that she was terrified, and when she commanded me to leave, I had to obey. I walked out of the dream wondering what she wanted of me, why she had called me up. In other words, the buffalo had the same questions I had as the dream-girl—"What's happening here? "

I felt, in the words of Tanis' poem, that the beast was indeed "waiting my command." I had a feeling of deep compassion for that frightened little girl and also for the buffalo, called up and then turned away. Surprisingly, I also had some sense of amusement, a lightness of heart that only made sense to me when I thought about the deer that danced out of the snow and inspired me to play. If I had allowed buffalo to dance, I might have lost my terror.

My experience as the buffalo opened the dream up wide and I could understand beastly figures from an altered point of view, not only in dreams but in folktales as well—and also everyday living with its many overwhelming aspects. The dark beings that rise from the depths of our imaginative unconscious can be, among other things, sources of power, waiting to be asked to share their imaginative strength with us. This is an effective method of finding the creative power in distressing dreams instead of rejecting them as nightmares. After all, we ourselves generate and empower our own beasts, and we deserve to find out what they have to offer. That is, what are we trying to tell ourselves that might be of creative value? Or to put it in artistic terms, what creative problem are we struggling with that requires a new perspective from us? For certain there is a gift being offered, when we are ready to receive it. My friend Gail Beck had one full night of animal dreams, first finding herself in an odd animal farm and then at an animal show:

> So this was either a festival or a circus, I'm not sure which, and there were at least three animals but I don't have a clear recollection of all of them. One of them may have been a puma. I was concerned about the way the animals were being treated. I became aware that one of them was a huge buffalo, elephant sized, who had black, woolly hair, curly, with splotches of grey that gave him a salt-and-pepper appearance. He was huge! I saw that this buffalo was chained and penned, the chain was around his neck as far as I could tell. I was most concerned about this magnificent animal being held in captivity like that. I was not afraid for myself even though this animal was huge, not even when the pen disappeared, which it did eventually.
>
> As the pen disappears, this animal communicates to me (not in speaking), "Don't worry, I know how to handle this." And the chain he was tethered with began to diminish in size so it became like a piece of jewellery, and about that point he began to walk away from me, and riding on his back up near the head, with legs dangling down like a bareback rider, was a woman with dark hair. He leaves behind, for me, a carved egg that's probably ivory, and on the top over the broad end of the egg, is carved a long-petalled flower. If I had to name it, it would be a poinsettia, two layers of long petals and some leaves hanging down. I had an incredibly good feeling when I woke up, very warm and satisfying (conversation, December 1999).

Gail shifted into present tense in the second half of the dream, as she became more caught up in remembering the details—the tethering chain that become a necklace, and the parting gift of the carved ivory egg. When she told me the dream initially, she ended her description by saying, "I have got to paint that egg." When I asked her to retell the dream so I could put it down here accurately, she forgot the ivory gift, and was surprised when I reminded her. She immediately got out her sketchbook and began a pencil drawing, commenting as she drew, "Well, the egg is life, and life is flowering." I saw, in her quick sketch, the unique fruit born by the tree in "The Water of Life."

It is intriguing that such a massive primeval beast would still be appearing in dreams today, straight from the walls of ancient cave paintings. The bison, of course, was also a central figure in North American aboriginal sacred narratives and dreams. I recall the story but not the source of a dream related by a Plains Cree dreamer who was also pursued by a buffalo. The dreamer ran as fast as he could but heard the beast thundering along behind him. When at last he collapsed in utter exhaustion, the buffalo caught up with him, leaned over him and said politely, "Why are you running? I just wanted to tell you something." This dreamer did not reveal what the buffalo told him, as this information is a gift for the dreamer only; telling it may cause the gift to lose its potency. The challenge for me and for the Cree dreamer was to overcome fear so that the beast could deliver the message. For Gail the challenge was to take the gift into her waking world of artistic expression.

Dark and dangerous creatures in folktales drew me in much the way I was fascinated by the bad sisters and evil witches. Traditional folktales offer more human-like figures as the true villains—giants and ogres, trolls and goblins, devils and demons, hags and sorcerers. In contrast, the beasts—lions, bulls, bears, serpents, and other savage beings, may look like villains, but they are almost always positive figures awaiting a transforming touch to reveal their true nature. In the Grimm tale of "Snow White and Rose Red," for example, the sisters meet two intimidating figures, a bear and a demanding dwarf (Grimm #161, and AT Type 426). The dwarf is irredeemably evil and is eventually vanquished by the bear, who then becomes a prince. You know the ending, of course. In this case he conveniently has a younger brother, so both sisters can live happily ever after.

My dream bears have had a similar potential for positive transformation, but I am usually too busy running away from them to find out whether they might turn into princes. Although they are rarely aggressive when I look back into the dream from the waking world, I have been unable to stand my ground. One clue I have used to identify "good" and "bad" creatures is to notice whether or not they take an aggressive stance. If animals leap at me with teeth bared and claws showing, I realize that I am not ready to meet them. In these dreams I try to run, or to wake myself up. Even with the most threatening of these dreams beasts, I feel that if I could just manage to stay in the dream and face them, even they would offer another side. For example, several years ago I had a series of dreams in which pumas were leaping out, chasing me down streets, appearing menacingly at my windows. I decided that I had been watching too many nature programs. But they did not go away, they simply began to offer other possibilities when I was able to stay in the dream, keep myself in my own picture.

One night I dreamed that I was awaiting a visit from my brothers and sisters, none of whom had ever visited me in Canada. I was looking with anticipation out the front window and saw my younger brother Terry coming down the sidewalk, and right behind him was a very hungry-looking puma. I banged on the window to get Terry's attention but he did not notice or seem to care that he was being stalked. I opened the door to get him inside safely and slammed it shut before I realized that one of my cats was trapped outside. Reluctantly I went out again to find her, and saw that the puma had leapt up to the top of the roof and was looking sadly starved, not threatening at all. I had not been feeding my beast. My fear turned to compassion, and I ran back in and took all the meat out of the refrigerator, including frozen steaks, and began to throw it up to the puma piece by piece. I was feeding the beast instead of rejecting it, and understood as I drifted back to the waking state that I was, at the same time, feeding my own imagination.

Some months after this I had a surprising dream that gave me an entirely different view of pumas, and of the problems of beastliness. While visiting my favourite childhood park in North Miami I was unexpectedly transformed into a puma, caught, and put in a cage. I had become the monster, and was filled with a monstrous rage at being imprisoned. I was saved from this hellish state by a monkey-like figure who resembled a creature from another dream that took a similar liberating role. There was a cage directly across from mine, with a small ape sitting on a swing reading a large book, like a child's alphabet book.

When the creature saw that I was looking, it turned the book to face me, and I saw what I thought was an apple that became a glowing red circle that slowly revolved clockwise. This focused my total attention and completely soothed my fury. As the last of my rage died, the bars of both our cages faded away and we were free. I woke up feeling as if I had truly been released from some long captivity. Aside from the exhilaration of emancipation, I was taken with the strong colours and movements of the dream, appreciating it as an impressive dance-drama.

Monkeys have appeared as helpful creatures in other dreams, but Puma and Buffalo no longer visit. However, their archetypal slot as overwhelming beasts had been filled by Bear, who appeared for several years and refused to be sent away. My first bears kept their distance, appearing as dark figures on the horizon. Though they did not approach me as closely as the buffalo and the various pumas, they still inspired terror, and I kept them as far away from me as I could. Perhaps because of this, bears have been my most persistent dream "monsters," beginning with the ones hiding under my childhood bed and imitating my father snoring.

Archetypal bears, while unpredictable and potentially dangerous in both dreams and waking life, also function as figures of great power and generosity in dreams and in folktales, sacred legends and myths. Prehistoric bear cults flourished in Europe eons ago, and are still alive among the Ainu people of northern Japan. Like that of any monster worth its salt, their power is a combination of negative and positive forces; if treated with respect and approached properly they are generous and helpful, while improper behaviour calls out destructive wrath. It was my fear of this overpowering rage that prevented me from accepting them and allowing them to approach more closely. During my mother's two-year illness, and after her death in 1991, I participated in sessions with Jan Ellis, a Winnipeg counsellor who specialized in using dreams in grief therapy. She pointed out the feminine nature of archetypal bears, which had an immediate effect on my dream bears, who seemed less threatening. To think of this awesome figure as a feminine nourisher and protector instead of as a threat not only relieved some of my dread, it also opened the potential for nourishing my imagination. I was able to see this more clearly in stories about bears, and was delighted to discover that this more open attitude fed my dreams.

When I heard a transformative bear story in a legend with shamanic associations, I saw the full power of this archetype. The story, "The Man Who Wintered in a Bear's Den," was collected by Kira Van Deusen during her work in Siberia (Van Deusen 1999, 79-81; also in Yashinsky 1998, 227-229). In it a poor man who herded reindeer lost them in a storm, and decided to follow them into the tundra. He expected to die, but instead he fell into a deep hole and found himself in a bear's den. When he saw that the bear had a cub, he was certain that he would be killed, but the bear did not attack. He stayed in the den for some time, with the bear protecting and even feeding him. Still, he was uneasy. One day he said to himself, "Whatever will happen, let it be," and at this point the patient bear allowed him to get on her back and climb out of the hole. He returned to his village and the people were amazed he had been gone the entire winter. "'The bear saved me," he said, and told the whole story (Van Deusen 1999, 229).

After years of running away, like the reindeer herder, I finally met a bear who was determined to get through to me. As with my long-ago buffalo dream, this one began peacefully. It opened as my long-recurring dream of trying to buy something in a department store. This time I was in the fancy clothing section of The Bay (Hudson's Bay Company), one of Winnipeg's upscale department stores. Everything was on sale at ridiculously low prices so I wandered along draping things over my arms to try them on, saying, "Only $4.00 for a $400 dress! I can buy all the dresses I want." In fact, I suddenly realized that I could buy anything I wanted in the entire store. Somehow that realization made me feel sad instead of elated, so I stopped in the middle of the aisle and said, "This isn't what I want. What DO I want?" I put down all the clothes and went up an escalator to a hall with a windowless wall on one side and three open doors on the other, yet another one of my recurring dream halls. But this time I was not lost. I knew that I was looking for something beyond material satisfaction, and there was none of my usual anxiety of trying to find "the right thing."

I saw that movies were showing in each room. In the first one it was a Disney movie, light and fluffy, and I said out loud, "No, not that one." I looked in the next door to see a romantic movie from the 1940s, which I also rejected. In the last room a nature film was showing in the familiar little theatre that I have visited in the Urban Gallery of the Manitoba

Museum. "Yes, that's it!" I said, and I went right to the front and sat down in the middle seat.

The tiny screen was filled with a forest scene, entirely peaceful. That should have been my warning for something unexpected, but as usual I missed it. Suddenly I was right in the middle of this forest. The bushes in front of me parted and a huge grizzly slowly lumbered out. Terrified, I began to run, and this time my feet did not stick to the ground. I found the tallest tree I could see and climbed up as fast as I could, forgetting, as I had in the buffalo dream, that I could have flown away. When I got to the top I remembered that bears could climb too, and sure enough, I looked down to see the bear coming up slowly and relentlessly. All I could do was to wait, paralysed with fear. When the bear's head was level with my knees I reached down and hit it on the nose as hard as I could, powered by utter terror, and the bear fell. But as soon as it hit the ground it started right back up again, so I hit it again and again and it fell, and started back up. The third time when I leaned over to strike it, the bear looked up at me and said in a strong but calm voice, "Why don't we go down and talk about this?" This was a command, not a request. My bears had never said a word to me before, and I was so stunned that I climbed back down the tree without question. When my feet reached the ground the bear put one heavy paw on my left shoulder in silence, and I woke up feeling the challenging and somehow comforting weight of that touch.

Though we did not get to "talk about this," I woke up, as I had after feeding the puma, understanding that a dream pattern had changed, that bears could become less threatening.

This is what I would call a "sea-change" dream. As in "The Golden Woman," it opens to fuller creative potential because I stop the pattern early in the dream: In "Golden Woman" I ask the mirror for a true image, and here I ask the dream to show what I truly want—a request from the soul, the psyche. It is a "big" dream, using patterns from four different long recurring dreams to develop its gift. Dreams arise from our private language of creativity, and the better we understand this language, the more we can benefit from "speaking" it. The first recurring image is the department store, where from childhood on I was trying to find "the right thing" and failing. This time I realize that "the right thing" is not in the store. Here it echoes an earlier dream from my first days of university teaching, in which I free myself by putting down what I am carrying (in this case a stack of exams) and go up to the next level, literally climbing out of an unpromising situation.

When I go up, I find myself in a hallway familiar from years of dreams, but this time I am not anxious. I feel that I am being guided to the door that will open to an imaginative solution that answers my request for something beyond material pleasures. I feel at peace, another familiar theme that is an omen that a surprise is coming —as it was when I faced the buffalo, when I suddenly transformed into a puma, when I dove into a blue pool where a dark shadow resolved into dolphins. The calm before the storm, so to speak.

When I find the room, I sit down front row centre, just as I did in the dream of hearing the "famous storyteller." In both dreams I am pulled into the action as soon as I sit down, in one by the teller announcing that I, not he, will tell a story, and in the other by suddenly finding myself standing in the movie forest I had been passively watching. And here the main action begins with my age-old recurring beastly archetype, here once again to test my creative imagination. At first I fail, running away again, but this time I stay in the dream and receive the bear's invitation to "talk about this." I accept, not without trepidation, and am rewarded with a touch that feels like a blessing. Only as I wrote this paragraph did I notice that the bear places a paw on my left shoulder, as my brother Kenneth did in the dream where he said "It's okay, Kay," a blessing indeed.

Recurring dreams continue to give us opportunities to test our creativity. In another dream in which I was running away from a much smaller bear who, I thought, was chasing me down a city street, I was told by my mother that the bear would not hurt me. I believed her because she was reading *True Story* magazine, her favourite reading in actual life, so I knew she must be speaking the truth. I turned around and saw the bear standing up in the doorway, no taller than I was. Still a bit afraid, I took heart from my mother's words, walked over, and gave it a true bear hug that felt wonderful. I did not send it away. My "mother" in this dream echoes some of the earthy figures from other dreams, women with profound wisdom who offer it when approached correctly. The challenge here is to realize that the wisdom is our own, arising from our creative depths. My bear cannot hurt me precisely because it is my bear, patiently waiting to be spoken to, touched, released into waking life. The cage bars disappear and the beast walks free. You possess your daemon.

This trapped power waiting to be released is exhilarating. I know this quite intimately from the few dreams in which I have actually been the beast; the puma in the zoo cage, the monster with the gigantic head of a Chinese lion described earlier, and, more than once, a fierce eagle. The power is tremendous and potentially creative, all the more so if we can get inside the skin where the beast moves, thinks, sees, and even dreams. Reviewing dark figures, as Tanis MacDonald did in her poem on Medusa, gives new perspectives to creative imagination.

The art of beastliness of the sort I discuss here brings the opportunity of overcoming our inmost fears, the sense of disquiet that often gets in the way of artistic expression in any form—those voices of "prissy Criticalness" Brenda Ueland described earlier. The authors of an aptly named book, *Art and Fear*, stress how our fears can be paralyzing, whether they are fears about ourselves or about our reception by others: "In a general way, fears about yourself prevent you from doing your best work, while fears about your reception by others prevent you from doing your own work" (Bayles/Orland 1993, 23). If our interior beasts embody our deep terrors, then facing and transforming them can inspire our best work and our own work.

This was my experience in the alligator dream I mentioned earlier, where I tried once again to run away. I was visiting my family in Miami, sitting alone on the old sofa at the end of the enclosed front porch. I saw a small movement at the other end of the porch and went to investigate. I found a tiny alligator, white and glowing, and bent down to stroke it. It nipped my finger fiercely and I stepped back—and noticed that it had grown larger. I dashed back to other end of the porch, leapt up on the sofa, and turned around. The alligator was now several times larger and still growing, so I knew I had to get out of there somehow. The heavy front door into the living room was closed but I knew my family was home, because I could see the blue glow of television through the front window. I managed to leap to the door and shove it open without my feet touching the ground, similar to the method I used in getting into bed as a child to avoid "the monsters."

I was now safe inside the living room with the door firmly shut behind me, but I could see by the white glow shining through the window and under the door that the alligator was still growing, and that it would soon be large enough to break through. My family kept watching television, oblivious to danger. I understood that somehow they could not see me, that I would have to deal with the beast alone or it would destroy everything. I put my hand on the familiar metal doorknob, painted silver by my father, and turned it to the right as I whispered in resignation under my breath, "God help me!" I pushed the door open slowly, and was stunned. The beast that stood before me was a pure white unicorn, with the same glow and the same fierce look as the alligator. Let me stress here that unicorns in oral tradition are not those sweet and innocently helpless creatures of popular imagination, but quite fearsome beasts capable of harm. It would not be very convincing if a savage alligator evolved into anything less powerful. The gift of this dream is a beast that is transformed instead of rejected.

I describe this in detail because it is the clearest experience I have had with the immediate benefits of confronting a creature fully instead of just looking at its hooves and sending it away. I accept responsibility for my own creation, at least unconsciously; I made the creature so I am able to transform it from awful threat to awesome beauty. This is not as much of a leap as it might seem, since unicorns in their fullest archetypal power are quite fearsome beasts, neither the cute pastel horse-toys of the 1980s nor the symbols of purity and innocence of medieval Christianity.

Monster dreams can be particularly distressing because there is often a sense of betrayal. I have heard from a number of other dreamers who, like me, felt abandoned because people around them did not help when they were in danger. I usually tell them the alligator/unicorn dream, and explain that it took me years of dreaming to figure out that people were not helping me because they could not see my problem—after all, it was my dream, not theirs. I stopped being hurt and angry once I understood this.

Since each dream evolves within a personal realm of imagination and builds on a lifetime of dream patterns, the art of dreaming responds to conscious awareness and practice as much as does any other art. Because I was able to see my transformed beast in this dream, my later experience in "The Golden Woman" could take me to a more subtle level of understanding. The mirror showed me the beauty first and I insisted on seeing the beast—my own aging face. I accepted the beast and thus could move on to transformation as the golden woman.

Beasts respond to being recognized, accepted, touched. Some of them even demand it, as we saw in "The Black Bull of Norroway" where the heroine has to accept the bull as husband and publicly recognize him as such when she visits each of his brothers in turn; she has to touch him by climbing on his back, and later by accepting him in her bed at night. Like the bear in my dream who says, "Let's go down and talk about this," the beastly husband wants to find out if communication and communion are possible.

The imagination that creates our beasts in stories and in dreams, not to mention in our daily lives, exposes our fears and challenges us to experience inner transformation. Conversely, in waking life our willingness to follow our dreams releases our interior creator from the fear that binds it and invites our beast out into broad daylight. The water of life we gain from touching personal dragons gives us energy for creativity.

Follow your Frog

In a Grimm tale aptly named "Lucky Hans," a foolish young man wants to go out into the wide world to seek his fortune but has no idea what this means. In order to finance his adventures he works hard for a stingy farmer for several years, and is rewarded with a sack of coins or a lump of gold too heavy too carry, so he trades what he has for smaller and smaller things—the coins for a horse, the horse for a calf, the calf for a pig, and so on. He finally ends up with a stone that he accidentally drops down a well. Instead of being dismayed, he says to himself happily, "How lucky I am! That stone was too heavy anyway." And he sets off once again to seek his fortune.

This popular tale is Grimm number 83 (Zipes 1987, 329-334) with similar stories (AT Type 1415) found across Europe and North America. There are some good Appalachian variants, for example, a Kentucky story called "Foolish Jack" (Roberts 1969, 143-147).

Hans is the epitome of the fool who seems destined to fail in the practical terms of the materialistic world of ambition. His common name is typical; depending on what country the story comes from, he can be Jack, Ivan, Ti-Jean, or Jan, for example. One author has published two books of his own retellings of Jack tales from the southern United States (Chase 1943 and 1948). A more recent book (McCarthy 1994) examines tellers of these kinds of stories in North America today. Jack and his cousins are still alive and well.

We know Jack well from "Jack and the Beanstalk," a story so familiar that it still inspires jokes, cartoons, and various other modern reworkings. In the Disney version, for example, Mickey Mouse takes the role of Jack, and in Bugs Bunny, Elmer Fudd is the giant. No matter what form the story takes, the foolish character is as fortunate as Lucky Hans.

I used this story when I was interviewing children and adults during dissertation research in the early 1970s. Invariably people got into debates about Jack's silliness. One group of 12-year-old girls jokingly suggested that a girl might do things differently: "I bet she'd ask for more beans," said one, and another added, "Yeh, girls expect more for their money!" They all agreed that a girl "wouldn't just count on luck, she'd plan everything out" (Stone 1975, 365-66). They not only talked about the girl's practicality but also on the problems she might have climbing the bean stalk in a skirt, and whether she would kill the giant or let him live. Yet if Jack had indeed decided to plan everything out and decided not to trade the cow for a few special beans, there would have been no beanstalk to climb nor the giant's treasures as a reward.

Over the years I had similar discussions with my university students, who wanted to know why characters like "Jack" won out in the end even when they seemed to do nothing to deserve success. Their achievements were popularly described as arising from "dumb luck." Many students thought that winners should be those who went after what they wanted, the kind of heroes who got ahead of the crowd by being active and independent. But others were delighted by the Jack-like characters whose very foolishness was a defiance of conformity, the very opposite of doing what was expected.

It is no accident that traditional tales throughout the world favour characters who win out over those who are practical and ambitious, like Jack's older brothers. One student who pondered Jack's situation decided that he had a lot more than dumb luck going for him: "for results that are truly amazing, fantasy and imagination are needed, not just hard work" (Pound 1996). He was inspired by a variant of a "Jack" tale I told in class, a Scottish variant I had heard from Stewart Cameron at the Toronto Festival of Storytelling in 1985. In this widespread European story, three brothers are given feathers as guides on their quest to bring back magical objects (Stone 1998, 166-176). The final quest is often for the most beautiful woman in the world, and her identity is always a surprise (this is AT Type 402). Here is a summary of Cameron's story:

A king called for his three sons to give them tasks in order to determine which one would be resourceful enough to inherit the royal realm. They were each given a white feather and told to follow it as it floated in a particular direction, and to bring back the finest ring in the world. The two older sons tossed their feathers high and followed them east and west, but Jack, who loved to stay home and play in the mud, threw his up half-heartedly and was delighted when it fell into the mud. As he sat down and began to create elaborate mud constructions, a small green frog hopped up and offered to lead him to her home, a cave filled with thousands of frogs of all sizes. The king of the frogs, upon hearing Jack's task, offered him a mud-covered ring that seemed quite beautiful to Jack—and of course it turned out to be more beautiful than Jack's brothers' rings when the mud was removed. The angry brothers demanded another contest, so they were given three more feathers with orders to bring back the finest piece of cloth. Jack again was led to the cave, and this time was presented with a mud-covered cloth, which turned out to be silk woven by a thousand spiders. He won again, and the jealous brothers demanded a final test.

This time they were told to follow their feathers and bring back the smartest woman in the world as their bride-to-be. Jack followed the little frog to the cave for the last time, where the frog king offered his clever daughter as bride. Jack was surprised but accepted his helper, and proudly carried her home to the king and queen. The king proposed riddles as a test, one for each: "How far is it between the earth and the stars?" "Name the tiny green sword that holds the earth together." "What am I thinking right now?" The two women brought by the brothers failed to answer their riddles, but the little frog easily answered all three. To the last she responded, "You're thinking that I'm only a frog, but I'm not!" at which she leapt out of Jack's hand and transformed into a lovely young woman. They eventually became king and queen and ruled their people efficiently, generously, and playfully, since, as Stewart put it:

> His wife was as smart as Jack was a little bit soft [foolish]. She was as industrious as he was, well, maybe a tiny bit lazy. And besides that, every time when the affairs of state got a little beyond his control he would nip out to the back door and go play in the mud in the back garden (Stone 1988, 175).

When I began telling Stewart's story in Winnipeg, a group of 12-year-old girls in one school were bothered by the final task of finding the most beautiful woman, and wanted the brothers to find the smartest woman in the world instead. We brainstormed on riddles that could be used to test the women, and these are now part of the story. This put the heroine in a much stronger position in the story, and when Stewart heard of this change he decided to include it in his further tellings.

Most students who heard me tell this story in my folklore class were more practical. They seemed to agree with Jack's ambitious brothers who complained, "We went all over the world searching while Jack just sat here and played in the mud," and were unwilling to accept the possibility that Jack's good-hearted nature was revealed through his seeming inability and lack of ambition. Richard Pound was an exception. He insisted that Jack went well beyond what the king demanded, and that more than luck was involved:

> In one sense Jack is lazy and lucky—his friend the frog bails him out. But in a different light Jack somehow transcends the competitive structure of the quests and achieves magical results. The hard-working brothers do find nice rings and good tablecloths with much toil, but Jack—by focusing on enjoyment and imagination—delivers to the king unbelievably fantastic works of art (Pound 1996, 6).

He concludes that the moral of the story is "that imagination does have a place in the world." He was so inspired by the story that he reviewed his nightmares of working in a demanding restaurant called Earl's (he called them "earlsmares") to see if these dreams could be transformed by active imagination, since his dreams were unpleasant replays of his daily work.

> In the dreams everything seems very real to me, so real that my body reacts to being out of control in the dream in the same way it reacts in my real job. I'll wake up from an "earlsmare" with my hands clenched, my jaw tight, and that same gnawing sensation in my stomach. As a result of believing in dreams I feel very real tension (Pound, 3).

While working on his class essay he began to challenge these dreams: "If the dreams themselves refuse to be out of the ordinary, it doesn't follow that I must act realistically as well—I myself can be what is exciting and odd in the dream." The story of Jack, who was certainly what was exciting and odd in his own story, inspired Richard to give his imagination a freer rein. He found that his dreams did indeed transform:

> I realized for the first time not only the annoyance of an earlsmare but also the opportunity it offered. It is, quite literally, a server's dream to be able to act in any way they desire while dealing with customers. As long as I was able to realize I was dreaming, I could now strip naked in the middle of the restaurant or paddle a canoe through the prep kitchen. I could do anything my mind could think of (Pound, 4).

He became increasingly excited by the potency of imagination in the story, his dreams, and his daily work, sensing that even mundane work could be an expression of artistry:

> With the story seen from this viewpoint, the frog that seems so instrumental in Jack's success could be read as Jack's faculty of imagination—the extra ingredient that was lacking in his brothers. This helps illuminate my dreams [and reality] of working at Earl's. I try to work as hard as I can and I never seem to live up to my own standards. Seeing those dreams as opportunities for creativity will, I hope, shift the whole framework of emotions around. I can see now how I should be able to enact the same sort of transformation in real life (Pound, 6).

Richard reported with a smile that he actually felt "a bit like Jack." He was following his frog. I have quoted his words at length because they are such evocative examples of my point that we can be artists in life and in dreams, and that other forms of creative expression, like folktales, for example, can affect us positively.

It seems that these old traditional stories of apparent fools are more than wish-fulfilling escapist fantasies (unless the Disney corporation gets control of them). Their purpose is more soulful, directing us to less materialistic and opportunistic views of life. Also, they emphasize the value of doing things your own way even when others might consider you odd, impractical, lazy, or just fooling around, accomplishing very little in a goal-oriented "real world" where success is measured by external things. Sometimes playing around in the mud, metaphorically speaking, is exactly what we need to do.

The pragmatic reproaches of Jack's brothers are familiar to artistic creators, who have to spend a lot of time "playing in the mud" like Jack in order to bring their work into being, whether in dance, music, drama, writing, painting, cooking, or, in my case, dreaming and storytelling. To be recognized for our true nature as artists is deeply satisfying, but not more important than our self-recognition and trust of what we are doing. Like Jack, we sometimes have to follow the unlikely frogs in our lives, and go on with things when others disregard or even denigrate our actions.

Another aspect of these stories, of course, is that Jack and his counterparts would undoubtedly be the troublesome kid in the classroom, suffering from various modern ailments that result in learning disabilities. I have learned a lot in the few years of telling stories to the group of troubled 11-year-olds at a Winnipeg school I mentioned earlier, so I know these are very real problems that create significant disruptions. But I also see the spontaneous creativity that often emerges when these students begin to trust their own out-of-the-ordinary way of seeing and doing things. One extremely insecure girl who barely said a word the entire year—she was doing her own version of Jack's silent playing in the mud—presented me with a gloriously colourful and joyous drawing inspired by one of the stories I had told. She seemed to have found her frog, at least temporarily.

The frog is an utterly common creature, lacking the dramatic character of a dragon or a beast, and perhaps that is exactly where the frog's power lies. It takes an unusual person to treat a talking frog with respect, as Jack does. Ordinary things like tablecloths and rings, for example, challenge protagonists to see that these might be much more than they seem. This is true of people in ordinary waking life as well, as I discovered in working with the various children in the "difficult" classes. I was looking for treasure in hidden form. It is no wonder that some of the magical characters in stories appear as ragged old men or ancient crones, not to mention frogs, waiting to reward those who see more than Jack's brothers were able to see.

Similarly, in some stories the protagonist receives a mundane inheritance that seems utterly without value. This may be small and insignificant, like a doll (in the Russian tale of "Vasilisa"), a crude cloak (in an English Cinderella tale, "Mossycoat"), or an ordinary animal like a cat, a dog, a horse. If there are older siblings they usually refuse the objects, but the fools take what is offered and go out into the wide world with curiosity rather than ambition. Even when they set out to "seek their fortune" they are looking for adventure rather than material gains, often not understanding what "seeking fortune" means.

In variants of the popular "Puss and Boots" and "Dick Whittington's Cat," the hero is left with only a crafty cat who succeeds in gaining fortune for his guileless owner. Variants are found throughout Europe, with different animals as helpers. "Puss-in-Boots" (AT Type 545, "Cat [or Fox] as Helper) and "Whittington's Cat" (AT 1651) turn up in Finland, Estonia, Sweden, Denmark, Ireland, Italy, various Slavic countries, and of course France, Germany, and England. In other tales it is an unlikely horse who guides the hero to success. My favourite is "The Golden Feather," an unusual Jewish variant of a complex European tale known in Russia as "The Little Humpback Horse" (Weinreich 1988, 142-47). The unpromising youngest son is given the youngest horse as his inheritance. Both are seen by others as ugly and witless, but the horse's wise guidance leads the inept young man to unexpected success over a threatening witch. The story concludes with young man and horse farming together, and providing their neighbours with the fruits of their labours.

With all the horses in my background it is not surprising that I am fond of stories where horses play a role. In the tale "Ösküs-ool and the Three Arts," from Kira Van Deusen's collection of Siberian tales, horses are secondary, but still important (Van Deusen 1996, 31-34). The Tuvan hero, Ösküs-ool ("Orphan Boy"), is so unsophisticated that he does not even know how to count the small collection of animals he has. He only knows that his favourite horse is important. Though this horse does not speak or guide him, as does the horse in the Jewish tale, somehow his relationship to the horse plays a part in his eventual success as he trades the animals—except for the one horse—to gain wisdom. Here is a summary:

When his father died, Ösküs-ool was left with a small herd of animals—10 goats, 10 cows, and 10 horses. Since Ösküs-ool could not count it seemed like a lot to him, though it was not much by Tuvan standards where a herder might have hundreds or thousands of animals. He did not know what to do with his animals, so decided to trade them for wisdom, which his father had told him was precious. He had no idea what wisdom was so he set off to find it. Like Jack and other European characters of similar nature, he was going out "to seek his fortune" without any idea of what this might be.

He visited three different domed yurts in succession, where he traded his animals for the wisdom of chess, the wisdom of sleight-of-hand magic, and finally the wisdom of counting. Because he had learned to count, he understood that he could subtract one horse from the ten. As he continued his journey on this horse he met the cruel Karaty Khan, who owned huge herds of animals and many enslaved herders who he had defeated at chess. Ösküs-ool was the first ever to best Karaty Khan, using sleight-of-hand magic to distract him and newly learned chess skills to defeat him at his own game. He won all of Karaty Khan's sheep, which he counted, and then handed over to the herders. Perhaps since both stories focus on the relations between human and animal, romance is not an issue. Instead the Jewish and the Tuvan heroes benefit others instead of living happily ever after by themselves.

Characters like Ösküs-ool are appealing not just because of their role as apparent losers—what we feel like on our bad days—but also for their resourcefulness and tenacity. They are often misjudged by other story characters, Karaty Khan, for instance, but their openness, patience, generosity and ingenuity turn the tide in their favour. Like Jack in the earlier story, imagination is the key to victory over an apparently superior force. Ösküs-ool exemplifies the type of character who progresses from inexperienced novice to knowledgeable initiate, now able to successfully face the world with new understanding and skills.

This is often the case in dreams as well, as we find creative solutions to symbolic issues. In 1983 I had an unusual two-part dream, "The Cave," that covered different time periods: I was an anxious teenager in the first part and became a more confident adult in the second, though not without a bit more Jack-like ineptitude.

I was standing with several other young people in a large cave filled with amber light, looking into a deep pool that the others had already leapt into. Although I was apprehensive, I was about to follow them into what seemed to be an initiatory rite of passage. As I prepared to jump, I heard an older woman's voice telling me not to jump, and I trusted her. The voice directed me to a flat, white stone that seemed to glow as I touched it and picked it up.

Suddenly the dream skipped ahead, or I might have unconsciously connected two dream-stories while asleep. I was now an adult, attending some kind of conference, still carrying the stone in my pocket. I felt warmth there and reached in to touch it, and somehow knew that it was now time for me to return to the cave. I perceived that this was to be some sort of test of my abilities and was anxious again, so I asked a male friend to accompany me. Using the white stone as a guide I found the cave but entered through a different passage this time. I was guided by the same woman's voice to a narrow rocky arch over a bottomless chasm. I was directed to pass over this bridge with my eyes closed, but I was terrified of falling and asked the man to cross first. He walked safely to the other side but I was still frightened. Humbly, I knelt down and closed my eyes, wrapped my arms and legs around the narrow arch, and inched slowly across. I reached the other side exhausted but relieved, sensing that this was literally a rite of passage, a bridging of a gap between youth and maturity. My success was not in the least dimmed by my lack of boldness. As I reached the other side I saw that the white stone had become smaller and dimmer, and knew that I no longer needed it. Instead of clinging to it as a symbol of my success, I put it on a ledge where it could be found by someone else who needed it.

Like Jack in Stewart Cameron's story, I was willing to look foolish and not be stopped by it as I crawled across the stone bridge. Also, I found something in a cave that seemed common but turned out to be precious—not a ring or fine silk or a frog princess, but a glowing stone that seemed to guide me and give me strength. And like Ösküs-ool who frees the shepherds and gives them the sheep he has won, I gave up the magic stone for the benefit of someone else who could use it.

Incidentally, fear of falling—of failing—is a very familiar theme, as I discovered after hearing similar dream situations described by other dreamers about crossing bridges, mountains, rivers and other daunting obstacles. I was interested to find an example reported in a book on lucid dreaming:

> I was walking along a gradually ascending mountain path with a friend. As far as the eye could see, the only thing moving was the silent mist that veiled the majestic peaks in mystery. But suddenly we found ourselves before a narrow bridge that precariously spanned a chasm. When I looked down into the bottomless pit beneath the bridge, I became dizzy with fear and could not bring myself to proceed. At this, my companion said, "You know, Stephen, you don't have to go this way. You can go back the way we came," and pointed back down what seemed like an immense distance. But then the thought crossed my mind that if I were to become lucid, I would have no reason to fear the height (LaBerge 1985, 100).

At this point he began to realize that he was dreaming, and in this lucidity regained full confidence and crossed the bridge, back into his waking world. If I, too, had realized I was in the dream world, I could have walked easily over the narrow bridge without fear—or even danced across.

My real-life experience with fear of falling happened on our honeymoon hike, when I tried to follow my husband up a rock face on Mt. Washington in the White Mountains of New Hampshire. I had never ascended anything higher than the hill in Greynolds Park in North Miami, and found the real mountains entirely daunting. My husband still insists that the "cliff" we were climbing was only 12 feet or so, but in my memory it was Himalayan. He scaled it easily, like the man crossing the chasm in my cave dream, but I crawled up slowly, hanging by fingers and toes and growing increasingly panicked but unwilling to admit it. Halfway up my panic became full-blown hysteria as I was certain I was going to fall and die. I was entirely unheroic in my screaming at Dan for bringing me up the mountain, and he managed to calmly talk me up, pointing out where I could find finger holds. Though I was still sure I was going to fall, I managed to hold back my hysteria long enough to finally crawl humbly to the top, undignified but alive. All was well until I discovered that I had lost my wedding ring, which I had put in the kangaroo pocket of my jacket to protect it from scratches. It is still there somewhere on Mt. Washington, waiting, like the white stone in my dream, for someone else to find it.

Perhaps it was this stone that attracted me to the speaking stones on the mountain in "The Water of Life," though of course these stones were anything but helpful. With Jack in mind, too, I can see more clearly how the youngest sister in the story succeeds where her brothers fail, precisely because she does not listen to the voices of challenge and despair. She makes her own stumbling way to the top of the mountain, but while she does not allow the stones to stop her, she does hear their voices of suffering. And also, she has her "frog" in the form of the small red fox who tells the truth about the talking stones. Both fox and frog speak in that still, small voice that can be heard through the cacophony of inner and outer voices that can persuade us to stop ourselves, and bring about our own stuck-in-a rut suffering.

And that reminds me of another story. Suffering abounds in folktales and sacred legends as much as in dreams and in life, and following one's frog can certainly lead to difficulties. In one particular story, "Sorrow in Youth," misfortune is at the very heart of the story. This is my version of AT Type 938A, "Misfortune in Youth," developed from a single variant (Lang 1967, 167). The woman, like me, had to scale a cliff, but with quite different results:

A rich merchant whose wife died giving birth to their child was determined to protect his daughter from sorrow. He kept her confined to his large estate, allowing her to explore a bit more widely each year. On her sixteenth birthday he gave her a ruby ring belonging to her mother, and allowed her full freedom on his vast estate. While exploring far from the mansion one day, she found a young eagle crying in distress, and carried it back up to its nest high on a cliff. In gratitude the eagle-mother offered to reward the young woman by giving her the choice of having her sorrow in youth or later in life. Since she did not know what sorrow was and was curious, she chose to have sorrow in youth. "So be it," said Eagle, telling the young woman that she would reappear when the sorrow was coming to an end.

When she climbed down, she discovered that she was lost, and by the time she found her way back to her father's home he had left, fearing that she was dead and would never return. Not knowing what to do, she left her father's gates for the first time, and sat down outside and began to weep in desperation, feeling sorrow for the first time in her life. A woman passing by offered her work, and she gratefully accepted, learning everything she was taught and working very diligently. All went well, until one day she broke a fine crystal bowl and was so distressed that she left without a word, filled with sorrow. After this, she went from one place to another for some years, leaving each time as she had made one mistake after another. Now she certainly knew what sorrow was.

One day as she was wearily on the road once again, she decided in desperation that no matter what happened she would not run away again. She soon found a job at a bakery where she worked hard, getting up early every morning to light the ovens so that she and the baker's wife could bake the bread. As they worked they talked about the dreams they had each night. Early one morning she dreamed she saw a woman with outspread arms standing at the top of a tall tree, and woke up mystified. When she told her dream to the baker's wife, she was instructed to leave immediately in order to find that tree. After searching far and wide she found the tree behind the bakery, and was this time instructed to sleep under it that night.

In the early morning she had the same dream of the woman with outstretched arms at the top of the tree, and awoke to find Eagle with outspread wings calling to her. Eagle dropped her a ball of silk thread, which she took to the old king in exchange for its weight in gold. Light as it was, the silk did not balance on the scale until the king put his crown on top of the gold and silver he had heaped there. He held out the crown to her, and when she accepted it he saw the ruby ring. He looked at her more closely and asked, "Who gave you that ring?" When she told him, father and daughter were joyfully reunited at last. She became queen of her own realm, all the wiser because of the sorrows she had suffered.

This struggling woman makes an interesting contrast to the playful Jack we met earlier. In the first part of her life she seems more like Jack's hard-working brothers, striving to do things correctly and giving up when she fails. Still, she is not an ambitious opportunist, and thus is willing to do whatever work is offered, not worrying about rewards. Only when she finally decides to stop running away is she able to experience a prophetic dream that leads her back to the eagle. Like Jack, she is rewarded because she is willing to follow the guidance of a creature, and also because she does not reject the seemingly ordinary ball of thread she receives, and with this fulfills the king's request.

This story seemed to have unusual depth and breadth to me from the first time I read it, but for several years it resisted my attempts to retell it. I was stopped by these failures and kept giving up, as the woman in the story did. One day I was looking at one of Henry Moore's strong, flowing sculptures in Toronto's Art Gallery of Ontario and had a flash of realization that stories, like Moore's challenging sculptures, needed to be viewed from every angle. I returned to the folktale with Richard Pound's enthusiasm about re-viewing his frustrating dreams of restaurant work in mind, determined this time not be so discouraged. I played around with different images and actions until the story began to come alive, and gradually to take on its present form. Like Öskus-ool, I had figured out how to trade what I had for wisdom, giving up old ideas to see new facets of a story I thought I knew. In this long period of experimentation, I gained more respect for the woman's apparent foolishness. One thing I know about fools in folktales, dreams, and in life as well, is that things happen when they are meant to happen. That is, it seems to me that ineptitude, lack of ambition, and other seemingly negative qualities that make us look foolish might eventually lead to unexpected outcomes. Some of these are positive, all of them are challenging. One example from my own life is the long passage in academic life from sessional part-time lecturer to part-time tenured full professor, as much by accident as by design. But that would be a very long story.

I am wondering what might happen next to Jack as the King, Öskü-sool with his new wisdom, or the woman now queen of her own realm. In many stories, characters who have risen above their hardships and gained wisdom might begin to practice their skills in unexpected ways. The wise fool might become the clever trickster.

8

Trickster was out walking one Day

We have already met Jack and his counterparts, whose seeming foolishness and dumb luck most often led to success. In some of these stories the fool seems to be at least a little clever as well as lucky; a little resourcefulness goes a long way, and the line between fools and tricksters is a very fine one, with considerable stepping back and forth between folly and wisdom. Often these stories begin with Trickster out walking, looking for adventures. And very often he seems exceptionally foolish. Let me demonstrate with a story from China, "A Wonderful Nose" (Ming n.d., 1-8).

A man named Hung Mao (Red Cat) trades all his goods for wild geese who fly away, so he tells his wife that he has traded everything for a wonderful nose that can find anything. He easily finds the food she has put away, and then is asked to find things for the neighbours, who have always called him Dah Shadze, Big Fool. He retrieves everything he is asked to find, and his reputation spreads to the emperor, who asks him to locate the missing great seal, which turns out to have been stolen by the servant that has been sent to fetch Hung Mao. He and the servant make a deal, the great seal is found, and now Hung Mao is asked to guess the contents of a closed chest in which a cat has been hidden. He says in dismay, "Oh dear, Red Cat (Hung Mao) is surely trapped now." The surprised emperor is impressed and rewards him well and he returns in triumph to his village, where no one ever calls him Dah Shadze again.

Is Hung Mao truly a Dah Shadze, a Big Fool, or is he a resourceful trickster? These kinds of protagonists are enigmatic characters throughout the world, sometimes falling into wisdom almost by chance by never admitting that they are wrong. In Islamic tradition we meet the foolish wise man The Hodja Nasrudin (or the Mullah Nasredin) who is asked to determine whether sun or moon is more important, and chooses the moon because it shines at night when everything is dark, while the sun shines all day when everything is already light (Yashinsky 1990, 13). He is correct when you think about it, using the trickster's delightfully skewed logic.

The characters of Spider and Hare, in various African traditions, devote themselves to foolish trickery with amusing and sometimes dire results, as in the well-known "Tar Baby" story where their overly clever greed causes them to be caught firmly in the sticky figure set out to trap them (Harris 1974, 7). But occasionally their foolishness brings a gift to the world, as when Anansi the Spider loses control of a box of stories and they fly free throughout the world (Yolen 1986, 24).

They are matched by their distant North American cousins, Coyote and Raven, and also by a host of tricksters in more human form, like Nanabush, Manabojo, Napi, Kluskap, and countless others. All of them are led into trap after trap by their insatiable hunger for food, wealth, sex, and prestige. It seems that these foolish figures never learn from their mistakes. Yet their persistence in world mythology suggests that they are far more than amusing characters. Paul Radin, who investigated trickster tales extensively, points out the profound ambivalence of this archetypal figure:

> Trickster is at one and the same time creator and destroyer, giver and negator, he who dupes others and is always duped himself. He will do nothing consciously. At all times he is considered to behave as he does from impulses over which he has no control. He knows neither good nor evil yet he is responsible for both. He possesses no values, moral or social, yet through his actions all values come into being (Radin 1975, 254).

I have been intrigued with these kinds of characters for a long time, probably because they seemed so completely different from my life and my dreams. They were bad and good at the same time, and though they often suffered for their foolishness they were never destroyed. And sometimes good came of their bad acts, as Radin notes. They consistently went against the grain, and did so with humour, unlike the naughty girls and the challenging hags of folktales. Tricksters were not quite rebels, but something more. I sensed early on that there was more to them than simple foolishness, greed, or sly wit.

I was pleased to learn through reading Jungian works that the trickster/fool is a complex archetype with a bewildering range of attributes, negative in some stories and positive in others. For example, the same characters I just mentioned appear in other stories that expose their cleverness. In a Norwegian tale a seemingly foolish young man wins the hand of a princess who is a famous tale-teller, who equals his outrageous lies (Yolen 1986, 28). The Mullah Nasredin, who does not seem to understand the functions of sun and moon in the example above, cleverly smuggles donkeys across a border for years without ever being caught (Yashinsky 1990, 19). Both Coyote and Raven, for all their foolishness, play central roles in indigenous creation stories, even being responsible for bringing the first human beings to the earth (though this may not seem so positive, given our human history).

Actually, the trickster is an apt archetype for us fallible humans, so full of complexities and ambivalence, trying to hold an uneasy balance between wisdom and folly, cleverness and stupidity, equanimity and rage, great generosity and appalling greediness. In world folklore and mythology, Trickster, in both negative and positive form, is by nature a disruptor, a disorganizer, one who turns the world upside down. Just when you think you have your life in order, Trickster will be there in some form to throw a wrench into the works. Sometimes this agitation is positive, bringing about life changes that might not happen otherwise.

I think another reason I was fascinated with these kinds of characters was that my brothers, Allen and Terry, provided living examples. Both were consummate pranksters, finding endless ways to make their four sisters' lives more interesting. They also became masterful tale-tellers, describing their own exploits with humour worthy of the most unrepentant trickster anywhere.

My older brother Allen was the rebel of the family, "born to be bad," as someone used to say. Earlier I mentioned one of his early accomplishments, stealing hubcaps from the bus that took him to school every day. His creativity took less disruptive forms as well. In high school he built a table-wide miniature town with all sorts of odd things happening in it. He created an aggressive cartoon character, The Slumgullion Kid, who beat up our favourite movie cowboys. Sometimes he drew The Slumgullion Kid on my feet in India Ink while I was asleep (obviously I am not ticklish). These would eventually be discovered by my classmates when I sat barefoot at my desk with the soles of my feet turned up. Today a wind-surfing pensioner, Allen has completed a book-length cartoon, *Yahoo Junction*, that evolved from his teenage cartooning days.

Precocious Terry began his career even before he could talk: Janet and I were often left to take care of him when my mother went grocery shopping, and 18-month-old Terry would manage to slip away from us and head off down 101st Street, shedding his diaper as he went. We would get a call from Mrs. H. across the street or another neighbour further on, and would have to go searching for our naked baby brother. At three he managed to start a small fire in the weedy field west of our house, and still later he accidentally blew up his pet turtles by trying to extinguish a smoking cherry bomb in their bowl.

As Trickster's antics go, these are all very innocent exploits, but they prepared me for my future as a folklorist exploring archetypal stories. I can recognize aspects of my brothers right away and appreciate the creative side of the trickster. This archetype, like all others, draws its deep power from ordinary human life.

Animals can also take Trickster form in real life, as I know from all the real-life cats I have had over the years. And of course horses, too, the ones who would dash under low tree branches knowing that this might knock me off, or inflate their bellies while I was saddling them so that the saddle would slip and toss me to the ground after we got into a good trot. Here is a fine example from my friend Gail Beck, who told me about a troublesome pony that belonged to a veterinary doctor she knew:

> Britt had a pony and two horses that he kept out behind his veterinary hospital. One night at 1 a.m. the sheriff called him and said, "Britt, your horses are out." He got up and saw that the corral gate was unlatched, so he went out and found the horses, got them all back again. A while later the same thing happened, and when it happened the third time he decided to find out what was going on. He sat up all night watching the corral, and about

> midnight he saw that pony crawl under the barbed-wire fence at a low spot, then walk back to the gate and unlatch it so the other horses could get out too. He was amazed! He fixed the fence and the lock and it didn't happen any more, but he told stories about the pony for a long, long time (conversation, June 2001).

This pony would fit well into Slavic tales of the clever horses I mentioned earlier. In fact, now that I think about it, many of the animal helpers in stories have more than a bit of the trickster in them, like the sly cat in "Puss in Boots" who tricks a giant and a king in order to benefit his master, and the frog in Stewart Cameron's "Three Feathers," who cleverly hides her identity from Jack as she leads him off. But these are secondary figures, and they are performing their tricks for someone else's gain.

In contrast to clever animals, the archetypal trickster is initially interested in his own gain, though he may accidentally accomplish some good as well. Here is an unusual example, a story that arose during a storytelling session in Winnipeg in the late 1980s, when members of Stone Soup Stories composed a spontaneous group tale featuring Coyote, a favourite trickster figure. Group stories are usually too nebulous to last longer than a single session, but this one had enough coherence and form that individual members continued to tell it, and even gave it a title, "Coyote and the Twinge of Loneliness." Though it is not a traditional tale, it captures the nature of this contrary archetypal character. It begins in the traditional way, with Trickster on the move, looking for trouble.

Coyote was out walking one day and noticed a strange plant he'd never seen before. He wasn't hungry but he wanted to have it anyway, so he gathered it and took it back to his den, put it in a dark corner, and forgot about it. After some time, Coyote began to have an odd feeling he'd never felt before, and he went to his friend Bear to ask what this might be.

"What's it like?" asked Bear.

"It's heavy and empty at the same time, like being in a deep, dark well. I don't like it."

"Oh. That's loneliness. What have you been doing?"

When Coyote remembered the strange plant and described it, Bear said, "Oh, foolish Coyote, that was a Twinge of Loneliness. It grows best in the dark, so we'd better find it right away."

They returned to Coyote's den and found the Twinge growing very well in the dark corner, so they took it out and scattered it in the air. So it's

Coyote's fault that everyone, even the happiest of people, occasionally feels a twinge of loneliness now and then (Stone Soup Stories, 1988).

Are Coyote, and his trickster relations around the world, simply fools, or do they have something more to offer? In this case it does not seem that Coyote has benefitted anyone, including himself. But if you look at this simple story as a playful explanation of the familiar human feeling of loneliness, it turns things around—and that is exactly what Tricksters do. More by accident than design they turn the world upside down one way or another.

Trickster is a complex and powerful archetype, involved in a continuing swirl of creation and destruction. I wondered why I could not recall any such characters in my dreams, until I read an article by Jung suggesting that the trickster archetype often appears as twins, expressing a dualistic nature (Jung 1964, 112-118). This was a surprise. I had met many twin figures, almost always male (as Trickster usually is in the stories) and assumed that these arose from my Gemini astrological sign. Also, my dream twins were never in animal form, and were usually common figures like meter readers and janitors, who often did nothing obviously trickster-like. The closest I came was a dream with a couple of vociferous loggers who wanted to throw me out of my house so they could cut down all the house plants with chain saws. In the dream I was distressed, but I was laughing when I woke up.

When I reviewed past dreams I saw that some of these enigmatic characters, when challenged, changed from hinderers to helpers. For example, the two school janitors whom I asked for help responded by taking me to a large room and giving me a pile of old clothes to sort. I was annoyed and started to complain to them when I suddenly understood it was a dream, and said, "Hey, I don't have to do this." They both smiled at me and pointed to the door. When I went out I found a glorious swimming pool that I immediately dove into, forgetting that I was afraid of water. Two pure white dolphins came swimming up to greet me. Dolphins, of course, are the tricksters of the ocean world. I was elated.

In another dream that I referred to in an earlier chapter, I had been sent to a junior high school class to tell stories and arrived discovering that the teacher was not there and the class was in chaos. I managed to get the class calmed down and was about to tell them the stories I had chosen for that difficult age group. I was prepared—and this will almost always be an invitation for Trickster to make his disruptive powers felt. The class was sitting quietly in readiness to hear my story when the door burst open and two large, dark men stomped in laughing. I thought they were drunk, could see they would send the class into a chaos again unless I acted quickly, but I had no idea what to do.

Luckily for me, I chose not to show my dismay, and instead of challenging them I said calmly and respectfully, "You're disrupting the students and you really need to leave." As I said these words, similar but much calmer than those I had spoken to Buffalo all those years ago, I gently took the wrist of the man I identified as the leader of the two and slowly eased them out the door. As we stood on the threshold, the man I had touched looked down at me, smiled, and said, "You're Irish, aren't you?" I nodded my head in stunned agreement, and he said, "I can teach you an old Celtic psalm." The three of us stepped out of the room and walked over to a large cylindrical pillar, where we were joined by another woman. The four of us circled sunwise around this pillar chanting an achingly divine melody of such beauty that I said to them, "Oh, I wish I had my tape recorder!" That tossed me out of the dream too suddenly for me to bring the "Celtic psalm" back to the waking world. I would have to wait another few years to hear a song of such profound grace.

Trickster tales in dreams, life, and oral tradition often point us to the door where we might find a pool with white dolphins or a profoundly simple psalm, or the creation of a new animal. In a story I am fond of telling to junior high school classes, the gift of the tale rises from the ashes. I found this story one year when I was looking for an unusual example of a particular "Jack tale" to use on the final exam for my folklore class, similar enough to one we had read but different enough for comparison. In the Appalachian tale Jack managed to trick every character in the story and end up with unexpected wealth. I was surprised to find a similar tale from an entirely different tradition, the hill country of Burma, in a collection of world tales (Dorson 1975, 281). The teller was a young man from the tribal peoples near the Tibetan border in the north. His intriguing tale, "Liar Mvkang," portrays a wily trickster who might have been able to outwit Jack himself.

In a certain village, the rich farmers decided that they were going to get rid of an annoying young man who they called "Liar Mvkang," named for all the stories he like to tell. One day when he was away, they burned down his shabby hut, leaving him with nothing at all. They hoped he would leave the village, and were delighted when he came to them and said, "Someone's burned down my hut and I have nothing, so I guess I'll go somewhere else. But first, can I have your permission to take some of the ashes?" "Of course!" they said happily. "And I'll need some salt, too." Only the rich people had salt, and they agreed to give him some. He mixed salt and ashes together, put them in a small sack, and went on his way.

When he came to the next village, he put down the sack of salt and ashes and went inside. The villagers greeted him warmly, asking him to stay and eat with them and then to tell them stories. Liar Mvkang was happy to oblige, but was worried about his sack. They promised that their cattle were far away and would not bother the salt, and that if any of their cows did eat his salt, he could take them—if he could identify them.

Liar Mvkang kept the villagers occupied with stories all day, until the cattle came home and, finding the sack, broke into it. When he discovered that his salt had been eaten, he reminded the villagers of their promise. They brought all the cattle together and Liar Mvkang began to identify them—easily, since those who had eaten the salt were marked with ashes. He returned to his own village with a small herd, and the rich men immediately accused him of stealing the cattle. "Oh no," he said with a smile. "There's a certain village that will trade cattle for ashes." The rich farmers all ran home immediately, burned down their large huts, stuffed the ashes into huge sacks, and set off to find that village, dragging the sacks behind them. They are still looking, but Liar Mvkang is home enjoying his wealth.

My logical university students were not as taken with this trickster as I was, insisting that he deliberately misled the rich farmers. I pointed out that Liar Mvkang was not truly lying, since in fact the village he visited did indeed trade cattle for ashes, though they were not aware of this. He simply let the rich farmers, inspired by greed, leap to their own conclusions. Now they are where he was before, with no possessions other than a sack of ashes. Ah, but they are missing the salt.

I have noticed that many folktale tricksters, Coyote and Liar Mvkang (and my brothers) for instance, are in open conflict with those around them. It is as if the external world is in need of a good turn-around, and they are there to provide it. The new animal created by Coyote is certainly going to change the world profoundly, and on a smaller scale, Liar Mvkang's village will never be the same. In contrast, the trickster-like characters who have appeared in my dreams seem to be less antagonistic when recognized and treated with respect, like the janitors who point the way to the dolphins, and the disruptive men who teach me a "Celtic psalm."

But even at his most disruptive, Trickster usually does not respond directly but uses his wits to turn the tables, in story after story. Even Liar Mvkang, sorely provoked by the farmers, does not march off angrily and accuse them of arson. He finds a way to turn them against themselves. Trickster's role in my dreams is similar, since the twin figures are more playful than threatening. If I could manage to be lucid as soon as The Twins appear in a dream, I would know that something unusual was going to happen and would be more ready to welcome it.

But perhaps a confrontation is acceptable on my part, perhaps even necessary in dreams, as if I am being tested for flexibility and wit. I led the two large and disruptive men out of the school classroom gently and respectfully, and challenged the twin janitors politely when they ordered me to sort a huge pile of old clothing. Perhaps the trickster just wants to see how far he can go, and what you might do about it in a way that reveals your essential character. A rigid or angry response will not work, since it would indicate that you were determined to have things go your way only, and no tricks, please! That would be inviting trouble. If, on the other hand, you are willing to flow with the unexpected, you might hear a sacred song or be visited by dolphins. The trickster's motto would be "Expect the Unexpected."

I was delighted to receive a dream by e-mail from a friend in Colorado that seemed to support these observations. Folklorist Carol Mitchell and I have been exchanging dreams for 20 years, in person and by mail, but this was the first time she had encountered trickster-type characters and she was fascinated.

This is a summary focussing on the trickster aspects, since the full dream appears in chapter 10. Carol is on a picnic where she encounters four crows, one of whom transforms into a naked man who attracts her attention. She asks, "was I visited by Raven? But not really sexy or scary" (e-mail communication March 1998).

Her confusion about the nature of this dream figure is valid, since he does not yet reveal his full tricksterish character. This ambivalence is one of the delightful problems with dreams in contrast to oral tales: in a story there is no doubt about the essential nature of the trickster, whether he is the easy-going Tuvan hero Ösküs-ool or the more cleverly vengeful Liar Mvkang. In dreams, though, how can you tell whether or not a janitor is simply a janitor or a crow just a crow? By his actions and reactions, and by what happens next. I was fortunate that my dream characters gave me elegant proof—the song and the dolphins. Perhaps if Carol had managed to stay in the dream a bit longer, her tricksterish crow-man might have been able to express another side of the trickster that I have not discussed here—his erotic nature. Carol's dream might have ended happily if she had remained asleep, but this is not usually the case in stories. Trickster is insatiably lustful, willing to do almost anything to have intercourse with whomever or whatever he desires, and it almost always ends badly. But he still manages to enjoy himself, and on his own terms.

Now that I have introduced the erotic side of Trickster, I recall one last dream that I have not told to anyone at all, not even to Carol Mitchell, who would surely enjoy it after her dream crow experiences. It is one of several I had in what I call my *Star Wars* period, in which my favourite character was the tricksterish opportunist Han Solo.

I was, once again, on a space ship, this time a huge space station. For some reason everyone was being evacuated, and I was looking out a wide curved window watching them board rocket ships to carry them somewhere else. I heard the door to my room open with that *Star Trek* swishing sound and turned to see a Han Solo-like pilot, dressed in black leather, coming in. He smiled at me suggestively and said, "We're next, but there's no hurry since I'm the pilot." I now noticed that there was an enormous round bed behind us, facing the window. I looked at him and smiled, and we walked to the bed together. As we were about to carry on, I heard a thunderous roar and looked up at the curved window in time to see a massive rocket rising into the sky just outside. I immediately recognized this phallic image from movies; we looked at each other and started to laugh, and I woke up.

Like Carol, I was awake before I could discover what this trickster had to offer. But one thing was for sure—he did not follow the rules, and he was not afraid.

Much earlier I discussed a book, *Art and Fear*, that illuminated how fear blocks imagination and prevents us from expressing our natural creativity. With this in mind, I suggest that the trickster archetype is crucial in helping us to find our way in this chaotic world. Trickster is not afraid of chaos, and in fact often brings chaos into being. He leads the way in asserting that a little chaos is necessary for creativity, and fear of disorder is our great betrayer.

As I said earlier, many Trickster tales begin with the words, "Trickster was out walking one day...," always on his way to new adventures. The constant and lively movement of this challenging figure inspires us not to accept the easy way out but to push ourselves a bit. We can walk too. Who knows what we might create next. One thing is certain—it will be a surprise.

some Day your witch Might come

I remember that stage of childhood dreaming where I could actually feel myself falling into sleep and trying to fight the sense of being enchanted by some unknown force. I also recall occasionally finding myself paralysed and unable to fully wake up, and in that state seeing odd things floating around in my dark room. There is one very clear memory of a hideous green face up in the left corner where the walls and ceiling met, a face that leered at me with the malevolence of the queen-witch in Walt Disney's *Snow White and the Seven Dwarfs*, which I had seen at age five. I knew I was awake, but I could not move out of the spell of that glaring gaze until I finally managed to move the little finger on my right hand. I used that spell-breaking method any other time I felt myself caught between sleep and waking, a state I later learned was called "dream paralysis."

Perhaps my long fascination with witches, crones, and hags arose from this very real experience. In waking life, dreams, and folktales, I was both drawn to and repulsed by older women who seemed overwhelming. While I was afraid of them, their fierce negativity always seemed to be only half the story, only one side of the coin, and I was curious about the other side. My fierce ambivalence was unconscious for a long time but finally rose to the surface when I began to work on "Frau Trude," a grim little Grimm tale about an unrelenting hag who destroys a curious girl in her fire. This folktale became very central for me, personally, and as a teller, and compelled me to explore my love-hate affair with powerful, threatening women. The story had double enticement for me: I strongly identified with the doomed girl when I first read the story, since she was the epitome of the "bad" girls in folktales even though she had no younger sister to mistreat. I was that girl, at least in my imagination, the girl with the curl whom we met earlier. It seemed to me that she was being punished for her curiosity about the world, as I felt I had often been. By the time I came to writing this book, I was old enough to be more concerned about the witch. Who was she, how did she gain her power, and did she always use it so negatively? My partial answer was in the bare bones of the Grimm tale, and what came out of it after some months of grappling with the story in performance. This story bedevilled me enough that I have told it in various ways, and have written three different texts and commentaries, trying to bring about my own disenchantment with the witch I had called up (see Stone 1994, 1998, 2000).

The story in the Grimm collection and as I tell it begins with a girl who was very curious and very disobedient who decided, against her parents' wishes, to visit a witch named Frau Trude. The witch punished her by turning her into a log and throwing her into the fire. The Grimm story ended there, but as I struggled with telling this ugly story over and over, the girl began to emerge from the fire. One day when I was telling the story to a group of women, she flew out as a shower of sparks, was turned into a fiery red bird, and commanded to search the world for a story that Frau Trude had never heard before. She returned with all the stories she learned but they were not enough, and she was destined to remain a bird forever. At this point in the story's evolution I remembered my dream, the one where I try to tell a story but have no words. What happened to me in that dream could happen to the girl in the story: When she opened her mouth to scream "No!" she was startled when other words slowly began to emerge. She found that she was telling Frau Trude her own story—which of course was the one that the hag had never heard. She was freed from her enchantment, but what happened next? That is another story altogether, and one that has its echoes in the continuation of "Light Kate and Dark Kate" in this chapter.

As an artist I sensed great potential in the archetypal figures of the naive girl and the all-knowing crone who had heard all the stories of the world. I knew I would not get at this through deliberate manipulation of dreams and folktales because these creations have their own voices, and leaping in too consciously with changes interferes with a more natural transformation. Patience is definitely a virtue, and not one of my stronger assets. The cruel tale of "Frau Trude" took quite a while to transform itself into the more promising story of "The Curious Girl," and it was worth the wait. Only after a story has found its own shape can I look back and see what influences arose like sparks out of the fire of imagination and memory. I was delighted to notice that the girl's finding that she could not speak evolved from my dream of finding myself without words. In the dream and in the story, words fly out on their own and an unknown story comes into being without conscious effort, as much a surprise to the teller as to listeners.

I saw, too, that in the figure of Frau Trude there were aspects of various cronish women I had known in my waking world, especially the woman across the street, Mrs. H., whose garden had seemed to me as a child to resemble the dark forests of folktales. I also saw aspects of my mother, of course, both as the story-mother who forbids her daughter to seek out the witch, and as the "witch" herself who punished the girl's disobedience and curiosity. What was more shocking was to see myself as the witch. You might think that now that I have entered the cronish half of life I might be free of the witch's threatening power, but apparently I have not yet faced up to this enchanting artistic potential in myself. I am not free of distressing dreams with threatening older women, and maybe I do not want to be. Here is one that was so disturbing that I woke up filled both with rage and terror:

In the dream I heard that a dangerous witch was threatening people and was looking for me, and I realized I had to seek her out before she could hurt anyone. I found her in bed, a wrinkled old hag with covers pulled up to her chin, a menacing figure with an ominous leer. I wanted to run but compelled myself to stay, as I had in other threatening dreams. I reached down and began choking her but she just smiled up at me, and I understood that I could not destroy her no matter how hard I tried. I woke up with her calmly intimidating smile still in mind, wondering who she was. Just before I reached full consciousness a name floated into my mind—Nameless Dread. It was so perfect that I laughed, and then saw the humour in the old hag herself. She was playing with me, waiting patiently for me to challenge her, and I had finally done so. She seemed like a deliberately ambivalent figure, waiting to test me and see if I was worthy, like many of the crones in folktales. Baba Yaga from Russian tradition is a very fine example. In two different variants of a folktale featuring the Russian Cinderella, Vasilisa, the witch, challenges but does not destroy the young woman. In "Vasilisa the Beautiful" she is sent by her stepmother and stepsisters to bring fire back from the witch, who agrees to help if all the work is accomplished. Not only does Vasilisa work as well as the good sister in "Frau Holle," she also feeds the dog and cat, who then help her escape safely. She carries home a skull with fiery eyes that are so bright that the cruel stepfamily is destroyed (Stevens 1967, 90-105).

Nameless Dread, far less challenging than Baba Yaga, had disappeared from my dreams after I called her name and thus had power over her. Or so I thought. My ambivalent crone was still with me, and made a return visit as a crudely disguised parody of my mother.

In the dream I was visiting my family home in Miami, and was trying to find my mother. I discovered her resting in bed, then saw that it was not my mother at all but a menacing hag with dyed black hair and sharp features. I immediately decided that I was going to sneak away before she noticed me. When I got to the living room I found that she had hidden my car keys, so I had to go back and confront her. Like Nameless Dread, she was lying there waiting for me with open eyes, the blanket pulled up to her chin and her gnarled hands lying serenely above the covers. I must have learned something because, instead of trying to choke her, I told her openly that I was planning to leave and asked if she had seen my keys. She smiled a Nameless Dread smile as she lifted her right hand to reveal them. She picked them up and tossed them to me with a laugh, saying cheerily, "I guess I'm just a selfish old bitch." I was amazed to hear myself answer, "Okay, Selfish Old Bitch." I woke up with a feeling of lightness and freedom, having given her a name and accepted her once again. Okay, Kay.

I began to recognize her archetypal form from earlier dreams: a threatening woman prevented me from crossing a bridge because I did not know the password; another woman kept me from going through a special door because she said that I was not ready; still another deterred me from packing a suitcase for a planned escape because I was not putting in the "right" things, whatever these might be. A particularly annoying woman informed me that my dream house was not perfect after all, but did not tell me what she meant. In general these women restricted my movement again and again. Twice they appeared as Darth Vader with that menacing heavy breathing and a threatening stare. But none of them ever attacked, or even threatened to do so. Instead they seemed to be waiting for me to do something. Tell them a story they had never heard, perhaps.

Jung described shadow figures that embody all the darkness that we reject in ourselves (Jung 1976, 144-48). Nameless Dread and Selfish Old Bitch and their many sisters represent her well. She will not go away, she cannot be destroyed, and she has the car keys. We cannot move without her, but we need to get our keys back. The only way to transform her is by accepting her, finding the story she wants to hear, and releasing her potential as a wise woman and muse. As I pondered Selfish Old Bitch masking herself as my mother, it occurred to me that perhaps her inadequate disguise was deliberate, that she wanted me to see through to the other side. I recalled my mother in a dream from years earlier, this time entirely recognizable and positive, and appropriately reading her favourite magazine, *True Story*. I was terrified by a bear who was chasing me, and went to her for help. She was lying in bed, much like Nameless Dread and Selfish Old Bitch years later. She looked up from her magazine and calmly told me that the bear would not hurt me. She was speaking the true story, telling me something I needed to know about threatening figures. Accept them and they do no harm. Lessons like this apparently need to be learned over and over again, hence the hag was not finished with me in dreams. It was my choice whether she told me the true story or stole my car keys.

This works in folktales as well. The hag can turn you into a toad or instead provide much-needed help, depending on how she is approached. And in the waking world? Two figures from my past come immediately to mind. One of them, as I mentioned earlier, was Mrs. H. across the street from my childhood house in Pinewood Park, who seemed to love her garden more than she loved people. For me and my sister Janet, she was "the crazy old witch" on our block, though I no longer recall what she did to deserve our misgivings other than water her garden early in the morning wearing her bathrobe. Outside! We were scandalized. We avoided her house on Halloween and sometimes tossed things into her yard that we knew she would never find since her yard was so covered with trees, bushes and plants that it was like the enchanted forest of folktales. Aside from being the neighbourhood gossip, she was odd to our childish eyes because she was not like the other mothers we knew. I only found out as an adult that she provided my mother with many of the plants in her own yard and garden, and taught her how to grow them. When I was an adult, I went over with Jolene to collect her mail when she was hospitalized after a heart attack. We almost went astray in her overgrown garden-grove, and I understood what it was like to lose oneself in an enchanted forest. While I never resolved my feelings of discomfort with her face-to-face, I feel that I have partly redeemed her (and myself) through the challenging figure of "Frau Trude." The story encompasses the forest-garden she struggled so hard to maintain, complete with unearthly servants.

My second cronish figure was "Harriet," an older woman I worked with at the encyclopedia company in Chicago. She took me under her wing, as she did all new employees, helping me find an apartment that she approved of, accompanying me in shopping for acceptable winter coats and boots (what did I know, coming from Miami?), and providing a constant flow of advice at work. Eventually her unrelenting advice became overbearing and I had to escape, rather rudely, as I recall. We had more or less reconciled when I left Chicago two years later, but I never felt I had succeeded in seeing the other side of the coin. I had not faced up to what bothered me most—a woman who was, unlike my mother, unabashedly bold and confident, unafraid of what anyone else thought of her.

Where does artistry come into this? With understanding and acceptance of one's own fears and one's own dark side, the force that Jung identified as the Shadow. If the Shadow is denied, it will find ever darker ways to make itself felt. If it is recognized, it might have something to offer. The writer Brenda Ueland, whom I have quoted earlier, is a fine example of a woman who accepted her cronishness and was quite willing to be outrageous in her enthusiastic defense of artistry. Her comment on a man who was proud that he had raised his children to be rational sceptics was that "he might as well have taken them out in the backyard and killed them with an axe" (Ueland 1987, 173). If Ueland ever appears in cronish form in my dreams she surely would not deny me passage.

Quite the opposite. She thought that we should all follow our creative bents in order to "learn about the powers that are in you, all the endless stories not only from this life but from all your former incarnations" (Ueland 1987, 163). For me, all past selves from my present life are former incarnations, and they all have their own stories and dreams waiting to get past the censor, the shadowy gate-keeper of the life I am living now.

We learn from our mistakes, in dreams as well as in life. Looking at stories and dreams as ongoing created works with limitless possibilities, you can see how re-viewing can be fruitful. For instance, here is a dream I had in 1984, "Old Woman," where I met an early version of the hag, this time testing me for generosity. I failed the first test:

I was lost after visiting a friend in the city and leaving with food and other gifts in paper bags. It was dark and I could not find my car, could not remember where I had left it (all too familiar from waking life). I gave up and started walking down a long road, now out in the country instead of the city, wandering aimlessly in the dark. I stopped, admitted that I was lost, and said to myself, "Where am I?" This was an invitation for help. I saw now that the road and the surrounding area were faintly silvered by a full moon that I could not see. A mist began to rise and I thought to myself, "This looks like Scotland or Ireland." I recognized the otherworldly quality of the surroundings and wondered where I was.

I now came to a fork in the road and stopped, not knowing which way to turn and vaguely sensing that this was a significant turning point. Like the curious girl, I thought I should turn back but really wanted to find out what was ahead. I heard a woman's admonishing voice from behind me saying, "You shouldn't be out alone like this. You'd better come home with me."

I turned to see a sturdy old woman approaching on my left. She silently beckoned me to follow her. I obeyed, almost as if I were under her spell—as the girl was when she was called to enter Frau Trude's house. We came to a small house in a forest clearing and went in. I put my paper bags of food and gifts on the wooden table in the kitchen. The old woman offered me a safe place to stay for the night and asked if I had food to share. Here my "bad girl" came into play. I took a small amount of meat and bread out and we both ate, then I began to put the rest away. "I want more," she said, but I did not want to give it to her. "I can take what I want," she threatened. I was annoyed, thinking I had shared enough already, but I grumblingly took out a bit more meat and bread and began to prepare it for her. "I'll do it myself," she said, and I figured she wanted to take it all. I was stingily trying to figure out how to give her more without really being generous, and hiding food in a corner of the bag. In the middle of my silent grumbling I woke up with a feeling of loss, not for the food but for the old woman. I wanted to go back and try again, but could not get back to sleep. Instead I stayed awake quietly and let the dream come back to mind.

When I understand a dream as an open creative expression, I feel freer to see its potential for further development. In both folktales and dreams (and of course memories), there is a fine line between allowing other possibilities to arise, and manipulating outcomes. When I allowed this particular dream to come back to mind, I tried to keep myself balanced on that fine line, truly wishing the dream to suggest its own alternative outcome. Like the girl who brings stories to Frau Trude in "Curious Girl," I wanted to bring something to the hungry hag. As I re-imagined the dream, here is what happened:

When the old woman asked me if I had anything else to eat, I decided to put all of my food on the table, and we both ate the entire feast. When we finished the old woman said, "Bring me one of the coals from the fire to light my lamp. Take the spoon to carry it in." I obeyed, taking a glowing coal out with the spoon and trying to carry it back to the table, but found I could not keep it balanced. It seemed to have a life of its own, suddenly flying out of the spoon and filling the room with blinding silver light that hurt my eyes. It flew right up the chimney and disappeared, taking the light with it. The room was now utterly dark and I could hear the old woman chuckling. "Well, you got the coal further than I thought you would. It doesn't matter. It's safe to go now." I left happily without even a thought of my bags, starting down the same road again. This time it was brilliantly lit and I could see the moon in the sky, just above the trees behind the hag's house, somehow connected in my mind to the glowing coal that escaped from her chimney.

One thing that allowed this dream to develop further was my acceptance of the hag as an enigmatic character. Witches can have transformative potential, as I learned from my son Nathaniel. My husband and I had taken him to see the Disney version of "Snow White" when he was almost six, the same age I was when I saw it in 1944. He found it as distressing as I had, but for different reasons. He asked me to tell him the story in my own words, knowing already, from hearing stories both told and read, that oral tales have lives of their own while written ones do not change. As I had guessed in the "hag" dream above, he sensed further possibilities and patiently let them develop. After a week of hearing me tell "Snow White" every night, he said, "Tell me that story one more time. But this time I want the bad mother to go to sleep for a hundred years and wake up a nice lady." As a storyteller I saw how he had creatively worked out a transformation, and as a mother with a short temper, I was touched by his generosity.

At this same age, five, I was seeing the green face floating in my room after a dream. If I had been able to see the face more than once, and perhaps have my mother telling me not to be afraid, maybe I too might have been able to see possibilities of its transformation into "a nice lady." The problem with witches, though, is that they do not transform. They are what they are, unlike the beasts who become men or the ducks and swans who become women. No self-respecting witch would want to become a nice lady no matter how long she slept. Perhaps that was the living centre of my fascination, that the witch could not change but somehow still had another side, some essential aspect of her character that allowed her to share some of her powerful art under the right conditions.

I had accomplished part of my quest through the evolution of "Frau Trude," where the girl was not destroyed in the end but gained her own shape back. This led me into the adventures of "Dark Kate and Light Kate," begun in the third chapter ("There Was a Little Girl Who Had a Little Curl"). I was now on new ground, moving further away from familiar folktales with no idea, but a lot of excitement about how things might go. I kept reminding myself of the inspiration I felt while listening to a man reading from Beethoven's letters about composition and how long it takes to bring a work into being, beginning with an idea that is carried around in the mind, taken on walks, played with, gradually written down, and treated to a lot of changing. Here, then, is Kate again, carrying on down the road following her toad, about to learn from her first mentor.

Kate galloped after the toad, catching it by its right front leg just as it leapt to the threshold of the crone's hut. Kate was astonished to find herself holding the right hand of the old woman, who smiled darkly.

"Welcome back, my dear. I've been waiting for you for a long time now."

Kate, terrified for the first time in her life, found that she had no control over her feet. She was compelled to follow the crone back inside.

"You've passed my first tests, let's see how you'll do on the third," said the crone. "I tried this on another impudent girl once, a long time ago."

Dark Kate was too frightened to move. The crone passed her hand over Kate's head and chanted strange words. She felt herself growing stiff and hard, unable to lift even her smallest finger. The crone had turned her into a log, which she then tossed casually into her fireplace. "Let's see what happens now." She cackled when a shower of sparks flew out of the fire and landed on the floor. Before they could scorch the wood, the crone transformed the sparks back into Dark Kate.

"Interesting," she said. "Have you met…no, that's impossible. No matter. You have fine potential, and I have a lot to show you."

Dark Kate did not go home again. Her mother wouldn't have liked the toads and snakes anyway. So she stayed to learn all there was to be learned from the odd old woman in that curious place beneath water and earth. Then she was sent on her way.

"My sister Frau Holle can teach you more. The apple tree might tell you where you'll find her."

Kate, older now, remembered with some regret that she hadn't treated the tree very well and expected no help at all. This time she approached more respectfully, but still couldn't resist reaching up and taking one sour apple without permission.

"Ah, you again. I see you still have your old spark."

"More than you know," Kate answered evenly. "You have no reason to tell me, but do you know where Frau Holle lives?"

"Oh indeed, she's the one who turned me into an apple tree. I'll tell, if you promise to find what spell will disenchant me and then come back here."

Kate agreed, intrigued with this challenge and certain that with her own new powers she could accomplish the task easily.

"Good. Follow the stream until you come to a hedge of brambles. Pass through them and you'll find yourself at the other end of the world."

"But where is that?"

"Just go on a bit further. It's right down the path."

Kate was sceptical that the end of the world was so near, but she followed the directions, came to the bramble hedge, spoke a spell that turned its thorns into blossoms, and passed through. On the other side she saw an old stone well.

"Oh no, not the well at the world's end again," Kate murmured. "Well, at least I know what to do. Here goes."

She dropped down into the well, heard the air whistling in her ears as she fell into darkness, and the voices of frogs and toads singing as she went. "Maybe one of them's a prince," she chortled to herself. For a long time, forever, it seemed, Kate's plunge continued, so long that she forgot where she was and where she was going. At last she fell into the water at the bottom of the well, sank until she felt solid earth beneath her feet. It seemed to be dry ground.

"Now what?" she said out loud, and was startled to hear a voice answer her: "Over here, over here."

She turned toward the sound and saw the merest bit of light, and in it a tiny brown toad that was beckoning her to follow.

"Well, it's not a white rabbit," she grumbled as she found herself once again following a toad. "My cousins told me to watch out for you," the toad said cordially.

And that is how she came to Frau Holle, was taught to shake the crone's feather bed so that snow fell in the right season, learned the language of the birds who could hear all the sounds of the world, and discovered which stones were the keepers of stories. There were other things as well, but she was diligent and mastered them all, and was even beginning to do things that her teacher had not taught.

"That's it. You're ready to move on. I have nothing more for you. You're finished here."

Kate was about to ask where she should go next when, all at once, the apple tree's request came back to her and she remembered her promise.

"Before I go, there's an apple tree..."

"Right. That one. It's been waiting for ages for someone to get this far and ask me to lift the spell. Simple. You have to pick every single apple from the tree, even the withered ones from all the past winters. That's all I'll say."

The tree stood on the path to Baba Yaga, the third sister.

"She has a kindly name, but my sister is anything but kind. That's her privilege as the eldest. You know what I mean. Watch out for her iron leg and her sharp fingers."

"But how do I find her? Don't tell me it's at the end of the earth, I've already been there twice."

"No. You go from the lowest to the highest place. Be off!"

The little toad accompanied Kate, showing her a shortcut back to the meadow where the apple tree stood, and then went to join all its toad kin who had scattered from Kate's bag a long time ago. She was now an aging woman, and her feet ached, her left knee was bothering her, and she noticed that she wasn't seeing as clearly as she used to. She began to wonder if crones lost their powers in the same way ordinary people did, or if they had ways of compensating.

The apple tree had aged too. Many of its branches were dry and dead, and it seemed to droop dejectedly.

"You came back. I'm amazed. Did you remember to ask?"

"Oh yes, but by the looks of you I'm not sure you're going to like the cure. I have to pick every single apple, including the old dried up ones from all the past winters. Your ancient branches won't take much climbing."

"But you don't have to climb. All you have to do is shake me, as I asked you to do before. You didn't listen then."

This time Kate listened, and began to push and shove the ancient tree with all her strength. Nothing happened.

"Not so hard," the tree complained. "Just touch my bark."

Kate felt the rough bark of the tree in her hands, touched it gently and began to sing a song about sitting under an apple tree that she remembered from childhood. "With nobody else but me," she crooned, as all the apples began to rain down on her.

Then a strange thing happened. The rugged bark began to soften, the tree slowly shrank, and gradually changed into the shape of a white-bearded old man who got smaller and smaller until he was half of Kate's size.

"That's what you get for spinning gold for silly girls," he grumbled. "It was the witch's gold, and she didn't like that one bit. And all I wanted was a child to call my own."

Kate had an unfamiliar twinge of compassion, and asked where he would go now that he was free.

"I'm not sure I can go anywhere after standing here for so long, but since I don't have anything better to do maybe I'll come along with you. I've never met the oldest sister, the one with the most power. Maybe she can do something for me."

They set off together, seeking the lowest and the highest place in the world. Neither of them had the slightest idea where that might be, but they had plenty of sour apples to eat along the way. They walked on for seven days and six nights, and on the seventh night they fell asleep in a low valley, under stars so bright that they seemed alive. "Oh," thought Kate as she fell asleep, "I wish those stars were truly alive and could help us."

To make a long story somewhat shorter, that is exactly what happened. Kate passed from the lowest place to the highest place as she slept. When she woke up she found herself in the sky, and there was the chicken-legged hut of Baba Yaga, surrounded by a fence of human bones topped with skulls with flaming eyes that watched her as she passed. Baba Yaga tested her with a necklace of crystal beads, which she broke and scattered to the winds.

"Find them and you won't lose your head," she snarled, and all the glowing skulls smiled.

Kate didn't lose her head. She was calm because she knew she had many helpers now, and she could call them because she knew the language of birds. Everyone from the smallest ant to the largest bear helped gather each bead. When the necklace was reassembled it had one extra bead, and no one knew where it had come from.

"Excellent. You have learned well if you have the help of the invisible ones, and now I can teach you the higher wisdoms."

Kate learned about the movements of earth, ocean, air, and the fire below them all. She understood the balancing of sun, moon, and planets, and which stars were truly alive. But in the end she wanted only one thing, to be back in her own realm with the good earth beneath her feet.

"Give up your hair and I'll weave a rope to lower you down," said Baba Yaga, "but you must not open your eyes until you feel the earth under you."

And so it was. Kate was lowered by a rope made from her own strong hair, and managed to keep her eyes closed until she felt her feet strike something solid. Alas, when she opened her eyes she had not reached the earth yet, but was trapped at the top of an immense pine tree. Dark Kate, with all her boldness and all her knowledge, was afraid to climb down by herself. She closed her eyes again and began to call for help from all the creatures she'd met in her long life. It was a bear who climbed to the top and helped her down.

The old dwarf who had been a crabapple tree was waiting.

"Time to move on," he said. And they did. They are travelling still, the dwarf and the crone, looking for curious girls who wish to learn more than is good for them.

The ambivalent crones in this story, and in most of my dreams, have one foot very strongly planted on the dark side, and perhaps only the toes of the other pointing to the light side. There is a balance, but one that is easily swayed depending on the nature of the one who approaches the crone. Kate, who in other stories would come out badly, earns her magical powers by learning how to learn. Since she is rash rather than dark-hearted, she can survive the crones' precarious ambivalence instead of being destroyed, turned to wood, or covered with tar like her less resourceful counterparts.

And me? I am respectful. I have sensed the dual nature of the crones I have met in dreams and stories, and note a bit of the trickster in Nameless Dread and Selfish Old Bitch, who teased me with their wicked smiles. But I had received no special gifts (getting your own car keys back does not count). Crones, of course, can take positive form as well. I found this when I began to have dream visits from an old storytelling friend, Katy Simons, 91 as I write this. Katy (whose story of "The Magic Drum" appears in chapter 13) had been a student in my folklore class in the mid-1970s, but had disappeared from my life except for infrequent spontaneous meetings. The last time I saw her, she was touring a public building with a group of seniors, and when I greeted her warmly, she did not remember who I was. We had both aged, but she was more easily recognizable to me than I was to her, with my brown hair gone white and my figure predictably less girlish. She acknowledged me politely, and when I said good bye I thought it might be the last time

I saw Katy. I was wrong. The next year an article on her appeared in the University of Winnipeg alumni journal after she had been honoured with the prestigious Righteous Among Nations award from the Holocaust Museum in Jerusalem for her family's part in sheltering Jews during the war years in Holland. I was delighted to see that she was still very much alive.

In a space of two months Katy visited me in three dreams, always in a public place (my other crones were always private), and always without the two aluminum canes she has used for years after failed hip surgery. In these dreams she was entirely articulate, knew exactly who I was and greeted me warmly, and had all of her old spark and boldness. In the third dream, Katy revealed the radiant aspect of the crone as an archetype of gift-giving power:

In this dream I was at a conference or a storytelling event, and was going up a flight of stairs to meet some friends. On the fourth floor I heard someone call my name, and turned around to see Katy approaching in one of her usual blue print dresses. "Kay, I brought you something," she said, as she handed me a glass box the size of an old glove box. The crystal clear box was transparent but its contents were obscure. Still, I knew that I was receiving a significant gift as I held it in both hands. "Katy, you always find such beautiful things," I said. "Oh yes, I know where the beautiful things are," she answered simply, and with a smile that was not ambivalent in the least. I awoke with a distinct sense of having actually received a fine gift, and when I told the dream to my friend Morgana, she pointed out that the crone who "knows where the beautiful things are" is me, of course. The gift is real.

When any archetype appears three times, an important change is taking place. With the appearance of a gift in this particular dream, maybe I have at last discovered how to listen and learn, how to accept what the crone has to offer, even when I cannot see what it is. Perhaps it is not meant to be seen, but felt in some other way. I want to emphasize here that familiar figures who appear in dreams are not actually the people we recognize from our waking world, but archetypal images taking on the appearance of those we know. Katy the woman is not a crone, but Dream Katy is. That is, the open archetype of the crone fills itself with a likely person who I happened to know, much like Selfish Old Bitch trying to look like my mother.

Like other gift-bearing dreams, this one asks to be brought to light in the waking world, and the dream was a reminder that I could do so. I had a roughly written memoir Katy had written years ago, and I was determined to get it into shape, to find the art in Katy's life and release it from the clear box. With this, the dream becomes real, transformed into the written word. Crones, skilled in true magic of all sorts, are at the heart of many transformations, as we will see in the coming chapter.

Transformations: Iron Fish and Naked Crows

Transformation, changing from one form to another, is one of the most familiar motifs in world folktales and sacred legends, not to mention dreams. People can become animals, birds, fish, insects, trees, or clouds, and of course animals and objects can also turn into people. While in the midst of a story or a dream we do not question such amazing changes, since anything can happen within the special logic of dreams and stories. For example, story characters do not find it the least bit surprising that frogs, lions, or swans can change into human beings in folktales, or that creatures in dreams can speak to you.

Transformation is often connected to the traditional four elements of fire, water, earth, and air. Change is sometimes brought about by an act of conscious or unconscious disobedience or outright audacity, and sometimes by compassion. The enchanted amphibian in the Grimm tale rose into daylight from the element of water, and became a prince only after being thrown against the wall by the spoiled, disobedient princess. There is no magical kiss in this tale, though there might be in others:

Both these transformational aspects—an essential element and an implied act of audacity—were present when I met the frog I dreamed up one night, a convincingly smelly green amphibian with a swampy odour. I was waiting for a bus with some friends, and noticed that there was a bus bench with a crudely carved graffiti proclaiming, "The Frog Sits Here." Sure enough, a sad-looking frog was hunched on the bench right under these words. I realized he needed to be in water, so I carried him to a large plastic baby bathtub that happened to appear a few feet away (what you need in a dream is usually there somewhere). As I placed him gently in I could smell his strong swampy odour and said to myself, "This is certainly a real frog!" Then, obviously not remembering that there was no transformative kiss in "The Frog Prince," I said to myself with a smile, "Well, this is my only chance. I can't resist." I leaned down and gave the smelly creature a playful kiss, and was stunned when he turned into an appealing and unclothed young man squeezed uncomfortably into the little tub. He was as amazed as I was. We looked at each other in disbelief, and then started to laugh. Alas, I woke up before we could seize the moment. But I did wake up smiling.

Note that the somewhat audacious kiss of transformation came only after I had placed him in the element of water, so I could not say what, in fact, really brought about the change. Nor did I care.

A folklore colleague and friend that I have shared dreams with over the years reported a similar dream experience. She, too, was too surprised to take advantage of the situation:

> I had a dream last night that I loved so I have to tell you about it. I was eating fried chicken, outdoors, on a picnic I guess, when I saw four naked crows talking together. (They were not plucked, but skinned—naked.) I was afraid they might get a bit cold. I decided not to eat all of my chicken thigh so I could leave some for the crows since I thought they'd need extra nourishment to stay warm until their feathers grew back—at least I was hoping they would grow back. They seemed quite healthy though and didn't seem to be hurting. So I took one more bite, leaving about half of a juicy chicken thigh, and walked over past the group and threw them the left-over thigh as I walked by. Suddenly, but not surprisingly, one of the crows became a tall naked man who started walking close behind me, sort of indicating that I should walk faster. And that's all I remember, but I thought it was kind of cool (e-mail communication, March 1998).

Carol commented that "instead of swan maidens, I have a crow man. Was I visited by Raven? But not really sexy or scary, so how could it be Trickster? Just some ordinary crow that metamorphosed into an ordinary man. I'd like to meet those crows again. The dream certainly left me intrigued."

I am not certain which transformative element is central, whether it is the chicken meat transformed by fire, or the crows who are creatures of the air but here stand on the earth, but most significant is Carol's feeling of compassion for the naked crows. This opens up the potential transformative action from crow to man. I am intrigued by how similar this is to my frog dream: naked creatures becoming unclothed men through acts of compassion that involve an offering (water for the unhappy frog, meat for the crows).

Water can be a source of surprising transformations: in various stories people emerge from lakes or seas, sometimes in animal form (seals, fish, even cattle), and sometimes in human form (seals, for example, may shed their skins to become men and women). In one of my favourite transformative stories, an ancient legend from China, an ordinary fish becomes an extraordinary mythological figure.

The story describes a waterfall on the Yangtze River known as The Dragon Gate. Here, golden carp gathered in the pool at the base of the cataract preparing to ascend. According to the legend, any carp that succeeded in leaping up through the pounding water, surviving the predators and fishermen who waited on all sides, would become a golden river dragon—Yu Lung—on reaching the top (SGI 2000, 28). As in "The Golden Woman," the river dragons become living gold, the pure element sought by alchemists in medieval Europe and elsewhere. Their task is to guard rivers from harm.

Dragons got a bad name in Europe after Christianity arrived, but in pre-Christian Europe and throughout Asia, these ancient mystic creatures were often regarded as spiritual beings. They were protective rather than destructive, as we saw in the Spanish folktale of "The Water of Life," where the dragon was the guardian of the sacred water. Archetypally, reptilian creatures have often been associated with water in both Old World and New, in part because of their natural abilities to change shape (tadpoles to frogs) or to shed their skin. In sacred tales this allows them to become immortal.

I mentioned earlier that water as an archetype is a metaphor for our unseen selves, our unconscious store of treasures. With this in mind we might regard reptilians in dreams as guardians of these treasures, protecting them from the conscious mind until we are ready to receive them and become transformed ourselves. In "The White Alligator" dream in chapter 5, the threatening alligator, a water creature, became an earthy, glowing unicorn only when I accepted its powerful presence and open the door to danger. Spiritual transformation in religious baptism gives another perspective on the profound archetypal symbol of water.

Even in the harsh light of day, the waking world can echo back to spiritual archetypes when we let imagination roam. I recall tiny fingerling salmon I saw in 1994, pushing themselves stubbornly against the current in a fish ladder tank at a dam near Whitehorse in the Yukon. These miniature creatures were already flashing their fine silver scales, inspiring me to envision them becoming sinuous silver river dragons.

Leaving dragons aside, fish might not seem likely candidates for folktale transformations, but they might have some surprises up their gills. In a traditional tale I read recently, described as coming from "a beautiful island that lies in the south seas," an iridescent fish has a very different sort of transformation, passing through the elements of water and earth into the plant realm (Lang 1968, 209-215). The story, entitled "The Bones of Djulung," begins with the familiar figure of mistreated sister:

On this island there were seven sisters, of whom the eldest was in charge and assigned all the tasks of cleaning, water-gathering, cooking, washing, and wood-gathering. The youngest was given the hardest and dirtiest task of collecting wood for the cooking fire every day, and one day on her way home she saw an iridescent fish and asked if it would be her pet. The fish, Djulung, swam into her hands and she carried it to her secret place, a small cave hidden by a waterfall. She put the fish in the deep pool inside the cave, brought it food everyday, and grew to love it as her only friend. When Djulung rose up to take the offered food, his iridescent glow lit up the water in the dark pool. The fish grew huge as she fed it half of her food, and one day a sister followed her and discovered the large and succulent creature. Djulung, as the fish was called, was caught, carried home, and eaten for supper by the elder sisters, without the knowledge of the youngest.

She learned from a dream what had happened and where Djulung's bones were buried, and immediately went to the place and dug them up very carefully, not missing even the smallest one. She carried the bones to her secret place and buried them next to the cave. As she sang mournfully, she saw a tiny green shoot rise up from the grave, and she continued to sing with all her heart. This shoot quickly grew into a magnificent tree with leaves of brilliant iridescent colours. One of these leaves was discovered by the chief of a nearby island, who came looking for the tree. The elder sisters, of course, knew nothing about it, but the youngest led the chief to the magical tree, sat down beneath it, and began to tell him the story of the magnificent fish, Djulung. And he listened.

Andrew Lang's nineteenth-century story ends with a marriage, but my imagination had been caught by the gentle love of the girl and the magical fish, and with his wondrous transformation into a tree with iridescent leaves, so I did not feel that the marriage had to be spelled out so literally. The fact that the chief listens and hears means that he is worthy of the woman. What happens next is up to the listener/reader.

It might be coincidental that Djulung is close in sound to Yu Lung; but since we do not know exactly where this "beautiful island in the South Seas" might be, no firm connections are possible. But the connection with water is not coincidental, since water is a sacred element, as we know from religious rites all over the world. In "The Golden Woman" dream I pass through air and then earth into the dark sea, where I become encased in a cylindrical mold, prepared for a golden transformation in the fire. In "The Water of Life," the sister frees her brothers and all others on the path from stones to people by touching them with a single drop of the transformative water. And of course she also brings new life to the Tree of Hope, which blooms again after the water soaks into the earth and passes up into the tree.

As I pondered the dream and the story, along with the Yu Lung and Djulung legends, I wondered why I had never dreamed of fish, those deep swimmers in the archetypal depths of our hidden souls. Later that week I had a fish dream, as if my dreaming mind was aware of my pondering. The fish in the dream, though, was not in its element, and could hardly move. This was an apt symbolic portrayal of my actual physical state at that time, after several days of flu that left me with a very stiff neck and an endless headache. Like the fish, I was not swimming very well.

The dream began with children playing games or reading stories, something light and merry. I was part of this but my role was unclear. I cannot recall if I was an adult caring for them, or one of the children. As we played, I heard a soft whirring noise coming from outside, and glanced out the window to see something moving slowly through the air just above the rooftops of houses across the street. At first I thought it was the Goodyear Blimp, a familiar sight from my Miami childhood where the blimp was based for part of the year. It seemed to be trailing an advertisement. Then I saw what it was. "It's the Iron Fish!" I yelled, as I jumped up and ran outside. The blimp-shaped fish was towing some kind of flowing abstract design almost as long as it was—that is what I thought was the advertisement—and it carried a much smaller fish in its mouth. All together, these elements resembled an odd floating weathervane figure.

As I got outside, the Iron Fish began to disappear around a corner, and I yelled in a child's voice, "Iron Fish, come back!" I was amazed when the fish immediately turned around and floated slowly back toward me, low enough now that I was able to reach up and pull it down. It was much too large to swim into my hands, but perhaps it would have found a way if I had not been so aggressive. I was reminded of the rainbow fish in the story of "Djulung," who trustingly swam into the outstretched hand of the kind sister, and indeed the small fish carried in the mouth of the Iron Fish was Djulung's size. I see now that it was just as likely that this small fish was a guide rather than prey.

Perhaps because I had grabbed Iron Fish instead of allowing it to present itself freely, it tried to struggle out of my grip. Its iron plating did not allow it the fluid movement of a live fish, so I was able to hold it firmly and to drag it inside. This was not easy, as the fish was large and weighty, and I felt like a two-year-old struggling to carry a huge stuffed animal. A cat leapt up and tried to catch the fingerling carried in the mouth of the larger fish, and when I protected it I noticed a few golden scales glimmering. "I want to draw your picture but I can't find my sketchbook," I wailed as I grappled with both fish, staggering around trying to find my drawing materials. As I began to drift out of the dream I could see that both fish were slowly transforming, becoming supple and alive, and that the abstract design trailing behind them seemed to have become smaller but even more beautiful, also with a life of its own, like a gracefully undulating sea plant.

I awoke frustrated that I could not find the sketchbook to do justice to the radiance of this image. I was also sad that the fish was out of its element, and thought I might have tried to get it into water and release it from its heavy armour, like the stones were freed in "The Water of Life." The stark contrast in imagery between the iron fish and the leaping dragon-carp in the Chinese legend has stayed with me, waiting for me to find my elusive sketchbook.

When I have a perplexing dream of this sort I do not try to interpret it intellectually but let it rest in the back of my mind, believing that it will present its own message when I am ready to see, hear, or feel it. I report it to a few sympathetic supporters and listen carefully to their responses. This is much like listening to multiple variants of a folktale for a fuller sense of its possibilities. I also find reverberations between archetypal elements of dreams and stories. For example, I know from narratives everywhere in the world that iron is a magical metal transformed by fire, and that early iron-workers were considered to be shamans and magicians. Thinking of the Iron Fish as having already passed through the transformative element of fire gave me another perspective; also, its iron encasement was similar to the encrusted cylinder that held me in "The Golden Woman" dream. In other words, the dream suggests transformation rather than imprisonment.

For a while I imagined what it might feel like to be a heavy Iron Fish out of water, dragging a long tail—lovely wordplay on "tale"—behind me, and carrying a smaller fish in my mouth. For a storyteller, this took on another dimension of meaning. The long tail/tale is heavy because it, too, needs to be changed. The small fish as a guiding voice is leading the way, not in danger of being swallowed after all. The whole story wanted to find its true element and become lighter and brighter. As the fish I swam hopefully toward the girl who called me down, but when I was grabbed I lost my direction and then had to go where she took me.

I could see how the dream was trying in vain to become art. It suggested sketching but could not provide the necessary tools; I could not draw and the fish could not swim, and it was truly agonizing. One of my realizations about dreams is that the frustrating ones sometimes stay in mind even more vividly than those that resolve beautifully. "The Golden Woman" is a rare exception, since I still remember the details of line and colour, the sounds (especially the echoing reverberations as I pass through the dark sea), and the clear sense of sinking slowly through air, earth, and water, and of the fire heating me to the edge of agony. But in most cases, pleasant dreams fade away all too quickly, leaving barely a trace or a wake behind. In contrast, The Iron Fish left a strong wake even though it could not swim. I carried the image of its cumbersome passage just above the rooftops, its slight movement that caused the trailing abstract tail to quiver slightly, and the motion of the tiny fish held in its mouth.

These images would make a fine little animated film if I had my brother Terry's skills in computer animation. I imagine the small fish swimming free and the iron fish flowing after it, both shedding flecks of black iron as they move faster and faster through the air and finally leap down into a deep pool, the abstract design turning into a shower of water droplets. The two fish rise to the surface through the dark water, and, like Djulung, they light up the water with their glow as they ascend. With these vibrant visions in mind I looked for and found my sketchbook, and did a series of drawings with metallic gel pens on black paper in which the two fish do indeed find their way back into water and achieve their full golden metamorphosis.

As I reviewed this dream three years later, I decided to do a mobile of wire and pieces of glass to try to do justice to the challenging contradiction of iron and fluidity. I remembered a similar fish in a small catalogue for an exhibit of Alexander Calder that Dan and I had seen in Washington in 1998. When I found that fish in the catalogue, I was stunned to see that it was the very Iron Fish of my dream, complete with an undulating tail of separate pieces and a small metal shape in its mouth. Obviously the dream had used this image held in my unconscious memory for two years, and found a way of making it manifest in a way that adroitly combined my internal and external worlds and provided new meaning to a fish that was, in the National Gallery in Washington, D.C., literally floating in the air. In this double transformation, Calder made iron float in air and I got it back into water, at least in my sketches.

Transformation is so central to folktales and sacred tales that I can hardly think of one that does not at least touch on this motif somewhere in its movement from beginning to end. The many varieties of Beauty/Beast tales around the world feature an astonishing array of creatures large and small, from bulls, lions, and giant serpents to frogs and mice. Some are male, others female. As we saw in Stewart Cameron's tale of "Jack and the Three Feathers" in chapter 7, these stories revolve around the recognition and acceptance of the creatures who bring about their transformation. Here is a Finnish tale, "The Forest Bride," similar to Stewart Cameron's tale. It is rewritten by Ottawa teller and writer Jan Andrews (Andrews 2000, 10):

A woodcutter told each of his three sons to go to the forest and cut a tree, travel in the direction it was pointing when it fell, and find someone who would agree to marry them. The two older brothers cut their trees and set out, but the tree cut by the youngest son, Veiko, fell directly into the forest. His brothers laughed as he dutifully set off into the woods, where he found a modest cabin in a clearing. Inside he found only a small brown mouse with sparkling dark eyes and a lovely voice. When she learned that he had been sent to find a bride she offered herself, and he happily accepted. He returned home, and said he'd met a fine lady dressed in velvet. His father was pleased.

Now the sons were sent to discover if their chosen ones could bake bread and could weave good cloth. Veiko was downcast by the prospect of asking a mouse to try to bake and weave, but she laughed, took out a tiny silver bell, and called hundreds of mice to help gather the needed materials, which she used to accomplish the proposed tasks. Her bread and her cloth were much finer than what the other brothers brought home, but the woodcutter was equally pleased with all of his sons.

He now sent them to bring their brides home for the wedding. Veiko was anxious about bringing home a mouse, but he kept his promise (unlike the princess in "The Frog Prince"). The mouse again took out her silver bell and called up a tiny coach pulled by six gray mice, and they all set off with Veiko racing behind. As they came to the bridge over the river near his home, the coach was knocked into the river. Before he could leap in, he saw six grey horses rise from the river pulling a handsome coach. The young woman inside had flashing dark eyes and a beautiful velvet dress...and what happened next is a familiar story.

This mouse achieves her transformation in water, but air can also be a medium for change. I am still bemused by something that happened in 1982 when we were spending a sabbatical year with my youngest sister, Lois, on Block Island, Rhode Island. One night I rescued a very nimble mouse from our cat by throwing a dish towel over the darting creature, wrapping it firmly, and tossing it out the door, thus creating a flying mouse. Lois was not as amused as I was, since she knew it would come right back in.

My flying mouse reminded me of the story of "Jumping Mouse," mentioned in chapter 4. At the end of the story the mouse leaps up into the wind and is carried on the air, where it experiences a startling transformation into an eagle. My mouse, in contrast, kept its rodent shape and most likely returned the next night for further adventures with the cat. Perhaps it was looking for Veiko.

The elements of air and sky figure prominently in stories from around the world. In many, heavenly beings descend to earth, sometimes to remain as husbands or wives, sometimes to entice humans into the sky. In other legends characters become stars or other heavenly bodies. Sky stories abound across North America. Among them is a Cherokee myth of disobedient boys who become the Pleiades (we will meet them later in this chapter), and rich variants from many different places about women or men who marry star beings. Among these is a particularly fine Ojibwa story we will see in the next chapter, about two sisters who unknowingly wish themselves into the sky.

What about fire, a common element of transformation? Fire is yet another major motif in world lore, epitomized by the Phoenix rising from the ashes of its consuming fire. Legends and sacred tales around the world feature a variety of protagonists who transform human life by stealing fire. Many are human or human-like, a well-known example being Prometheus from Greek mythology. The animal world is also a primary source of fire-bringers, particularly in the sacred tales of North America. Coyote, Hare, Raven, and other tricksters are fire stealers, but more modest creatures are also found in these narratives, like Water Spider in Cherokee sacred legends (Mooney 1992, 240-41). In practical terms it was a significant step in human development when it was learned that fire could transform food, metal, and the landscape—for better and for worse. It is not surprising, then, that fire in its destructive and transformative aspects would burn in human imagination, in new dreams and old tales.

For years I have dreamed of conflagrations threatening from a distance; as they got closer I would wake myself up, avoiding the possible experience of profound change. Thus transformation by fire in "The Golden Woman" was all the more powerful because it was so entirely unexpected. I had no time for fear since the four helpers rolled me into the flames so quickly that I could not react. Perhaps, too, fiery in element "The Golden Woman" was inspired by earlier dreams in which I allowed less obvious forms of fire to ignite my dreams. For example, it was a glowing red disc that transformed the puma in a dream I mentioned briefly in chapter 6. Here is a fuller summary of this significant dream with all its angry passions:

I was driving to spacious Greynold's Park, a very familiar place from my Miami childhood. I was going to the picnic ground we had often visited, but when I arrived and got out of the car I was surprised to hear a hypnotic voice chanting in the midst of a big crowd. I jumped back as wild animals of all sizes—rabbits, mice, squirrels, deer, bears, foxes and wolves—dashed out of the crowd and across the street into the safety of the woods. Suddenly I, too, became an animal, a powerful puma, and instinctively leapt away from the people and into the safety of the woods. As a beast I understood that I now had to hunt and kill my food, no more grocery stores or restaurants. In horror I screamed, "I can't do that!" and the response was immediate. A large net dropped over me and I was trapped. I was taken to the Crandon Park Zoo and put in a spacious cage with all meals provided—fresh sirloin steak on an elegant platter. It should have been ideal, but I hated it. I wanted out. A keeper appeared and began striking the bars with a metal-tipped wooden staff. The clanging sound and the sparks that rose from metal hitting metal enraged me. I crouched down determined to kill this keeper, and in that lowered position I saw that he was trying to get me to look at a cage across the way. A golden gibbon was sitting on a high perch, reading what looked like an alphabet book. But it was something entirely different.

This small ape, very much like the monkey-like creature in the kitchen in my earlier dream, looked up, saw me, and held the book up so I could see a red circle that seemed to be an apple. As I looked more intently I saw that it was an expanding disc of living fire, like the inside of an active volcano. I had a deep and very visceral understanding that I was looking at the centre of creation and that we, puma, keeper, and ape, were all an equal part of this creation. At that point, the iron bars of the cages melted away and we were all freed.

When I awoke and invited the power of the dream to stay with me, I recalled a waking experience with living fire that gave me a model for the glowing circle. In my final year as a geography student at the University of Miami, my industrial geography class took a field trip to a cement plant. When we were shown the massive rotating cylinder in which materials were transformed into a molten state, I could not pull myself away. Watching that constantly turning fiery mass mesmerized me completely, and the memory has been kept alive by seeing volcanoes in nature photos and television documentaries. Most fascinating to me were the volcanic eruptions that occur in the deepest parts of the oceans, a combination of fire, water, and earth, at the very centre of creation that makes its way up into the air.

Since artistic imagination is fed by an intricate weave of remembered experiences from dreams and life, I can see how my fascination with dream fire led into the consuming/transforming fire in "The Curious Girl." She simply had to be thrown into the crone's fire.

By contrast, I have rarely dreamed of earth as an element of transformation, though it is certainly vital in world lore and mythology. Burial in the earth is an ancient and wide-spread practice that builds on belief in resurrection, and in folktale and myth this belief comes to literal fruition. For example, both earth and water figure in a Russian story titled "The Rosy Apple and the Golden Bowl," a favourite of Toronto teller Carol McGirr. The kind youngest sister has been given a golden bowl that reveals the future in beautifully coloured images as the apple is rolled around inside it. Her jealous sisters crave that bowl so much that they take her into the forest and murder her, burying her in the earth beside a silver birch tree. Some time after this a passing shepherd fashions a pipe from reeds he finds growing under the birch, and the pipe sings the story of the murder. The sister's father begs the water of life from the tsar and rescues her, transformed, from the earth (Stone 1998, 197-200).

Transformations that take place in the earth element are usually much more prolonged than in fire or water, and the resulting change is often from the human into the plant world. Familiar examples of this come from Greek and Norse mythology, as well as from more recent peoples for whom the land was still a living entity. In a Cherokee narrative of the Pleiades I mentioned earlier, one of the disobedient boys who is angry after being punished by his mother sinks into the earth, while the others ascend into the sky and immediately become stars; his metamorphosis takes place slowly in the earth, only after his mother has watered the earth with her tears for some time. At last a small shoot appears and eventually it grows into the first pine tree (Mooney 1992, 258-59).

My experience with earth in "The Golden Woman" is not quite complete, since no obvious change happens to me in the earth. I move through it but do not stay long enough to be transformed, as I soon will be in the sea and then the fire. In a more recent dream earth is more central, though I am not the main character.

In the dream I was asked to tell a story to a group of adults, and wanted to find one I had never told before. As often happens in stories I try to tell in dreams, this one unwound itself as I told it. I did not know myself what was coming next. I began by describing a woman sitting alone at a large table after a Thanksgiving dinner, staring absently at the platter of turkey bones. All at once the bones began to move, coming together to form a headless skeleton that somehow spoke to the astonished woman. "I want you to bury me," it said, and when the woman responded that she had already planned to do so, the turkey bones then began to specify the burial:

"I want you to put me in a wooden box, and put your husband's gold cane in too. Dig a hole exactly three feet deep and three feet square."

The woman was preparing to do as the turkey commanded when I woke up, smiling at the talking turkey bones. It was still dark, so I decided to lie there and let the dream rest in my head instead of getting up to write it down. I tried to remember the precise words the turkey used. I was not sure exactly what gold object the turkey asked for, but it was somehow related to a royal treasure. That is, she was being asked to give up something precious to her not only because it was gold but because it was a memento of her husband, who was not there to give his permission.

Usually when I anchor a dream in my memory this way I stay strictly to the details of the dream, treating it as an actual experience. But perhaps because this was a story being told in a dream it felt freer, and I found myself spontaneously treating it like a story I was preparing to perform, allowing it to suggest its own details of plot and character development. It seemed to me that this was not a royal setting, that the woman really had very little in the way of precious objects. Thus the husband's golden cane spontaneously became a gold watch, and the wooden box was a chest carved by her father. These were the only cherished possessions she owned. The place of burial became clear—under an old apple tree—and the transformation implied by the dream took place through an accidental wish.

I went back to sleep confident that I would be able to remember the dream in the morning, and in fact I was able to tell both the incomplete dream and the evolving story when I woke up. In doing so I realized that I was carrying out what I have been going on and on about through this whole book, transforming a dream into waking art. It seems fitting to end this chapter with the story as it has evolved instinctively from the dream. The story will continue to emerge as I tell it in performance.

In a certain place at a certain time, a woman and her husband lived a simple life in a small house. They had just what they needed, not more and not less. One day after a modest Thanksgiving meal, the husband had gone to do errands while the wife prepared to clear the table. As she looked at the platter of bones, they suddenly began to move together and rejoin. When the turkey's skeleton was complete, it stood right up in the platter and began to speak to the woman.

"I want you to bury me," it said. "Of course," she responded.

"I want you to bury me in a wooden box," it demanded. She sighed, thinking of her only wooden box, carved by her father long ago, but she agreed.

"I want you to put your husband's gold watch in with my bones," it insisted. "Oh dear," she said sadly. It was her husband's only precious possession, his grandfather's watch, and he wasn't there to say yes or no. But the turkey bones were so certain of what was needed that she agreed.

"The hole must be exactly three feet deep and three feet square, under the old apple tree in the front yard." She thought of the tree that hadn't produced apples for many years, wondering how she could dig into the ancient roots.

"If you do all this, I'll grant you one wish," said the bones, and then they settled and scattered back onto the platter. The woman found the wooden box and the gold watch, and began to gather the bones one by one, not missing even the smallest. When she had finished, she carried the box outside, found the shovel, and began to dig under the tree. It was hard work, and when she was weary she thought, but did not say, "Oh, I wish this was done," and so it did not happen. When she finally finished the hole and had to climb down into it to place the box at the bottom, she thought but did not say, "Oh, I wish my husband was here to help," and so it did not happen.

As the box touched the earth she heard the bones rattle and thought of the poor turkey and without thinking said, "Oh, I do wish that fine bird was still alive." It was too late now, she had spoken her wish. All at once she heard a noise from the branches of the tree above her and looked up to see the turkey there. "Well," it said, "since you've used your wish to bring me back to life, I'll tell you a secret." "Oh!" she said in surprise. "Take the box out, get your shovel, and dig down just a bit more, and you'll find something surprising." When the turkey finished speaking it flew away.

The woman began to dig, and it was done in no time, as if her first wish had been granted. She set the box up on the edge of the hole and then began to dig down a bit more. Her shovel struck something hard, and she started to dig around it carefully. Just then her husband appeared, and her second unspoken wish was granted. When she told him what had happened, he climbed down and helped her dig out an old metal box and bring it up to the surface. As they were about to open the box they heard the loud gabbling of a turkey, and the woman woke up from a dream.

She sat up in bed, waking up her husband beside her. "Oh my, I've had the strangest dream," she said. When she had told it all to him the morning sun was already rising, and they decided to get up, find the shovel, and dig under the old apple tree. Sure enough, when they dug down just a bit more than three feet they found an old metal box, lifted it out and opened the lid to find a treasure that kept them healthy and happy until the end of their days. Even more wonderfully, the apple tree began to bloom again after the box no longer interfered with its roots, and they had fine sweet apples for the rest of their lives together.

section III–
DREAM WORLDS

Falling Up

Only recently I dreamed I was leaving an academic meeting with three friends, talking as we walked along the empty city street at night. I looked up and saw a perfect circle of radiant stars above us, so vivid that I was surprised they were not in the sky when I woke up. I was thrilled. In dreams as in waking life, seeing brightly shining stars fills my chest with a positive feeling that alternates between tightness and expansion, a deep heartbeat.

Gemini is an air sign, and while I do not take this very seriously, I admit that I have had a love affair with the sky since childhood, long before I even knew what "Gemini" signified. I could spend hours sitting on the swing in the side yard imagining shapes in the towering summer clouds passing overhead, or lying on my back in the front yard mesmerized by the night sky filled with an incalculable number of brilliant stars. In most of the places I have lived since then, stars are lost in urban hazes, now visible only in dreams. Floating into a star-filled sky, flying up to the clouds, and rocketing into outer space, have provided years of compelling dreams. And falling, of course, is an essential part of flying, as we shall see.

I read *Peter Pan* at age ten or so, and what remains with me all these years later is the evocative phrase in which Peter Pan directs the children through the night sky with the words, "second star to the right, and straight on until morning" (Barrie 1911, 49). I can still feel a thrill as I imagine flying through that night sky to another land, surrounded by diamond-bright stars.

It took a while to learn how to get up there, avoiding trees and electrical wires and other hazards of flight. The first awkward and ineffectual flights began after my best friend Betsy and her family abruptly left Miami in my last year of elementary school. I tried in dreams to fly north to Virginia to find her, but never succeeded. Usually I could not even get off the ground, just hopped uselessly up and down. Desperation drove me to new heights shortly after these first flights, when I was trying to escape from my dream parents, the ogre and the witch, who were always after me for some act of disobedience. In these early dreams I struggled to climb up on the back porch roof before they could catch me, where I would jump up as high as I could and sail into the air with my arms stretched out like Superman. The sensation of falling to earth was distressingly real, and I either woke up in panic before I hit the ground or I got tangled in my mother's clothesline, a kind of spider's web waiting to trap me. Quite by accident one night I learned to fly: when I had that familiar bodily feeling of falling, I held onto it instead of waking up, and managed to reverse it so that I was falling up—flying at last. After this my escape flying improved very slowly.

For years my flights involved trying to get somewhere and find someone—my cousins in Detroit, my brother Allen in Korea, or pen pals in Burma and Japan. But I was always getting lost, and did not dare fly over water because I would always fall in, which made it difficult to cross an ocean. Even with no obstacles, I rarely managed to arrive at my hoped for destination or, if I did, I never found the person I was seeking. My flying dreams greatly improved later in life when I studied maps as a geography major, because I could visualize what I was flying over. I could slow down, keep closer to the earth, and plan my flight path. I could often find my destination and land safely, but I still had to avoid looking down at water or I would fall immediately. Still later in life I freed myself from destinations and began to fly for pure joy, for the freedom of movement and the delight of being up in the air. I was even able to take others with me occasionally if they wanted to come, just by holding their hand. This was not always successful, though. Once, when I tried to show a friend how to fly in a dream, we fell into the ocean and she had to rescue me.

In one of my most satisfying dreams ("Dreaming the Sky") I did not go anywhere at all, I just hung in the air. I was in a car with my husband and children, driving home from some gathering, and I noticed that the car had left the road and was floating steadily up into the sky. No one else seemed to notice or to care when I pointed it out, until I turned to my daughter Rachel and said, "This is a dream! I'm going to get out and fly beside the car." She was alarmed and tried to stop me but I opened the door and floated out, assuring her that I was not flying away. I was so elated at the feeling that I floated over onto my back and found myself, for the first time in a flying dream, looking up into the spacious blue sky, a rich alive blue that filled the universe. In ecstasy and awe, I called out "Thank you! Thank you!" to the sky, a prayer of gratitude.

My flying dreams are far less frequent now, almost as if I were ready to come down to earth at last. But getting "stuck" in my waking life can still bring on a flying dream. Early in my teaching career when I was feeling overwhelmed by university duties, I had a dream ("Red Emergency Door") that expressed my waking anxieties exquisitely.

I was picking up a huge stack of final exams, including mine because the department required me to take my own exam. My answers had been marked by two colleagues, one who gave me a C- and the other an A- with the insulting handwritten comment, "Oh well, it's only folklore." Mortified, I continued down the hall feeling like a complete failure, unable to answer my own questions. By the time I reached the door to the stairs up to my third-floor office I was enraged. I yanked the door open and stormed up the stairs.

When I reached the landing I put the stack of exams down on the floor and yelled as loud as I could, "I don't have to put up with this!" Instantly the steps transformed themselves into a staircase spiralling up a tower. I smiled at the "ivory tower" implications and went on, my steps becoming so light that I was almost floating. I came to a small dome-shaped window with a shaft of bright sunlight pouring in, and as I passed through I was filled with the bright light, electrified and illuminated, more positive than my experience with the light bulb in the "Chinese Lion" dream. I was free of rage, helplessness, anxiety, or even yearning. My feet came off the stairs an inch or so and I floated on up joyfully. When I got to the top I found a bright red emergency door with a sign warning me that an alarm would sound if I opened it, and though I knew people would start coming up as soon as the alarm sounded, I had no fear or anger left. I pushed down on the bar that opened the door and felt the releasing click, heard the sound of the alarm and then footsteps coming up the stairs far below me. I flew calmly out into a landscape of gently rolling forested hills and green fields under a rich blue sky.

For almost a decade I considered this dream to have been a warning that I should fly away from university teaching and find my joy elsewhere, and I felt I had betrayed my creative self by failing to follow the message. One year I told this dream to one of my folklore classes when we were talking about towers in fairy tales, where they usually represent imprisonment. I was stunned when one of the students suggested that the dream was not about flying away but about flights of fancy, which he suggested was my teaching style. I had missed the creative artistry of my own dream. I went on teaching for another 15 years, keeping this dream in mind any time I felt stuck.

Soon after "The Red Door" dream, I decided I needed to keep my feet more firmly on the ground and to stop flying, but I just could not keep myself out of the sky. In particular I wanted to discontinue the dreams in which I skyrocketed right through the blue sky into black outer space, where I always got lost. These ecstatic dreams started in adolescence, not surprisingly. The flights took place when I sailed off the backyard swing as it rose to its highest point, and the too-rapid flight always propelled me into the sky before I could take any control. The erotic energy is obvious to me now, but back then I had no idea why ecstasy was so difficult to get a grip on. I finally made a conscious effort to stop these delirious flights by banning the swing set from my dreams. After my exhilarating adult experience in "Dreaming the Sky," it appeared once more, presenting itself enticingly as glowing, radiantly pure silver instead of rusted metal with flaking paint. I was lucid enough to see what was happening, and decided to let the dream ("Hole in the Sky") continue.

In the dream I consciously walked across the yard and sat down without swinging, waiting to see what would happen next. A thick knotted cord of white silk dropped down in front of me, an elegant transformation of the gym class rope I never managed to climb in junior high school. I started to climb slowly, hand-over-hand, and when I reached the top of the blue sky I saw there was a hole. I pulled myself up through it and held myself there for a moment, realizing that I always got lost because I was going too fast.This time, I was pleasantly surrounded by black space with radiant stars all around me. A glowing spaceship that resembled a 1940s silver diner floated a short distance away. But before I could climb out of the hole something external caused me to wake up, frustrated that I had missed something beautiful. Our dreaming artist sometimes remembers, and two years later the dream world created another space dream ("Silver Diner") that was so closely related to "Hole in the Sky" that it seemed like a continuation.

In this dream I was standing on the ground looking up at the vast night sky thick with the brilliant stars I remembered from childhood, before pollution dimmed them. The sky seemed alive with their light, and I felt a profound yearning to be up among the stars. A small silver rocket suddenly appeared in front of me, an elegant version of the children's rides in front of grocery stores. I laughed, but decided to see where it was going and climbed on, ascending slowly up and into the starry sky, finally stopping outside the silver spaceship/diner from the previous dream. I went in, finding that there was no one else there except a young man with light-coloured hair standing behind the counter. He looked like my brother Kenneth, imagined as an adult in "Okay, Kay." This time he looked at me, smiled, and said pleasantly, "Yes, this is all there is. This is it." I felt enormously comforted and woke up smiling, feeling that I had been given a gift. As if his words had satisfied my long yearning for dreaming the sky, I have had no more lost-in-space dreams. I still occasionally find myself in dreams gazing longingly up into a sky filled with luminous stars, but I am no longer compelled to fly up to them.

Not surprisingly, I was drawn to stories with magical flights: *Peter Pan*, and *The Little Lame Prince* with his magic carpet, were early reading. Later I read folktales as a graduate student, filled with magic carpets, flying ships, winged horses and other air-borne creatures, flying cloaks and boxes and tubs, not to mention magical birds who carried people from one end of the earth to another, or the north wind that carries the heroine east of the sun and west of the moon in a popular Norwegian folktale, one of the many variants of "Beauty and the Beast" (Thompson 1975, 113-122). There were also numerous stories in which protagonists were drawn up into the sky without knowing how they arrived there. One such story is "The Star Husbands" from Ojibwa (Chippewa) tradition (Thompson 1968, 126-27). This was the first story I told in public, to a class of 11-year-olds in a Winnipeg school. In it, two girls find the hole in the sky, as I did, but they move through it in the opposite direction.

Two sisters were sleeping out under the night sky, dreaming that the two brightest stars were men they could marry. They woke up in the land of the sky people, with the Star Husbands they yearned for. They discovered all too quickly that living in the sky was not as pleasant as they hoped, and grew homesick for their own people. One day as they wandered on the clouds, they found an old woman guarding a hole in the sky. First she reprimanded them, since this was a sacred and secret place, but then she felt compassion and agreed to help them get back down to earth by braiding a magic rope from their own hair. She told them that the rope would grow as long as they kept their eyes closed, and slowly lowered them down through the hole in the sky. The sisters descended for a long time, keeping their eyes dutifully closed, but when they thought they felt the earth beneath their feet, they opened their eyes and found themselves stuck at the top of a tall tree. They begged three animals in turn—Bear, Lynx, and Wolverine—to help them down, but only greedy Wolverine agreed to help if they would marry him. The sisters assented, but managed to trick crafty Wolverine and returned safely to their people, leaving wolverine wiser but nastier.

These sisters seemed to have the same problem with the world on the other side of the hole as I did—you cannot stay there comfortably if you are an earth creature. We yearned for the stars, for a transcendent experience, and discovered that the man in the silver diner was right—this is all there is. We get our feet back on the ground at last, finding the passage through the sky hole and returning to the familiar mundane world. But now we have the story of the adventure. I am quite sure that if I had not learned and told this story, I would not have had such a clear image of the hole in the sky and the experience. Art and life come together in the dream world beyond that magical hole. I imagine the scene: two thick ropes, one of soft white silk and the other of gleaming black hair, support us securely between heaven and earth as we slowly return to our element.

As I noted earlier, flying is related to falling, in dreams and in life experiences as well; falling through dark tunnels is reported as an experience by practitioners of shamanism, for whom this is a passage to the other world of reality. People who report near-death experiences also often report passing through a tunnel; my mother, for example, described but later denied feeling herself pulled along a black tunnel during her first hospitalization for cancer. I could never get her to say more, unfortunately. I was particularly fascinated because I had read quite a bit about both shamanic journeys and near-death experiences that had changed my thinking about falling. I remembered how I had learned to fly in dreams by deliberately falling up. My mother, not surprisingly, found it very distressing, given the dire situation she was in at that time, terrified of falling into death. And of course the shamanic journey is just that—a fall into symbolic death and then a triumphant return, often with a gift of wisdom for the community.

My interest in falling as a way of travelling to another realm of experience drew me to some of the traditional narratives Kira Van Deusen found that suggested shamanic journeys (see Van Deusen 1999, 2001). In an earlier chapter I mentioned the legend of a reindeer herder she collected, in which a man lost in a sudden snowstorm fell down a deep hole into a bear's cave. His bear, like my tree-climbing bear in chapter 6, was a helper, and in shamanic terms would have become his spirit-guide.

The fall through the hole in the earth is the reverse journey of falling up through the hole in the sky, or descending from it on a rope made of hair. Like the two sisters in "The Star Husbands," this man cannot stay in this other-worldly place, but he does gain power from it, as do the sisters. The story echoes shamanic journeys in which a human being falls or climbs into another world and is helped by an animal or a mysterious being of some sort. Falling and climbing are common motifs in dreams, and can be actual physical sensations in sleep.

I have experienced two startling falls, the first as a child and the next as an adult. Both certainly felt like other-worldly adventures, though in very different ways. Each provided a kind of power that remains with me, though certainly nothing as dramatic as meeting star husbands or cave bears. I must have been only six or seven and still new to Pinewood Park, at the time of my first fall. The surrounding scenery seems vague in memory, as if I was not fully familiar with our bleak new yard that had not yet experienced my mother's green thumb. Janet and I were swinging across the top bars of the swing, the "monkey bars," like Tarzan in the Saturday matinee serials. We decided to jump off like Tarzan—I was Tarzan, of course, and Janet was obviously Jane. We had done this once before when we were sure no one was looking and landed safely, but this time I fell, hard, and knocked the breath out of me. This part of the experience is still a clear body memory: I lay there on the ground unable to move, breathe, or even think. I was sure I had died, and was surprised to feel so calm about it. I wondered absently if Janet would be concerned. When I heard Janet crying I realized I was still alive after all, and tried to roll over and get up. I was overwhelmed with a pleasant dizziness, my first experience with a state of altered consciousness. I think it was after this that we learned to spin, revolving until we were too dizzy to stand and everything whirled around us as if we were flying to another world.

My second fall was far less pleasant. In 1998 I was climbing to the low porch roof of our cabin to lie back and enjoy the meteorite showers, a rain of stars. I had almost reached the top when the ladder threw me off. The split second that I was in the air, suspended between heaven and earth, was most other-worldly; my body told me it did not belong there and "warned" me to expect something unpleasant. I landed hard on our wooden deck, and, having fractured a lumbar vertebra, lay there in agonizing spinal spasms for 40 minutes waiting for the ambulance to make its way from the nearest town. As we waited, the summer doctor and the entire local police force of three stood over me talking about football. In the midst of excruciating pain, the irrelevant absurdity of their casual conversation actually allowed me to smile briefly between agonized moans. I had a better idea of what Alice had gone through in her Wonderland adventures, trying to keep some sense of balance in bizarre and sometimes painful predicaments.

One of the things that kept me holding to a mental rope of security was an urgent desire to return to this book, but writing was the one thing I was told not to do because sitting was not good for my back. After ten days of lying in a hospital bed and three months in a clam-like back support that had to be strapped on every morning, I returned to my everyday world and slowly began writing again. These experiences gave me very different perspectives on the unpredictability of life and the consequences of rising and falling. The girls in "Star Husbands" did not expect to find themselves in the sky, nor the reindeer herder in the cave with a huge bear. But what falls down must come up again. Unexpected experiences offer possibilities for creations like a book, a poem, a dance. Or for me, a story.

I read a lot while lying in bed, since I was unable to do anything else for weeks, and when I was out of bed I had to strap myself into my "clam shell." One of the books I read was a collection of traditional tales from Tonga that a student gave me years earlier, so exotic that I never felt I could tell any of them because there was no pull of recognition. This time when I read the story of a child born in a clam shell, where she remained trapped until womanhood, I had a clear sense of what it felt like to fall into immobility. Eventually she is transformed, but she has to wait a long time. I try to imagine what a clam might dream while awaiting a life without an imprisoning shell. We will meet this clam-child again in chapter 14, and perhaps discover her dreams.

Clam and Iron Fish might agree that both dreams and life proceed in random directions that move irregularly like water, rarely on a straight path from here to there, and with many unexpected convergences. Sometimes we fly, sometimes we fall, but all of our experiences present invitations to evolve and transform, and to create something new from these happenings.

Building a Dream House

Imagine that you are walking through the house of your dreams, down hallways and into rooms, up and down stairways to attics and basements, checking out the kitchens, bedrooms, bathrooms, looking out windows and doors. Imagining is not quite the same as dreaming such a walk, though, because dreams offer more surprises, not all of them to your liking. In 1999, the first year of my retirement, I had a long series of house and apartment dreams, creative responses to finding my place in a new way, outside of teaching, and discovering metaphorically and actually that this was not as easy as I had hoped. Surprises were always waiting around the corner, keeping me alert.

In one of the first house dreams of 1999, my husband Dan and I were standing in the large open hall of a brand new house with high ceilings, filled with light from glorious domed windows, warm aqua and peach colours on the walls. It felt so refreshing to be here. As we looked around enjoying our new home, an older woman with dark hair barged in the front door, looked at us sternly, and said crankily, "It might look good, but it needs a lot of work."

I woke up feeling let down by this woman I call "House Critic." My new house was somehow deceiving, imperfect, which is as often the case with dreamed houses as it is with the dream houses we actually build. Still, it had potential, though I did not find out what this might be since I believed the woman and woke up before looking.

I have explored many dream houses over the years, some large and elegant like the one above, others old and cramped. I roam through endless rooms in rambling houses, or the single room of a small apartment. Unlike my other recurring building dreams where I am lost in long hallways, I am never disoriented in these houses, but I am also never sure what I am looking for. I have climbed up into attics of all sizes and shapes, and down into basements of varying degrees of darkness.

Many acquaintances describe similar experiences in houses of all kinds, especially attics and basements. Some more often dream of bedrooms, others of living rooms, and some—like me—often find themselves in kitchens. My archetypal dream houses often relate to my state of mind, the various rooms representing where I am mentally and emotionally in waking life at the time of the dream.

Attics, for example, suggest the head with its intellectual concerns, so a visit to an attic room might be a pleasant, light-filled event or might instead lead to feelings of being up too high or disconnected. In a dream I had in 1996, I was watching a television documentary on houses and at the same time I seemed to be in it, as a teenage girl discovering her secret room in the attic. The room is still so clear in mind that I can feel the joy of being in it. It was a long, low room with steeply sloping sides, half of it painted pure white, the other half with dark wood on ceiling and floor. It had no furniture in it but a large bed, and no clutter—which would certainly not be true of my room in waking life. Built-in cupboards with doors lined the base of the walls behind the bed. As the television viewer, I watched the girl standing at the foot of the bed looking out the small attic window and then joyfully opening the many little doors in the cupboards. I knew she loved it there because it was a secret room that allowed her to escape from everyone else. And of course that was exactly how I escaped my own large family, hiding in the attic of my mind.

Dream expert Patricia Garfield reports a much less pleasant attic she dreamed up in turbulent adolescence:

> I am in the attic of an old, crumbling house. It is hard to find my way because of the darkness and great masses of piled junk. Everywhere I turn are boxes of trash, crates, and old, discarded household equipment. I pick up a box to clear a space and am shocked to find that it is coated with thick, gray dust, which clings to my hands. Now I feel the light, sticky touch of spider webs across my face. Shuddering, I try to push them away with

> the back of my hand. I struggle frantically to shove aside the trunk in front of me, and behold with horror a mass of swarming, crawling bugs, shining in the dark. They were hidden until now. I wake in terror (Garfield 1989, 21).

Garfield's distressing experience echoes a similar one I had in a dream basement filled with "great masses of piled junk." In archetypal terms basements are the opposite of attics, close to the earth and deeper in our unconscious. Yet even in their darkness they can shed light on unconscious preoccupations. I know that when my dream basements are expansive and neat, even when they are dimly lit, I wake with a feeling of being rooted and balanced. Dark, dusty basements overflowing with junk, like our actual basement in Winnipeg, leave me feeling heavy and overwhelmed, both dreaming and waking. Cleaning is needed.

I spent a lot of time in attics (and, of course, towers that might be ivory) when I was at the heights of academic life and scholarly writing, and more time in basements when I was in the dark depths of doubts and painful soul-searching.

In dream living rooms, the heart and the social centre of a house, I was usually with other people, most often my Miami family, feeling the pleasant support of social interaction or the tensions of conflict reflecting my waking world. My dream bedrooms were sometimes places of retreat, as they were in my Miami days when I had only my corner of the bedroom to find privacy in a big family. In later years they were also places of encounter; here I met Nameless Dread and a number of other intimidating older women. Given the threatening content of some particular dreams, it seems these shadow women often come to challenge me when I am trying to hide or escape from the world.

Kitchens and other food-related areas are central places of action in many of my dreams. Since I am not much of a cook in waking life, I can only assume that my kitchen dreams are not about food preparation of the mundane sort, but about eating as spiritual sustenance. In kitchens we prepare, create, transform, making raw materials into cooked form for ourselves and others. Countless kitchens, cafeterias, and restaurants, the silver sky diner among them, were places of symbolic nourishment that "fed" me when I was hungry for profound soul food. On the deepest level, kitchens were places of alchemical transformation through the element of fire, or heated water. It is from a kitchen that I began my passage through water and fire in the dream of "The Golden Woman." In my mother's kitchen I met the monkey-like "monster" sitting in front of the stove, who first frightened me and then elated me with a transformative message that literally sent me flying. A much larger challenger found me in a kitchen in a later dream that we will find in chapter 15. This "Ochre Ogre," as I named him, challenged me to find my trash can and presumably get rid of the junk in my creative centre.

And bathrooms? Most often in my own dreams these are places of relief, appropriately. They are also places of purification, and in this sense can have a deeper ritual significance. I am almost always in a public bathroom with other people around, and even when my reason for being there is discomfort coming from my actual sleeping body, there is always a sense of something more, of a shared experience. Thinking of the art of dreams, bathrooms offer a place of letting go of the creations we make in the kitchen. This might sound silly given the mundane surroundings, but remember that dream symbols always have open potential. What we make of them depends on our own associations.

Hallways and entryways promise to lead into rooms of all sorts, through open or shut doors, or up and down stairways. While I rarely know what room I am looking for, I am aware that there is a central room somewhere, as there is in the Grimm version of "The Water of Life," that we will see shortly. I have yet to find this room and the treasure it might hold. When I have been able to let go of the anxiety of searching and finding and just enjoy the exploring, I have found other remarkable rooms, some elegantly furnished and others modest and simple but filled with light and warmth.

Looking back over my dream house metaphorically as a whole, I see how the various rooms can be paired as opposites that together form a working unity: public living rooms with social interaction and activities balance with private bedrooms for more personal encounters and relaxation; kitchens are places of nourishment and creativity while bathrooms are for purification and release; attics for loftiness and spirituality, and basements for deeper quests into darkness.

The persistence of house dreams, both negative and positive, certainly confirms their importance to me as archetypal symbols, and as such, potential entryways to the creative core, my own internal edifice. This is not only true for me, of course, since archetypes by nature are transpersonal. Many of my friends, often but not always women, have reported dream houses in great detail. Both Morgana Graham and Gail Beck reported meandering through the rooms of houses that seem to go on forever. Gail's houses are often associated with water (a creek, pond, or sea) in some way. When I was visiting her while writing this chapter, in January 2002, she described a dream in which she explored a house:

> My parents are buying a new house—something they almost never did in their lifetimes—and Mom and a real estate agent are in the house. Mom wants me to look around and see what I think. (My father's there too but not on the scene.) I step outside to look. It's a very old structure, maybe hundreds of years old, like a European house. The lower floor is square-hewn logs with white chinking and the upper floor is larger (it's cantilevered), weathered clapboard with some dark trim up near the roof and small leaded windows, not square or diamond-shaped panes but rounded. It just comes to me now that these were like the windows in the Hobbit house that we just saw in the movie, *Lord of the Rings*.
>
> I go inside and start looking around and the whole house is full full full of things, and in one room there's a woman who's sorting things, apparently the owner getting ready to move. This room is full of dishes, and she's showing me glasses, clear glass tumblers. Our short conversation is gone now, but she was eager to show me her things, and very friendly. So I go looking in other rooms. One was mostly filled with tables of all sizes and sorts, just jammed together from one side to the other. After this there was a room full of chenille bedspreads, the old-fashioned ones, some hung up on bunk beds and some on blanket racks. Two I remember are very detailed: one is solid pink, that old peachy pink, and the other one is white with brightly coloured flowers. I start thinking what a neat place this is and wondering how I can get the woman to leave some of the stuff for us because it's such a big place and we're going to need a lot of stuff. It was fun being there, just a good place to be (conversation, 22 January, 2002).

Gail simply enjoys wandering around this dream house, but some houses offer adventures as well as real estate. North Carolina storyteller Gwenda LedBetter told me a dream in which a wise woman showed her something sacred that Gwenda decided to protect by taking both the woman and her treasure up to the attic. The attic became a tower similar to the tower I climbed in "The Red Door" dream, a place of both protection and escape. Retelling the dream allowed her to get the dream out of her attic and into the waking world, and perhaps into her stories in one way or another:

> In the dream there is an old Indian woman who is the keeper of a small velvet bag containing two pieces of cloth. The cloth has a spiritual power for the world. Someone comes to the house we are in, meaning to take away the cloth. I take the old woman upstairs, to hide her. We are in a bedroom and hear voices. I remember a tower…you have to squeeze up into it. I help the old woman up, squeeze through myself, and turn to help a third large woman. She can't make it [in]. I wait till all is quiet and slip out of the tower and down the stairs (conversation, February 2001).

All houses and their rooms have the potential to move us into artistic creation by symbolically revealing what our concerns and conflicts are in the waking world, showing where we might be stuck or where we might be freely moving. As I said earlier, my retirement in 1999 seemed to inspire a series of house dreams, some of them reminiscent of folktales in which houses figure prominently, from hovels to palaces. Sometimes these were dark places like the enticing witch's hut in "Hansel and Gretel," sometimes mansions filled with beautiful things tempted one to stop and get lost.

Getting stuck, no matter if it happens in a dark witch's hut or an elegant palace, is a common motif in tales. The hero of "The Twelve Dancing Princesses" makes his way through a fantastic grove where trees bear jewelled fruit, but he overcomes the temptation to stop and fill his pockets. He takes only a few as proof that he has been there, and moves on. This is also central to a variant of "The Water of Life" in which the hero wanders through endless rooms in a palace, each room more temptingly beautiful than the last. Unlike Gail in her dream house full of fine things that I described earlier, the hero is looking for something specific, the one room that contains the water of life. Success comes because he is able to keep focused on his quest for the healing water and to resist the temptation to enter other luxurious rooms. In some of the stories he, too, finds a woman in one of the rooms who is, like Gail's woman, the apparent owner. Here is a summary of my composite version (for Grimm see Zipes 1988, 388-392). This is entirely different from the story of "The Water of Life" we have already encountered here.

Three brothers in turn promised their father, the king, that they would bring back the water of life to cure him. The older brothers ignored the advice of a dwarf, always choosing luxury over plainness, and ended up stuck and unable to go on. The hero followed the dwarf's advice to choose plain over beautiful, and succeeded in finding the palace that contained the water of life. Inside he passed down halls leading into room after room of enticingly beautiful furnishings, and finally came to a dark, curtained room with a sleeping woman. When he stepped in, she awoke and told him that the water of life was in a fountain at the very centre—the heart—of the palace. He went directly to this place, found the flowing fountain, and retrieved the healing water and eventually the enchanted woman herself, but only after further adventures.

Stories, of course, are usually more coherent and consistent than dreams, which can be quite disjointed and incomplete. In dreams I rarely find such a clear source of living creative energy as did the young man in the folktale, but I sometimes come frustratingly close, guided by a strong inner sense that the room I am seeking is just around the corner if I can only stay asleep long enough to keep looking. Perhaps this was what the cranky House Critic was hinting at when she rudely entered the house dream that opened this chapter, warning me against being entranced by the superficial beauty of the entry hall in our new house. Maybe she wanted me to go deeper. From this perspective she resembles the dwarf in the Grimm version of "The Water of Life." If I remained captivated by the superficial beauty of the entry hall I would be stuck like the older brothers, unable to move on to the heart of the matter. In this dream I woke up instead of going on, disappointed at being stopped. Later that year I had a very different encounter with an older woman in a dream I called "Show Me the Wind":

I had been involved in some kind of Native ceremony and was walking back with Anne C., a Cree woman who had been a student in the last folklore class I taught before retirement. This time she was the teacher and I was the student. She was quietly explaining something, saying she wanted to "show me the wind." We came to a house, hers apparently, and immediately went in and up the stairs to a large attic room, a bedroom that had (like my own) a sloping roof and storage closet with small doors positioned behind the bed. She told me to sit down with my back to the wall where the closet was, and she then went into one of the small doors. I got a quick glance before she disappeared into the closet, and saw a large room lit with golden light and full of beautiful things. I wanted to look in and see everything that was in there, but I resisted, following her instructions to sit down with my back to that wall. From inside the closet, she began to whistle softly. I felt a wind surrounding me and lifting me up gently. There was no tangible treasure, but I woke up with a feeling of profound calm.

My sense of this dream and many of my other house dreams, and some folktales as well, is that some kind of initiation or transformation is at the heart of the matter. That I am indeed seeking one special room is fully expressed in this dream. Like the folktale hero, I receive one of the four archetypal elements (water for him, wind for me) instead of the material treasure that tempts me. This is even more obvious in a dream reported by Gail Beck, a long, involved dream in which she ends up in bed being approached by four women she finds menacing:

> I'm now on a bed dressed in black—everything else in the room is pure white, the walls, furniture, bed covering—and the man I've been with summons up four women who are somehow going to take me away. They are young women, each one a different race, and dressed in black like angels of death. They are standing at the foot of the bed pulling at my skirt, first all together and then one at a time. Then I see that they have different coloured eyeballs that they're spitting out at me, and I'm throwing them back and saying, "You're not going to get me!" (conversation, January 2002).

Because she finds the women disturbing, as I have in similar encounters, she wakes up without finding out if they want to show her the wind or some other potentially transformative element. It is interesting that she is aware of the strong contrast of the white room and the black figures, not unlike my dark and light attic dream I described earlier. These contrasting colours suggest a possibility of balance, since neither dark nor light dominates. Finding this balance can release a dream into fuller creativity.

Kira Van Deusen discovered this in a rich and complex dream from her own recurring dream house series. Having just heard of a friend's death, she was feeling closed in by the world, and her dreaming architect-self built a modest little house:

> Last night I had this dream. I was in a tiny little house, much smaller than any place I've ever lived. It had lovely windows in front. It was very funky and yet everything was in place—even an ingenious spot for the dishes on a beam overhead. I was slightly panicked that it wasn't big enough and then realized that it WAS big enough for now, and if I wanted more I could build it (Van Deusen, January 2001).

Kira's concluding words are significant, since they express her half-lucid realization within the dream that she was the builder of this house and could create more any time she wished.

That February, only weeks after receiving Kira's dream by e-mail, my husband and I were visiting his cousin Amy Stone in New York. I had brought my work with me, so she asked what I was working on, and after I described this chapter, I asked if she ever had "house" dreams. "Oh yes! All the time. House dreams and apartment dreams, all that. Just last night, as a matter of fact." She described a dream that, like Kira's, expressed the dreamer's anxiety about a house at the same time as it expressed her delight. She was watching a woman pass through the endless rooms of a richly coloured Cambodian house:

> The house was decorated with old, rich teak wood and wonderfully deep, intense, saturated colours, mostly reds and blues. But the house was also dangerous because it was booby-trapped, explosions going off all over the house. I'm anxious for the woman and I feel what she's feeling, really intense, but no one seems to be harmed. It doesn't make sense, and I only know the dream is over when I see movie credits rolling at the end. The first one credited Air Cambodia with the aerial shots, and someone near me—I'm apparently in a movie theatre—commented on how well they had done the intense tropical light of Cambodia (conversation with Amy Stone, February 2001).

Amy had been awakened early that morning by a fierce howling wind, wondering at how her dream combined intensity of colour and beauty with intense danger. She had repeated the word "intense" several times as she reconstructed the dream for me, not only in the descriptions but in her emotional responses to it, negative and positive. I asked her what time of night she thought she had dreamed it and she said it was the last dream she remembered early in the morning. I told her that I was also awakened early by trucks doing street repairs that sounded like explosions, and then kept awake by the howling wind. I wondered if these intense sounds might have added potency to her beautiful house dream.

I told her my "sunglasses" dream, created around the sound of a glass suncatcher tapping on my window, and we were both amused by the possibility of her dream house building itself around the noises of morning street repairs and wind. That is, taking discordant sounds and creating an entire beautiful house, booby traps and all. The fierce morning wind should have reminded me to tell Amy the "Show Me the Wind" dream. Had that wind come all the way from Winnipeg to Manhattan?

The folktale of "The Water of Life" provides the perspective of finding a treasure in an unfamiliar place by not allowing oneself to be distracted from finding the heart of the matter. I find this useful in bringing creative light into my disorderly dream houses. Similarly, Patricia Garfield, whose cluttered attic dream was so distressing, insists that even dark dreams can reveal "something of value midst the trash and dirt" if you persist (Garfield 1989, 27). I have sensed in many house dreams that there is something beautiful to be found, and have tried and failed many times even when I had direct guidance, as when I am told by an unknown man to look in my basement. (Yes, I am aware of Freudian implications, but this book is on dreaming as art.)

In this dream the stranger was unaccountably standing in my kitchen as I came in from a meeting. He said cordially, "I put something beautiful in the basement for you." I promptly went down the steps to see what it was. Instead of something beautiful I found a dingy, dusty basement filled with cobwebbed boxes and ancient broken toys, and an atmosphere of dread. I woke up as I was running up the steps yelling for my husband to help me.

Whatever erotic implications this dream might have, my deepest regret is that I let myself be distracted by ugliness this time, not beauty. I woke up in terror similar to that described by Garfield in her "cluttered attic" dream. The trick in house dreams is keeping eyes and mind open so that one is not diverted by either beauty or homeliness, and then the real treasure offered by the dream can be found. As Garfield notes, it might be "a brilliant blue vase, an old painting I didn't know was there" (Garfield 1989, 27). These dreams seem to assure us that our treasure is close by, in the house we are in, and not in a faraway castle, if we persist in seeking it. In both dreams and stories there is often someone who gives advice, such as the dream man who tells me there is something beautiful in the basement or the woman who shows me the wind, not to mention the crabby woman who tells me my house is not in order.

A popular folktale found in various parts of Europe carries exactly this message, building on a double theme of trusting your dreams and of finding your treasure at home after seeking it elsewhere. Here the advice-giver provides the message in a negative way, but the hero is alert. One story index lists a dozen story titles (Ashliman 1987, 278-80), including a popular English tale called "The Pedlar of Swaffham" (Jacobs, n.d., 98).

A poor man dreams one night that he will find out about his treasure if he travels all the way to a distant city and stands in a certain place. He sets out immediately, reaches the place and spends some time waiting in vain to learn about his treasure. On the last day a sceptical man asks him why he stands there every day, and laughs when he hears the man's foolish dream. "I had a dream that I'd find a treasure buried in the backyard of a man in a faraway place, and if I believed that I'd be a poor man today." The poor man listens to this negative advice and immediately returns home to find his buried treasure, as his dream promised.

Certainly we recognize the cliche "There's no place like home," even if we have not travelled to Oz or anywhere other than a dream to discover hidden treasure. But still we often miss what is under our nose or in our own backyard. Many dreams have told me this, but the most insistent one is an astounding dream featuring an amazing pendant that I kept refusing to look at. This dream, "Cameo Pendant," appeared as a fully developed creation in 1984. Details of sights and sounds are still in my conscious mind decades later. In a number of ways it prefigures "The Golden Woman" dream that will appear some years afterward. My parental home is central here, and this is the only dream in which every room in the house is mentioned. Here is the dream in full, including the surrounding situation and my state of mind as I went to bed that night:

I wrote: Dan's parents are visiting, so lots of talk about family members. Also, I've been reading James' *Varieties of Religious Experience* and pondering my spiritual frustrations, and also remembering my small satori experience several years ago when a crowd of milling commuters in New York suddenly seemed intimately connected with me, all of us one entity and yet separate individuals at the same time.

I've attended some sort of family-centred public function in Miami, apparently an academic conference on family relations, and have returned to my parents' house where I'm helping my mother do something, first on the back porch and then in the kitchen. She's talking to me about strong women she's known. I tell her about some discussion I was having with several younger women at the conference about my failure to "find" god because the image presented to me was too small and narrow. My mother nods but says nothing.

While this is going on my middle sister Jolene, possibly the most "religious" family member at this time, is in the living room settled into my father's brown recliner known in waking life as "The Throne," watching kids' cartoons with a small boy I don't recognize. My father comes out of the bathroom, having shaved, and calls me into the living room to talk. He's sitting at the end of the sofa near the hall instead of challenging Jolene to his chair. He seems to be deliberately disruptive, insistent on having my full attention, and though I'm annoyed I will myself to listen respectfully to his ramblings because he is, after all, my father (in waking life we aren't getting along well).

He asks what I was doing at "the gathering" but doesn't really listen to my answer, instead talking about things he's read, about his favourite brother Ed and various other relatives. All at once he stops talking and hands me a pendant from an earring or necklace that he says belonged to my daughter Rachel. I assume it's a cheap childhood trinket, and don't look at it carefully. Some part of it is broken and he's been trying to fix it but can't, so asks if I can help. I'm not really interested in the pendant and only notice that it's an oval of blood-red glass or stone, about the size of a quarter.

The television cartoons are getting louder and I ask Jolene to turn them down. When she doesn't, I get up angrily and go into the kitchen to help my mother with the dishes, putting the pendant down on the counter. Apparently I'm planning to wash it, since it seems dusty. My father calls from the living room to remind me not to lose it, so I pick it up again. He and I move out to the porch to avoid the loud television program. I'm still not paying close attention to him or the pendant, though.

Now we are on the porch, with him sitting on the sofa and me on the big lawn chair. He asks about the pendant again. I start to say that I've left it in the kitchen where apparently I had been washing it in a pail of water, though I can't remember. He points to the ledge behind me. I reach back to pick up the pendant but it falls from my hand. I have to search for it, which compels me to look at it more closely—in fact I see it for the first time, and can't figure out why I didn't notice sooner.

It is definitely a pendant and not an earring, and is very old. It is clean and clear now, having been purified, but it seems smaller, only the size of a dime now. Has it shrunk because I was ignoring it? It has a small red bead attached to it at the top and is cut in an oval octagon shape. I see that it's a cameo with a woman's face in profile and words engraved under it. As I study it, it enlarges slowly, growing to the size of my palm so that I can see it clearly. The woman is now facing me, and I can see her amber visage highlighted by the blood-red background. The words under it say something like "Quebec Frolics 1981." I'm puzzled since I don't recall being in Quebec in 1981, but somehow I know now that this proves that it is indeed my pendant and not some trivial thing without meaning.

I keep studying the engraved face, a handsome woman with strong, peaceful features and a simple hair style. She's of no definite age, but is definitely "mature." I hold the pendant up to inspect every detail, and realize with a start that it's my face! I accept this at the same time that I marvel at the skills of the artist who could make a stylized face so personal. Now the face begins to change, transforming very slowly into a series of other faces: women and men, young people and old, from one race to another. I watch in wonder, with profound understanding that all faces are one and yet each one is unique.

I want to show this marvel to my father but he starts talking again, and I wake up. Perhaps his talk deliberately wakes me up so I will remember the dream while the details are still so vibrant. I am still entranced as I wake, literally in a trance, as these details flow through my waking mind.

Years later I am still amazed and delighted to have given myself such a dream gift. It seems to be a response to my pre-sleep situation, both in the dynamics of family relations (Dan's visiting parents) and in my spiritual questing. The transforming faces echo my experience in the train station, where I had the fleeting sense that I was at the same united and separated from the crowd of people on the platform.

Even remembering this dream now, my chest fills the same way it did in the dream, and as it does when I am doing something I love to do—

making paper, sketching, creating a Calder-like mobile of wire and beads, telling a story, or writing. I thought at the time that if I were a skilled graphic artist I could have brought the pendant to life in brilliant detail. I was delighted to see just such a creation in an animated short that featured dozens of faces morphing into one another ("Canada Vignettes: Faces," National Film Board of Canada, 1978), amazed at how it replicated my dream.

Whatever it means psychologically, my stubborn refusal to look at the pendant is a denial of this wonderful creation that is determined to come into being despite me. How generous. Like "The Golden Woman," this dream is a full artistic creation, and as such it is commenting on the process of bringing something into being by accepting what is (my face on the pendant, and much later, in the hall mirror in "Golden Woman") and allowing this to evolve, to come into full fruition. Here I am using every room in the house, especially the kitchen as the place of creativity, and the living room as the heart of the psyche. The front porch, where I finally see the transforming pendant, is the entryway into the house, and on its threshold I had already met the alligator/unicorn of another dream.

Our house in reality had no basement, though this did not prevent me from finding one in any number of dreams. I am always searching for something there (why else would you go into a basement?), sometimes happily but more often not. I am wondering now about the dream in which the strange man directs me to the basement where he has put something beautiful for me. Though this dream came much later in my life than Cameo Pendant, I was still reluctant to find something beautiful. It seems that we have to keep learning the same thing over and over again until we get it all the way down to our deepest levels. This dream takes me to a deeper level of something beautiful, so I have to begin all over again, digging through all those dusty boxes in the dark basement, or, better yet, tossing them out. Psychological? Of course. But that is what we have to do as artists, too. Only then do we reach our own golden beings.

In any case, the pendant dream did give me that "something beautiful" to bring into the light of day. Now I have done so, graphically in words instead of in drawing, but with all the rich detail the dream had to offer. Treasure at home indeed.

Learning to swim in Tidal waves

You might think that anyone who could fly in dreams would have no trouble swimming, but I cannot recall a single dream where I succeeded in doing so. When I get anywhere near water in dreams I am sucked in or pulled down before I have a chance to react. Even in "The Golden Woman," where water was not hostile, I surrounded myself in a cylindrical shell as I sank through the dark underground sea. Water is not my element.

My water-loving friend Morgana, a fine swimmer in life and dreams but unable to fly, asked me jokingly to teach her. I tried for several months to get her into one of my dreams for a flying lesson, but only succeeded when I gave up. One night there she was, standing with me on the beach at Baker's Haulover in North Miami, site of many of my watery nightmares. In a brief moment of lucidity I announced joyfully, "Hey, Morgana, this is a dream and I can teach you how to fly!" She smiled. I took her hand and we started up, but I made the mistake of heading out over the ocean instead of staying over the shore. Of course I fell in, and Morgana had to rescue me. I woke up laughing, and so did she when I described her flying lesson.

Water has never been my preferred element, in dreams or in the waking world. I spent a lot of time in swimming pools and in the Atlantic Ocean, growing up in South Florida, but never learned to swim properly. My sister Janet and I failed swimming lessons twice, which must have taken a lot of determination. I preferred to play in water, to pass through it in my own idiosyncratic ways. I almost drowned three times, once as a child only a few feet away from my father and twice as an adult not far away from swimming friends who thought I was joking when I called for help. All three times I managed to stay calm enough to dog-paddle and seal-swim to safety, so my unorthodox methods were effective enough. But I did not manage to swim out of trouble in dreams.

Water in its normal state was bad enough, but when it threw itself up into threatening waves I was paralysed. If you can imagine a wave as a dream character, as animate in its presence as any a frightening beast, you might understand why the overwhelming forces of nature might be even more menacing than dream creatures; they do not present a solid form, do not speak in any voice, do not wait for any reaction, they just keep coming. Earthquakes, raging fires, windstorms and tornados, and worst of all, tidal waves, have played threatening roles in a number of my dreams. I usually took the cowardly way out by hiding, running away, or waking up in fear. There was no being whose voice or image I could bring back to waking life and give a name to, as I did with "Nameless Dread" and "Selfish Old Bitch," thereby mitigating their power over me.

The commanding tidal waves embodied water at its most devastating. In my first memorable one from several years ago ("Tidal Wave I"), a massive wave arose without warning from a calm ocean, crashing down violently and separating me from my husband and children. I woke up shaking, got up to make sure everyone was actually still safe in bed. When I told Rachel the next morning, she calmly suggested I jump up and ride the crest, artfully surfing the perfect wave. I managed to do exactly that in "Tidal Wave II" a few months later. I was riding a bicycle across a bridge past a young Rachel and other children playing peacefully in the water to my right, unaware of a tidal wave I could see bearing down on them. I managed to calm my panic and call back her waking words; in one fluid movement I kicked the bike away and leapt to the crest of the wave before fear had a chance to grip me in paralysis. Rachel and I rode the wave together as if it were a finely choreographed water dance. After such a joyful experience, I was sure I had solved this particular water problem. I was wrong.

Several years later, in the weeks following the devastation of September 11, I had a dream of awesome and terrible beauty in which an immense tidal wave stretched across the entire horizon. It was immeasurably more powerful than those of the earlier dreams. At this time, my waking imagination was filled with murderously vengeful fantasies and my unsettled nights with distressing and disconnected images that I could not bring together into a single coherent dream. I hungered for some sense of balance and peace, not as an escape from the ongoing horrors of a world in chaos, but as a way of facing the coming day as I woke up each morning after a restless night. I was pleading with my dream artist, as I had in that adolescent Buffalo dream, to create a scene of calm stillness. I still had not learned to recognize this pattern of asking for tranquillity and being presented with a challenge instead, so I was unprepared once again.

"Tidal Wave III" began with the calm I had asked for, a fine early summer day at Baker's Haulover beach. The day was very mild, with a pleasant breeze coming off the ocean, which was a very clear green under a cloudless blue sky. The beach was crowded with people having fun, me and my husband and children among them. Someone down the beach to our right shouted in wonder, "Hey, look at that tidal wave," and everyone stopped to look at the bulge of water on the horizon far out to sea. Then they all went back to their activities as if the wave was merely amusing. I was the only one who watched the wave build, saw how fast it was coming, and realized it was up to me to get everyone off the beach. I started to yell, "Let's get out of here," but no one was listening, including my own husband and children who had become rather vague characters, part of the crowd. I could feel my stomach tighten with fear as I saw I would have to get people to move somehow, pull them along by force of will.

My screaming and running and pushing people along did finally get them to leave the beach, but not with any enthusiasm. They ambled along as if they were just indulging this crazy woman. If I had been paying attention I would have understood they were letting me know that it was my dream problem and not theirs. By exerting tremendous psychic energy I managed to get everyone off the beach and moving to high ground. I decided we all had to be up on the third floor of our houses to be safe, and managed to get my family to our "house." It turned out to be a flimsy structure of wooden branches crudely woven into a tower. We managed to get to the top without it collapsing, and it seems to me now that Dan and the kids were laughing as if it were a game. The tower was three stories high as I demanded, but it was not exactly a place of refuge. The thought behind it seemed to be the same one that motivated the people—"So what's the big deal?" I was still yelling at everyone on the ground to get up higher, especially the elderly man who was tranquilly working in his lovely, colourful garden below us. He smiled up at me benignly and went on with his gardening.

I could hear the rush of water as the wave rushed toward the shore as I frantically and vainly tried to get Rachel's two playful cats into my arms so they would safe. As I turned to catch one of them, I saw the oncoming wave, and I was stunned. It covered the horizon, as if it stretched across the entire world, and it was so high that only a small part of the clear blue sky was visible. But it was no longer moving. What I saw was an awesome wall of crystal water standing straight up, its surface ridged as if it were composed of joined columns of water sparkling in the sun with diamond brilliance. What amazed me most as I drifted back up to the waking world was the completely tranquil power of the wave, a standing wall of pure living water apparently waiting for some decision to be made. I had no idea what that might be, but I did not turn aside the enigma.

Many people who have told me distressing dreams and hoped for some insight have asked, "what could I do?" Let me use "Tidal Wave III" as an example of answers I have come up with for my own dreams, using some of the techniques I have found effective. Some are from dream workshops I participated in over the last two decades, others are inspired by a variety of reading on dreams, especially the writings of Joseph Campbell and Carl Jung, but most of all they are intuitive, stimulated by my own and others' dream experiences. There are three basic ideas in approaching any dream, especially the distressing ones: first, trust yourself to understand your own dream instead of seeking outside interpretations; second, be prepared to take a dream seriously enough to accept whatever it has to tell you, no matter how unpleasant (or pleasant) it seems; last, consider the dream as an artistic creation, a story or poem you are creating for yourself. This allows you to get some necessary detachment from emotional responses.

In my infrequent meaningful dreams, "Tidal Wave III" among them, I try to lie still, without opening my eyes or moving, in order to invite the dream to stay with me as long as possible. Returning too quickly to the waking world often snaps the connection. I pay attention to the whole sweep of movement, sounds, and action. In "Tidal Wave III" I patiently recalled details like the colour of water and sky, the sounds of the gentle surf moving back and forth on the shore, the people's laughing voices, the temperature of the air on my bare skin, the smell of salt water. Often a single detail can call back an entire dream. I also take care to recall, as well as I can, the flow of emotional states as a dream progresses. "Tidal Wave" began with a sense of tranquillity and moved quickly into fear, anger, frustration, and finally awe. Allowing that sense of awe to stay with me was the key that opened this dream to its full majestic beauty.

Once I have the dream firmly in mind, I might get up and write it down immediately. I used to do this regularly, but now I depend more on memory to keep the dream intact until I can tell it to someone. The oral experience anchors the dream fully, often revealing aspects that might be missed in simply going over it in my head or writing it down. For example, when I told "Tidal Wave III" to Morgana, the swimmer, I heard my description of the tower as "rickety," which allowed me to see just how flimsy it was and to wonder why I had not created something stronger. The sound of the word "rickety" was somehow very evocative, almost ticklishly playful. I explored the possibility that the wiser part of my dreaming mind wanted to make sure that I would not give in totally to fear, nor would I get away safely into a sturdy building and miss the astonishing wave. Each time I told the dream I noticed, or my listeners pointed out, other aspects of the dream, and it took on greater depth and breadth without the story changing. Morgana, for example, noticed the element of eroticism in the fantastic upright columns of water.

When the Tidal Wave dream was standing in memory more firmly than a rickety tower, I began to explore what might have inspired it to arise. I looked first at my immediate external world, thinking of the disasters of September 11 as a motivation for the overwhelming wave, and of the vulnerable tower so close to collapsing. But if the dream was primarily motivated by such a negative and destructive force, why did the wave stop? I kept this question floating in mind to allow other possibilities to surface, finally remembering that only a few nights before I had watched the undersea epic film *The Abyss*. It concludes with a world-wide tidal wave sent as a warning by undersea beings. Their curtain of hanging water, spanning oceans around the world, is withdrawn only when humans agree to discontinue threats of nuclear violence. My dream wave seemed to be directly inspired by the movie image, having both the power and the magnificence of that wave as well as some sort of warning.

I sensed that I was getting closer, but that something was still missing. With patience, another puzzle piece found its place. At the time of the dream I was rereading the Chinese classic, *The Journey to the West*, preparing for a storytelling event in Vancouver. I had been reading and rehearsing the opening chapters for several months. In my portion of the epic, the Monkey King, the protagonist, first admired the beauty of the cascade and then leapt through it into a huge cave that became a primate utopia. Perhaps because I was focusing on the action instead of the poetry, I missed the connection between my dream and the poetic description of the waterfall:

> A column of rising white rainbows,
> A thousand fathoms of dancing waves
> Which the sea wind buffets but cannot sever,
> On which the river moon shines and reposes.
> Its cold breath divides the green ranges;
> Its tributaries moisten the blue-green hillsides.
> This torrential body, its name a cascade,
> Appears truly like a hanging curtain (Yu 1980, 69).

And that is exactly what I saw, a hanging curtain of water made of columns of rising white rainbows. The description was so perfect I wondered how I had missed this image the first time around. But that is how dreams work, arising from our personal underground sea of the unconscious mind, reaching the surface when the time is right. As I see it, the dream was influenced by all three of the forces: The September 11 destruction provided the tremendous fear and sense of responsibility that compelled me to get myself and everyone else off the beach, while the images of radiant standing water arose from the film *The Abyss* and the poem in *The Journey to the West*. But this was only the beginning.

I wanted to connect my internal and external sense of what a tidal wave was. From my training in geography I understood that tidal waves are born far out to sea in deep water, ordinary wave action growing to uncommon magnitude, usually as the result of ocean storms. These waves increase like snowballs rolling down a hill, and by the time they approach land they gain ominous force. In a tidal wave, or tsunami, the elements of water and earth are in direct confrontation; water leaps beyond its limits and pushes onto the land, sweeping away or blasting apart anything in its wake. This natural force gave my dream wave its awesome potential as an expression of overwhelming emotions.

I moved from the natural world into the archetypal nature of the wave. Jung regarded water as a profound archetypal image for the unconscious as a whole—an entire ocean of life that cannot be seen clearly by the conscious mind. Movements in dream oceans, then, offer lucid symbols from our own depths. In the case of a tidal wave, the surge and flow of water certainly had the feel of deep emotional turbulence, not to mention erotic potential. In contrast, my experience in the depths of the sea in "The Golden Woman" is entirely serene and comforting. There I accepted the movement of the gentle and supporting water. In "Tidal Wave III" I was resisting the water from the first instant that I saw the wave beginning to grow on the distant horizon, and this resistance gave the water strength—much the same as resisting beasts and monsters instead of facing and accepting them provides them with greater power. My own inner turmoil, magnified by my responses to the violent world events, grew into a monstrous wall of water. The unconscious archetypal forces were obviously trying to get my attention.

With both natural and archetypal worlds in mind, I reviewed the dream's personal images, characters, and emotional tone in comparison with similar dreams and relevant folktales. One of my abiding overall dream patterns is a great fear of being overwhelmed—by buffaloes, bears, threatening people, and natural forces. In particular, I pondered all of my tidal wave dreams, and found that seeing them together as one long dream revealed their slow psychological and artistic progression. All three involved the strong sense of being overwhelmed and separated from people I loved.

In "Tidal Wave I," the wave I created gave no warning and struck with such terrific force that I had no time to react, and the surge and flow of its emotional impact was too strong for me to brush aside as "only a dream." The advice of my daughter in the waking world motivated me to send myself the message that I accepted this as a creative problem and was open to alternative solutions. In "Tidal Wave II" I was alone and not even near an ocean, but still managed to call up a tidal wave that threatened to crash down on a water-play area filled with children. The fear of being overwhelmed was still there, but because this wave was smaller and slower and more distant, I had a chance to react, to ride the wave with Rachel. My creation of these two waves allowed me to find a temporary solution to the water problem. To put it in a more positive way, fear inspired creativity.

It took the world crises of 2001 to inspire "Tidal Wave III," a wave worthy of a disaster movie and well beyond any simple dream solutions. It was much more commanding than other waves, and involved many more people. Friends I told it to offered their own insights, not as contradictions to mine but as expanded views. One woman asked a question that stirred me: "Why are you so afraid of your own power?" If dreaming is an art, this question is equally relevant psychologically and artistically. Artists afraid of their own talents will be overwhelmed, as we saw in the book I mentioned earlier, *Art and Fear*. I could see how a fear of my own power was apparent in the dreams featuring angry crones like Nameless Dread and Kitchen Woman, both challenging me to take stand. I understood, too, how the immense Ochre Ogre might be seen as "Tidal Wave III" in the flesh, and though I listened to his words I was not letting him in the door.

I also recalled a much earlier dream in which a huge dam with a crack down its centre was threatening to burst. In the dream I was walking with my family across a dry river bed, and looked up to see the massive dam about to unleash all its held-back water. Certain that we would be destroyed by the deluge, I woke up with the same terror I felt in "Tidal Wave I." Why was I so terrified of all that power I was creating? The water I kept calling up and then holding back was persistent, even patient, at finding endless ways of flowing into my unconscious through dreams. It was not going to go away, because it wanted to live in the light.

I needed a traditional story to help me get more perspective. It is no accident that I strongly favour folktales in which women must confront a beast whose supernatural powers and physical strength threaten to overwhelm them. My long struggle with fear of overwhelming forces gave these stories even greater potency, since they suggested resolutions that transformed both me as dreamer and me as tidal wave, much as beauties and beasts both change in the folktales. As with dreams, I have learned to trust pertinent stories to arise from the sea of the unconscious, never knowing what might appear. I knew that I needed a story with an overwhelming force, with water as a transformative element, and with a woman who survives the challenges. As often happens, this solution arrived serendipitously. One afternoon I found myself with extra time while telling stories at the Manitoba Museum. My storytelling venue was in the arctic gallery, so I decided to tell an Inuit story, "The Magic Drum," that I had not told for several years (Metayer 1972, 15-18). It answered my call for a story with the three elements I was seeking: Bears are the overwhelming force, water is one of the transformative elements, and the woman survives and triumphs. Here is my bare-bones summary:

For a long time, a young woman refused to marry the hunters her parents presented her. One day she was courted by two brothers, and decided to accept them as husbands. When they left her parents' igloo with her, the brothers put on their fine fur parkas and became white bears. They pulled the girl with them to an icy sea, dove through ice into dark water, and then left her alone to sink to the bottom. Small sea creatures came to nibble away at her clothing and then at her flesh, transforming her into a walking skeleton. The skeleton woman went on walking until she saw that the ice was thin enough to break through, so she rose up and came out onto land. She built a small igloo and lay down to sleep, wishing she had a large and comfortable one like her parents, and awoke to find herself in just such an igloo. Each night she silently thought about what she needed—a stone lamp for light and heat, some food and clothing, and human company. Each morning she found what she needed had been provided, and was excited to hear hunters walking over the snow. When they saw the skeleton woman, they ran away in terror to tell their old father about her.

The old man, unafraid of dying, went to find her, was invited and fed, and then asked to make a small drum. She played the drum, danced, and chanted, and was transformed into a beautiful young woman again. She chanted again, and the old man became a young man. They returned to his sons to reveal themselves, where the father announced, "This is that skeleton woman, and I am your old father. Now we are together."

I first heard this story told 20 years ago by Katy Simons, the Dutch woman I described in chapter 9. Katy was a trained nurse who had cared for Inuit children at a tuberculosis sanatorium, and loved telling stories from that culture. When I met her she was almost 70, an elderly woman who still felt very young at heart, like the man in the story she told.

Because of the nature of Katy herself, and the powerful images of bears, skeletons, and astounding transformations, the story has resonated memorably for years. The bears, of course, were significant to me from my own dreams, so their actions were hardly surprising. While they are not nearly as positive as my dream bears, they do act as the agents of the heroine's transformation by carrying her into the water, the element of birth and rebirth. Because she does not give up, she rises with new strength and power that allow her to return to her own form, and to find a man worthy of her new powers. I was inspired by her determination not to be overwhelmed.

You would think, considering my problems with seas and oceans, that the creatures inhabiting them might also be threatening. But this is not so. The rare dreams I have had, each involving whales of one sort or another, were quite benign. In fact, in one lucid dream I had the ecstatic experience of being propelled into the air on the back of a leaping orca. Poet Tanis MacDonald reports her own orca dream in a poem, with very different results. She introduced it by linking it to her stressful waking life of the moment:

> I had this dream while I was still doing front-line AIDS support, and I think this is an AIDS anxiety dream; the whale is a killer whale, and I keep working to stay out of reach, though the beast is not fooled and can locate me in a second.

Her poem, "At Sea," takes on new meaning as Tanis is relentlessly pursued by the determined killer whale (orca), symbolizing her fear ofAIDS.

At first I brace against the wind
on the harpooner's deck, jutting
like an arm out over the dark ocean

but I know the strength and size
of the hunter, so I climb the mast
and cling to the yardarm. Sails flap

against me, canvas for a burial at sea,
but I wind my arms around the rope
tied to my perch of hard pine.

A hundred feet below, the ship's deck
rolls, and the whale arcs its body up
from the waves, a predator's leap,

a black-and-white arrow of salt flesh
and teeth, grinning wide, soaring up
to me like Romeo vaulting the balcony.

He closes his maw on my frayed rope
and falls back, one huge eye fixed
on me as he splashes down, pulling

the rope and me with it. I roll off
the crossbar and fall into the leering
mouth of the sea and the beast

I sailed here to love.

While you can see the entire dream in her poem, Tanis as poet plays skilfully with the words, transforming the artful dream into an elegant poem without losing the dynamic balance between fear and fascination with the beast. Since I am no poet, I look to stories for my transformations, like the legend of the young woman carried off by polar bears.

Supplied with all my musings and this story and Tanis' dream-poem, I could now return to the "Tidal Wave" dream in my imagination, placing myself back on the wobbling tower with my face to the wave much like Tanis clinging to the mast, acknowledging the commanding beauty of what was below me. When I could see the wave clearly, I climbed down and walked back to the beach, with trepidation and also with curiosity. I stood on the sand at the edge of the water and looked up respectfully at the brilliant columns. I asked it what it wanted but did not receive an answer, so decided I needed to commit myself further. I waded slowly into the water until I was standing right at the base of the wave and could look up into its radiant light, but still received no response to my request. More was needed somehow. I remembered the grand cascade, the water curtain in *The Journey to the West*, with Monkey King leaping through it into a great cave. Inspired, I dove into the standing wave and felt the living water, the water of life, all around me, lapping at me like the sea creatures in "The Magic Drum." But the dream still felt unresolved. This playing inside a dream was more work than I expected.

I tried again, standing at the base of the wave and imagining the Golden Woman standing with me. I hoped that this dream figure, who had been transformed by air, earth, water, and fire, might have good advice on the watery element. This shimmering figure seemed to be dancing slowly with the movement of the water, so I imagined myself moving with her. Perhaps this was enough acceptance of the powerful water that had carried her down to safety, because I seemed to get a clear response. This was intuitive rather than verbal; the tidal wave resembled the earlier dream of the cracked dam with all its potentially threatening water, but this time with no dam to hold it back. That was it exactly, but a different response was needed, since each dream presented different artistic challenges; in a waking vision of the dam dream, I was able to walk safely across the dry river bed, and then to imagine myself as the dam and then as the water breaking free of it. Since the constraining force—the dam—was obvious, and the dried course was already formed, this was an easier exercise in imagination.

In "Tidal Wave III" the water was still holding back and waiting for release, but it had no dam to restrain it and no place to go that would not threaten destruction. Still, I had to try some sort of release. Heartened by my trust in the Golden Woman who I kept beside me, I invited the wave to let go. Instead of crashing down on me, it settled slowly back into the ocean, sending a strong but gentle surge of waves to the shore, enough to swim in without fear of drowning. At last the dream felt as if it had completed its message. For the rest of that week my "mantra" became, "Let the water go," and after several days I was rewarded with another water dream, quite unlike any other I had experienced.

In the dream I decided I needed to talk to a strong woman healer, and called a doctor I knew from years ago. She invited me to come immediately and I did so, without getting lost. That was already a clue that this dream would be different. I found the waiting room full of women who had apparently been part of a recent ceremony they were discussing. My doctor was describing the last part of the ceremony in a limestone cave filled with animal shapes sculpted by water. One of the women jokingly remarked that the cave was too dry, and set a glass of water in the middle of the green carpet. Another remembered how underground water began to rise slowly up into the cave, and I saw that water was gradually seeping into a corner of the carpet. No one was the least bit worried, including me. I awoke both perplexed and somehow comforted from this "Rising Water" dream, feeling that what happened was exactly right.

As I recreated the dream just now I saw how it contained echoes of my much earlier cave dream, the one in which I was preparing to leap into a deep pool in an amber-lit cave but was stopped by a woman's voice. It seems to me that the guiding woman in that dream has become visible in "Rising Water," and that she is the positive side of her dark sisters "Nameless Dread" and "Selfish Old Bitch," among others. The caves, as womb-like places of change with their elements of birth-water, is evocative. Perhaps in the first cave dream my dream-artist was not quite ready to dive, or to see the woman. I was still afraid of that power. In the current dream she is certainly ready to be seen, but I am not with her in the cave where the water is rising. Or am I? I recognized that the placing of the glass of clear water, and the water seeping up in the room, were the beginnings of another ceremony. My valuable underground water was coming to light in a less destructive form.

When I thought of letting the water go, I still had the dammed water and the tidal wave in mind, forgetting that underground water is an even more powerful symbol of the unconscious mind—the kind of water that Joseph Campbell called "the river beneath the river." This is the very water that the Golden Woman passed through and that the Golden Dragon released from the well in "The Water of Life." Something was moving in my dreams. I had the same solid feeling of energy in my midsection that I have had in the midst of writing or storytelling that is flowing spontaneously.

In dreams, as in all forms of creativity, spontaneous flow, balanced with lucid consciousness, can have surprising results. Being awake in dreams might have the same results as the young woman wishing for what she needs in "The Magic Drum." What you need is there, you just have to ask. It helps, of course, to be aware that you are in a dream of your own making, and thus have full power to ask for exactly what you want and need. We will see just how this works in the following chapter on lucid dreaming.

Stone Lions Are Real: Lucid Dreaming

When a tree floats horizontally in the sky or stone lions step majestically off their guardian perch in front of a library, the clear illogicality of the situation can inspire recognition that you are in a dream. In childhood dreams it might be terror that inspires the fleeting realization that you are dreaming and can thus escape by waking up, as I did in both Rat and Buffalo dreams. With Buffalo I actually made the lucid statement "This is my dream," but did not fully believe it and failed to act on this early brush with lucidity.

Even the most ordinary occurrences can signal a dream, as in an example from expert dreamer Patricia Garfield. She was driving on familiar streets making mundane plans for her day when she realized she was in a dream:

> Still driving, I command "Up!" and my body lifts from the ground. The car is gone. I now whiz through the air as I lie on my stomach about ten or fifteen feet above the earth. I'm no longer driving but I still grasp the steering wheel, which has become huge, a great circle. I hold the top rim, and the lower part rests on my thighs, above the knees. I feel the sun and the wind. I see the pavement clearly as I sail along. Everything is sharp, bright. It's a glorious sensation. I ask myself, "Are you happy?" and I know that I am. "And you know that you're dreaming?" and I know that I am (Garfield 1989, 4-5).

Garfield used the great circle of the steering wheel to begin her dream mandala, as I, following her example, used the great circles of the mirror, the sea-cylinder, and the fire in "The Golden Woman" to begin my own.

Lucid dreaming is now sufficiently well-known that it turns up in popular media. I was visiting a friend in Atlanta in 2002 when I read with delight the "Raising Duncan" cartoon I mentioned in the preface, where man and dog float in the night sky. The man is aware he is dreaming and says, "I know this is a dream but I love it!" The dog, enjoying himself in flight, thinks with dismay, "What? This is a dream?!" The simple cartoon captures the paradoxical joy of being aware of a dream and the contradiction of experiencing dreaming as an actual but fleeting experience. And what difference does it make to be lucid while asleep? It means that you are aware of yourself as the dream-artist and can see exactly how your work is developing. If I had managed to be awake in the dream of "Rising Water" I described earlier, I might have been able to enjoy it longer, perhaps ask the dream to re-enact the ceremony the women had been discussing, and to put me in the midst of their experience in the limestone cave with its fantastic shapes.

It is exhilarating to "wake up" in a dream, to understand that you are in the world of dream reality where anything can happen. It can also be a very comforting experience if you are in peril, since you can easily avoid danger by literally rising above it in a flying dream, or by realizing that there is nothing to fear because it is your own dream creation. You can end the dream or allow it to go on unfolding, and perhaps to transform. You can do anything you can imagine, as I discovered when I met the stone lions.

Some time ago I was walking down a street in a dream city with no particular destination in mind. On the other side of the street there was an old library with two stone lions crouched at each side of the entrance. As I approached, the stone lions suddenly stood up, stretched, and leapt gracefully down from their pedestals. I was terrified as I watched them stalk down the street in the opposite direction, but instead of following my inclination to run away, I decided that I had to go warn people about the lions. For some reason this decision shifted me into lucidity, bringing the realization that stone lions cannot really jump down and walk away. "This is a dream," I said to myself, "The lions aren't real," and went on my way in the opposite direction. I had just read a book on lucid dreaming, so decided to try what the researcher had instructed his lab subjects to do—actually signal to the waking world from inside the dream. I rolled my eyes to the right and then to the left three times, and had the physical sensation of having done so. If I had been hooked up to the REM machines this movement would have been recorded, but I was satisfied with the feeling of exhilaration. I said aloud to my dreaming self, "If this is a dream I can do anything I want. What do I really want to do?" Since lucidity for me is short-lived (a matter of seconds) I made a fast decision to do a back flip, a movement I had never succeeded with in junior high gym classes. I awoke with the physical sensation of having done a perfect, joyous flip.

I had already guessed that dreams were physical and not just mental experiences from my own and others' reports, and also from watching my various cats growl, meow, and "run" in their sleep. So I knew that in some way, however subtle, I had actually done something that my body felt. I wished my junior high gym teacher, Miss Horn, had been in the dream to witness my belated success.

Many of these dreams have been, like this one, potentially frightening. Earlier in life I used my momentary awareness to wake myself up, as most children do. As an adult I began to understand how fearful events could trigger lucidity, and tried to stay in dreams to see what would happen next. In this I was encouraged by the dream of a woman I met years ago, who described being threatened by a knife-wielding man on a dream bus. She startled him by yelling happily, "You can't hurt me, this is a dream!" He smiled and gave her a bunch of red roses instead of attacking. Like her, I found that a menacing dream could turn into something more pleasant, and the more I was able to stay asleep but alert instead of waking, the better these dreams got.

Perhaps my best test of this was the bear dream I described in the earlier chapter on beasts. Remember that I was in a local department store with my arms full of expensive dresses when I realized I was dreaming and could buy anything I wanted. I understood that material things did not satisfy me and asked for something deeper, so I was carried up (symbolically this takes me to a higher spiritual level) where I met the largest dream bear I had ever seen. At this point I lost my lucidity and ran, but the bear apparently stayed lucid, patiently followed me up the tree I climbed and invited me politely to come down and talk. I am still amazed and grateful for the generosity of the dream in not letting me get away. It is quite an experience when a character in your dream informs you that you are dreaming.

Despite the above examples, and of course the strikingly lucid "Golden Woman" dream, I do not regularly manage to become lucid. I have tried but rarely succeeded in asking my dreaming mind to be more awake, giving myself pre-sleep instructions to expect a lucid dream. Invariably I get caught up in the flow of a dream and forget that it can be wilfully changed, and before I know it the lions are real and I am running again.

This is not surprising, since a lucid dream is a delicate balance of unconscious and conscious states of mind. Some dream researchers even claimed that such a state was impossible, that you could not be conscious and unconscious at the same time. The work of other researchers, notably Stephen LaBerge, proved that it was indeed possible and even desirable. The waking mind steps into the dream and looks around, though as an outsider it is not invited to stay for long, nor is it given full power over the dream. Often this state of lucidity surprises a dreamer into waking up instead of keeping a conscious presence in the unconscious world. In my experience, lucidity is usually a brief experience, no more than a few seconds, and decisions are hard to make in such a short time. Like the characters in folktales, I have only a flash of a moment to make my wish before my mind is caught up in the dream again. "The Golden Woman" is the only dream in which I was lucid for the entire time, aware and accepting of every moment of the dream actions.

I had what I called "waking dreams" for years before I had any other name for them, or any idea that lucidity could be wilfully developed. In 1985 I heard a radio interview with Stephen LaBerge, who had just written his first book on lucid dreaming. He confirmed what I had only guessed—that dreams were actual physiological experiences and thus could be used by athletes, actors, dancers and others for physical training. One of the dream examples he used was a woman who noticeably improved her skating from dream practices. I was intrigued, and bought the book hoping to learn how to be more lucid. I was not disappointed. As I mentioned earlier, LaBerge taught his sleep-lab subjects to use a pattern of eye movements to signal when they were conscious of being in a dream. These signals were registered on a polygraph machine as actual communications from dream world to waking world, and proof to me that a dream was a real experience. He was also able to measure changes in brain waves when lucid dreamers carried out dream exercises in singing and counting, first imagining and then actually doing these activities:

> When we looked at imagined singing and counting we found that neither task produced any consistent shifts in brain activity. But singing and counting in the lucid dream produced large shifts equivalent to those that occurred during the actual [waking] performance of those tasks (LaBerge 1985, 96).

He concluded with the suggestion "that lucid dreaming (and by extension, dreaming in general) is more like actually doing than like merely imagining" (LaBerge 1985, 96). This was exciting information for me, confirming that a lucid dream is a direct experience with the full act of creativity. Dreaming is an art in which we are artist and creation at the same time, and the more you are aware of that, the more ingenious you can be.

I was delighted to read LaBerge's challenge to Freud's comment that an unexamined dream is like an unopened letter. LaBerge proposed another model in place of the view of dreams as psychological self-communication: "In essence, dreaming is more like world-making than like letter-writing." He went on to say, "If I am right, dreams have more in common with poems than they do with letters" (LaBerge 1985, 225). If this is so, then we are fully responsible for our world-making dreams and everything that happens in them. In lucidity we can enjoy this responsible creativity to the fullest and accept the surprises such creativity has to offer.

For example, I dreamed I was invited to a dinner party at a friend's river-front home, familiar to me from Enneagram workshops in waking life. For some reason I did not go into the large room where everyone else was already seated at banquet tables. Instead I was wandering in the next room filled with long tables covered with clothing and other objects for sale, and I was busy sorting through them. Another woman came into the room and said, "Oh, a garage sale!" and something about this triggered my realization that I was dreaming. I told the woman we were in a dream but she did not seem to care, so I ran into the next room where the dinner was taking place. I went directly to my friend and said with elation, "Carol Ann, this is a dream," expecting her to be as thrilled as I was.

Instead, she looked at me with a level gaze and said with the hint of a smile, "So, how does it feel to be god?" It felt quite wonderful, but I was startled into wakefulness before I could enjoy my divine status, a little humbled but still smiling. I was happy to be told by my own dream character that I was the creator of this small world, even if I could not enjoy it for long.

A dream, of course, is less tangible and permanent than other artistic expressions, but not necessarily less satisfying. This one was an interesting variant that combined and built on two recurring patterns, my dream house and my department store dreams. I was not quite lucid enough at first to recognize these familiar dream patterns, but eventually I got the message from the dream itself. But who, in fact, is the "god" of the dream? Obviously not the lucid dream character; if that were the case, another character could not startle a creator out of its own creation. My older brother Allen reported a similar dream, discovering in a lucid moment that he was the creator of the various people in the dream he was having. "Hey, you guys," he said to them, "I made you all, so you have to do whatever I want." It did not quite work out as he expected. His "creations" looked at him and yelled back, "Oh yeah? Watch this!" and started to chase him. He ran. Such moments of rebellion happen in other artistic expressions as well, when what we have made takes unexpected turns that we can either accept or reject. In a dream, however, we are the art as well as the artist, so we can run or we can change the pattern.

LaBerge felt that the actual lived experience of dreams, and particularly lucid dreams, made them potentially effective not only in artistic creativity but in healing as well:

> This is because lucid dreams are not merely experienced as being very realistic and very vivid; without exaggeration we can say that lucid dreaming is the most vivid form of imagery likely to be experienced by normal individuals. Thus what happens in lucid dreams has an understandably powerful impact on the dreamer, both experientially and physically (LaBerge 1985, 172).

As the architects of our dreams we heighten our experience in lucidity because we are more aware of the shifting interaction of conscious and unconscious states of mind. These are not polar opposites but instead are constantly weaving dreamed and waking experiences, drawing on remembered day-time activities that affect the dreams as well as on remembered dreams that affect waking life. Also, earlier dreams can be remembered and responded to within other dreams, much as artistic expressions can refer to other works of art. Here is an example that draws on my waking experiences on a particular day, as well as on the library lion dream from years earlier. At the time of the dream I was visiting a friend who had showed me around her lab at the University of Florida.

In the dream I was walking down a long corridor, lost as usual, and saw a long counter with three white-coated people at the end of the hall. I went directly to them and started to ask for help and suddenly realized I was dreaming. I said to the first person, a man, "Hey! This is a dream and I can't hold this for long so please tell me something!" Immediately he began to talk to me, but I could not understand what he was saying. In growing desperation I said, "You're speaking dream language and I can't understand it." The second man looked at me and began to gesture instead of speaking, then picked up two vials and poured a liquid back and forth while looking at me meaningfully, but I had no idea what his gestures and actions meant. I could feel lucidity slipping away as the last person, a woman, silently indicated that I should follow her into the lab room, which was set up like the one my friend had showed me earlier that day. She sat down at one of the high lab tables and began to speak clearly and slowly, as one would speak to someone unsure of language:

"I went downtown today and I saw two young lions playing in the fountain. I said to myself, 'They're not real!' But they were real."

I woke up mystified about her message, then realized with a start that she was referring to the lion dream I had some years earlier, and was challenging my denial of the lions' reality in that lucid experience. This dream character was demanding from within my own created dream that I accept dreams as actual experiences, another kind of reality. She might have gone on to echo LaBerge's advice about our creative role in dreaming to "Control yourself, not your dreams" (LaBerge 1985, 117). In other words, find a balance between the objective detachment of lucidity and the deeply subjective experience of being in the dream. Too much control can destroy artistic balance. She seemed to suggest that I had lost the power of my lions by denying them. Like the deeper truths of folktales and mythology, the dream lions were "real" after all. Who knows where they might have taken me. But if the woman scientist in my dream is correct, and I trust that she is, it is never too late to accept and act on dream reality and its artistic potential. After all, she remembered the lions from the previous dream, and kept them in mind for me for several years, until my lucid dream self managed to ask the right question.

Lucid experiences can give us the chance to see ourselves in action as creators of our dreams, so long as we remember that we are just one of the characters. I learn this lesson again and again, usually with good humour. For example, while writing this chapter I spent weeks trying in vain to re-experience lucidity. Several dreams even felt like they were teasing me, presenting increasingly absurd situations to prod me into lucidity, but I kept missing the clues. When I finally gave up, the lucid experience slipped in. Oddly, there was nothing at all absurd about the dream. I was simply walking down a perfectly ordinary city street, no library lions in sight, and noticed a perfectly ordinary man moving ahead of me. He was in his mid-forties and was solidly built, with short curly blond hair. For no reason I can now recall, I realized I was dreaming and yelled to him, "Wait a minute, I want to talk to you." He obligingly turned around, and I now saw that he was on a scooter or a skateboard, but not in a hurry. I walked up to him in the middle of the sidewalk and said, "This is a dream, but I don't know what I want to ask you." He smiled, and waited patiently for me to figure it out. Then I remembered something. "I can fly," I announced, ready to share my gift by teaching him, as I had others. He surprised me by answering serenely, "I can too." I laughed, and suggested we fly up to a nearby hill to decide where we might go next, and we took off together. When I woke up I understood once again that I was only one character in my dreams, and that other figures would continue to surprise me with their own independence. This was the first dream where someone other than me could fly on their own, and for some reason it was highly amusing to me. I found that I was ready to give up my ego-position as divine creator and solo flyer in favour of interacting with someone else on an equal basis. This dream act somehow cleared away the undergrowth of my writer's block and I was able to get to work with new energy, talking back to my internal critics. They, apparently, cannot fly and do not trust the joy of it.

If lucidity in dreams can lead to insight and freedom of flight, what about waking lucidity? I struggled to find examples from my daylight life and wondered why it was so difficult. Hard enough in dreams but nearly impossible in waking. Ah, yes of course, awakening is enlightenment. This is what meditation is all about, retraining the wild wandering mind to sit still for a while and observe the world outside and the world inside without the usual projections and protections and wishes. A dream has the advantage of being a dream, something we can clearly identify as our own projected, protecting, wish-fulfilling creation that we can catch ourselves at: "Aha, I'm dreaming, so now I can do something different." But what comes next is as difficult in a dream as it is in the waking world. What do we really want to do? When the dragon asks the young woman in "The Water of Life" what she has come for, she knows. Unlike her, we often do not know what it is we want most deeply.

I have described earlier my brief experience with waking lucidity in Grand Central Station in New York, when I lost my protective anger and all the barriers between "me" and "them" disappeared and we became one huge flowing movement with no separation from anyone or anything, and yet each one gloriously separate and unique. It was so exhilarating that I still feel the potency of the gift decades later.

I have thought about this experience many times, but only now see how dreaming and waking lucidity connect. In both states of mind lucidity has been called up by a realization triggered by a distressing situation: being frightened by stone lions stepping off their pedestals in a dream, and by the presence of hundreds of strangers in a train station in waking life, for example. Lucidity challenged what I considered to be reality when asleep and awake, and arose only when I was able to let go of my limited ideas for at least a moment, and experience another truth, a further reality.

Many people believe that only the waking world is "real" and the dream world is "unreal," a fantasy. But in fact dreams are not fantasy, not fiction at all, but symbolic portrayals of our deepest true selves. In contrast, our waking life is often a kind of mirage of our own making, our own wished-for world that does not actually exist as we wish it to be. So lucid moments that come during both wakefulness and sleep offer the opportunity to see with new eyes, hear with new ears, comprehend with a more open mind. And from the truths we find, we begin to create our own great beauty.

One of the dream characters that has sometimes triggered recognition that I am dreaming is a figure I call "The Wise Child." It is sometimes a very precocious baby who can already walk, talk, and reason, much like heroic characters in epics and sagas. For example, I was with my sister-in-law Liz in a 1986 dream, riding in a car with a father and his baby. Liz held the baby and then passed it to me in the backseat, and I was amazed to see what a mature, wise, and utterly joyous face it had. It began to talk, telling me about "grandma and grandpa," at which point the father called back proudly that the baby was only eight months old. I felt this child could tell me more, but I woke up too soon. I have also dreamed of delightful older children, perhaps four or five, with very mature faces and eloquent speech. They have been so remarkable that I should have realized I was dreaming, since most waking-world children would not reveal such maturity, apparent wisdom, and pure joy untouched by fear.

In folktales, on the other hand, precociously wise children are less unusual, and in general the kinds of anomalies that might signal lucidity are so common in folktales that they are merely part of the logical development. I was excited to explore lucidity in folktales, then. I kept in mind that on the deepest level these stories, like dreams, are metaphorically true and not merely fictional. Folktale protagonists have the same challenge as dreamers, perceiving their situation clearly and then acting on their perceptions. In fact lucidity, seeing things as they are, is a quality of folktale protagonists in general. They seem to have a clearer view of reality than do the other tale characters. For example, Cinderella knows somehow that she is not the abased creature her stepfamily believes her to be; she is able to see white doves as helpers and not just as ordinary birds, as her opportunistic sisters do. Similarly, foolish Jack knows he is more than a simpleton; even when his mother throws out the magic beans, he knows where to look for them the next morning. And the sister in "The Water of Life" is not swayed by the voices she hears from the stones even when they are her own brothers' words; thus she is able to follow her path, encounter the dragon, and benefit the people turned to stone. Because these characters act from their lucidity instead of sitting around pondering it, as I have, they gain what the other characters want but cannot get because they are too opportunistic to see clearly.

Even though such characters are not seeking materialistic gains, as are their siblings, they triumph in the end. Cinderella wins the prince, Jack finds the giant's treasures, and the sister in "The Water of Life" retrieves the precious water that revives the tree and frees the stones.

In a more challenging example, a story character overcomes seemingly impossible odds by keeping a clear view of who she is as she matures. Earlier I summarized a tale described as coming "from the south seas" in which a sister sees the rainbow beauty of a fish while her sisters only see a fish supper. Here is another "south seas" tale, "Daughter of a Clam," from the island kingdom of Tonga, told from the point of view of a sea-creature itself (Fanua 1975, 13-19).

A woman who longed desperately for children was told in a dream to eat the peeled fruit of a certain tree as the first rays of the sun rose above the horizon. In her excitement she forgot to peel the fruit and gave birth to a daughter enclosed in a clam shell, who was thrown into the river. Clam, moving with the water as she grew, one day found herself in the royal pond, where she fell in love with the king's son who bathed there every day. As a clam, she could only express her love silently by sucking the water of the sponge he bathed with.

One day Clam discovered that she was pregnant and returned immediately to her parents' home, where she chanted to them. Her remorseful parents to took her home to care for her, and in time she gave birth to a perfectly formed daughter, who she named "Bathing Sponge." Clam asked to be put back in the river and directed her parents to care for the child and to bring her to the water each day.

Bathing Sponge grew into a beautiful young woman who cared lovingly for her clam mother. One day the king's son, now the King of Tonga himself, passed by and heard singing. He was taken by the beauty of Bathing Sponge, and asked her grandparents for permission to marry her. When Bathing Sponge reported this to Clam, she rose from the water in a fury and told her daughter that this man was her father. When the king heard this, he haughtily ordered both Bathing Sponge and her mother to appear before him and his court. Clam, undismayed, instructed her tearful daughter to break the clam shell on the rocks. When the shell shattered, a lovely woman stepped out and announced that she was ready to visit the king. Together they appeared in the royal court, where the king was astounded by their beauty. He said in wonder, "I thought your daughter beautiful, but she is only like the moon, while you are like the sun." They married, and from that day on Clam was called Sunbeam, and their daughter Bathing Sponge became Rising Moon.

Clam never has any doubts about her true nature, both as a clam and as a woman. She does not waste time on fantasizing even when she falls in love with the prince, but lives out her clam's life until she is able to get free of her shell, and the spell that held her there. She seems to me to be lucid throughout the story, and she thus is able to recognize the moment and the means of her transformation. As with dreams, traditional stories rely on action and on concrete forms to express abstract ideas. To open the clam shell of any story or dream, I have to let go of pre-set ideas and interpretations and allow them to offer the tools for their opening. If I pry or force, by trying to decode them intellectually, a shell will only close more tightly.

A special tree was central to Clam's story, and of course to "The Water of Life." Unusual trees have appeared in two of my lucid dreams as well; one was floating in the sky and the other wanted to swallow me. In the first dream I was frustrated at having to sort a huge stack of papers with no help from others who were at some sort of meeting with me. It was so absurd that I realized that it must be a dream, so I carried the papers outside and said, "If this is really a dream these papers will turn into white birds when I throw them up." I gave them a good toss into the air, and sure enough they transformed into white birds flying off in all directions. As I looked up to watch them I saw a tree, in the style of a cartoon tree or a child's drawing, floating horizontally in the sky. I woke up laughing, but when I told it to a friend she pointed out that trees are our counterpart in the plant kingdom, so the tree was saying something about me. "You'd better get your tree rooted," she commented.

Some time later, after sadly watching a city crew cut down the magnificent but diseased elm tree directly outside my bedroom window, I met a very different tree. I awoke in my familiar bedroom and heard my cat, Alix, scratching at the closed door. I got up to let her in, but when I opened the door I saw to my horror that the entire hallway was filled by a massive tree trunk. As I watched helplessly, the tree began to lift its huge root system, and I could feel its power trying to draw me up into the tree. At that moment I realized I was in a dream, and began to tell the tree a spontaneous story about a wonderful tree that lived in the very centre of a great forest. The tree outside my bedroom door began to relax its roots as I joyfully described the tree in the story. I ended with "and it had a long and happy life," and woke myself up.

My floating tree came to earth, but still not quite rooted. This unfinished business with trees gave me a fuller perspective on the tree in "The Water of Life," and in fact after having these two dreams I began to see the tree in this story as a full character in its own right. That is, as I became more lucid in the story of "The Water of Life," the tree became more deeply rooted. I wonder, now, what transformation might have occurred if I had managed to stay lucid in my second tree dream, and allowed the tree to swallow me up into its trunk. I am still waiting for another chance.

I keep coming back to the transformational moment in the lucid "Golden Woman" dream when everything shifts. This is not the dramatic transformation at the end of the dream, but the opening moment when I see my 25-year-old face in the mirror and sense that something is not quite right. I do not know what it is at first, but allow a moment of puzzlement to rise up, and that leads me to the lucid understanding that this is a dream. Like the "Cannibal Tree" dream, I was in familiar surroundings, and because there was nothing threatening me I was considerably more comfortable staying in the dream and maintaining lucidity. I was able ask the mirror to speak the truth, and saw my "true" face as it was in waking life. If I had been able to maintain the same lucidity in the tree dream, (and in my childhood buffalo dream), I could have asked what the dream figure wanted—or what it wanted to offer as a dream gift.

The story of Clam is complex, since she is both locked in her shell and aware of herself. Like Clam, I accepted who I was with clear eyes in "The Golden Woman," so the dream world was able to change and carry me down through the four elements and into the shell-splitting fire. With the threatening tree, I almost got to experience what the woman in the clam shell felt in her imprisonment, but chose to "run away" into the waking world instead. In lucidity I might have remembered that it was the confinement in the shell-like accretion (and for Clam, the actual shell) that brought about metamorphosis.

The stone lions are symbolically real, as are the trees and the buffaloes and all the other dream symbols that we create for ourselves, and they all have gifts to share. "This is a dream?" Duncan's cartoon dog asks. Yes, and I love it.

15

"A sacred voice is calling": Dreams as spiritual Experiences

At the most profound level, creation is a sacred act. If dreams at their best are our artistic creations, then dreaming itself can be a sacred act. This was all the more so among people for whom vision quests and dreams were sources of transformational power. Certainly not every dream has transcendental quality, but those that do can give us a direct encounter with spirituality in surprising ways.

In 1979 I had a compelling dream experience that has stayed with me as vibrantly as if it were last night's dream. Late one morning I fell asleep on the living room sofa while waiting for nine-year-old Nathaniel to come home for lunch. I dreamed that I was napping on the living room sofa waiting for Nathaniel to come home for lunch, quite unaware that I was not actually awake. I woke up in the dream thinking that it was almost noon, got up and went into the kitchen to fix Nathaniel a peanut butter sandwich. I glanced out the kitchen window at a blissful scene of green rolling hills, thinking how lucky we were to live out in the country in such a beautiful place. Something struck me as odd, and I said to myself, "This doesn't look like Niagara Street in flat, prairie Winnipeg. I must be dreaming!" I reluctantly let the pleasant scene fade as I accepted its unreality, but then realized that if I was dreaming, I did not have to make lunch after all. I chose to return to the sofa and continue my morning nap and go back to sleep inside the dream. In doing so, I had unconsciously asked the dream to take me deeper, as in "The Golden Woman" dream that would come to me several years later. In that dream, too, I recognized the illusory quality of an enticing image and let it fade, thus allowing for something deeper than surface beauty to arise.

When I fell asleep again inside the "fixing lunch" dream, I immediately had another dream. Instead of recognizable scenery, there was a luminous environment that had no beginning or end, no horizon, nothing to indicate depth or breadth. It was simply spacious, measureless living light shimmering with soft iridescent colours. A large pink-tinged flower bud floated in the exact centre, ready to open into full bloom. There were two hands on either side of the opening flower waiting for the blossoming. I felt them and I witnessed them at the same time, as in the climactic scene of "The Golden Woman." As the petals began to expand outward the hands opened too, following the movement exactly. This was the entire dream, a "haiku" dream of great depth—a flower opening and the hands opening with it in a delicate and intimate dance.

As I drifted back to wakefulness, I still watched with the eye of the dreamer and with that lucid eye of the waking self as well, sensing that the movement of hands and flower was intimately connected and somehow deeply related to universal wisdom. This was a distinct feeling, a bodily sensation, not just a thought. I had the same feeling as I experienced in the "Caged Puma" dream mentioned in the chapter on beastly creatures, where I was staring into the fiery red circle held up by the small ape and sensing its profound sacred power. Both dreams, separated by several years, highlight the colour of red and build on the circular image that echoes the form of the sacred mandala, a circle within a square that indicates the four directions. The vibrant red colour of the caged puma dream, alive like the heart of a volcano, felt like the very essence of life. When I put this image into words, it reads: "This is the heart of the matter." The blooming flower says to me, "It's all in your hands."

When I woke up that day to greet Nathaniel and serve his lunch, I told him the dream without comment or interpretation of any kind. This had been our practice for a few years, and we both benefitted from sharing nightly ventures and puzzling out their meaning, so I was curious to know what he might make of it. As usual he perceived the depth of the dream and saw its negative potential: "That's scary," he said, worried that a person's hands might be responsible for universal balance, and might be unable to maintain it. I reassured him of my strong sense of connection with some vital principle. That sense has remained with me, along with the brilliance of the opening flower and its luminescent milieu. It was a profoundly spiritual dream, but I had nothing at that time to help me put it into perspective.

In the poetic biography *Black Elk Speaks* (Neihardt 1961), a Lakota sacred healer, Black Elk, described a deeply significant visionary dream he had as a precocious young child, much like "The Wise Child" in my dreams. In his dream he saw two men who transformed themselves into geese. They sang to him as they flew away, "A sacred voice is calling you." A few years later when he was seriously ill, his vision-dream recurred in greater detail, so much so that he could recall it vividly in his old age. The geese-men came to him again to lead him into an elaborate vision filled with horses of various colours, bison, and eagles, each of them revealing different aspects of the sacred nature of the world all around him. Black Elk understood this as a vision for his people as well as for himself, and tried to live by its teachings throughout his difficult life.

Black Elk lived at a time and in a place where dreams and visions were taken very seriously by his people, where archetypal forces had their full potential to literally change one's life. In shamanic practices among the Lakota and elsewhere in the world, various animals and birds represent the shaman's soul in passage to other realities or are the spiritual guides into these new worlds. Soul journeys were taken as actual experiences. Even in the weakened form such archetypes might take in our dreams today, all sorts of creatures can still speak in the soul's voice, offering a passage into our unseen but strongly felt sacred selves. Birds in particular are soul-filled archetypes.

Several years ago I had a surprising dream. I was walking toward people who were having a joyful picnic when one of them, a handsome young man, came out to greet me. As soon as we touched hands we both became skeletons. I had a brief moment of terror and then felt my soul free itself, flying out through the top of my skull—the crown chakra in both Hindu and Buddhist traditions—as a small eagle. I had a strong sense that I had a mission but did not know what it was, so I flew in circles around a group of people below calling out to them for help and asking them where the man had gone, since I wanted to make sure he was safe. I could not get even one person to look up, and I felt entirely lost and alone. Even in the dream I could not understand how they failed to notice an eagle. As the dream creator, of course, I was the one who was failing to notice this beautiful flight of the soul, but I did remember it and respect it. This experience was both disquieting and exhilarating. While I had failed to get their attention (that is, failed to let the dream fly fully), it was uplifting to have become an eagle even for a moment.

After hearing me describe this dream, my friend Gail Beck, who reported the hell-and-back dream earlier in this writing, related her own evocative bird dream that revealed an even more obvious spiritual quality, and a more complete resolution:

> So, I'm sitting outside with someone, like I sit out there in the yard in the early evening, and this bird comes and lights on my head. Whoever is with me remarks on how pretty it is, so I sit there very still, wanting to see the bird but not wanting it to fly away. I finally decide to get up very carefully, and it stays with me. I go to a mirror where I can see the bird. It is indeed beautiful. When I first see it, it has some black stripes on its wings like the goldfinch. So then I put my hand up slowly and the bird gets on my finger. I can feel it. It's a soft, blue-grey colour, lighter on the head, with a yellow—and for an instant a pure gold—spot on the back of the head.
>
> So, I want to keep the bird around, and now my children—still young in the dream—want to put it in a cage. We have a large wooden cage with screening, like on the porch here. I put the bird on a perch in the cage. The front screen is hanging off, like the porch screen. I'm thinking the screen needs to be fixed so the bird can stay in the cage.
>
> As I'm standing there thinking about that, the bird speaks to me, tells me I don't need to worry about that because it's not going to go anywhere. I can hear the soft voice of the bird, but it's almost like thoughts are being transferred rather than speaking. I hear the voice, a soft, human voice, but the beak isn't moving (conversation, December, 1999).

If we think of this bird as a symbol of the soul or psyche, the dream takes on added beauty. Her description of the bird "lighting" on her head hints at a luminous essence, divine light. Gail's soulful bird is first seen by someone else, a witness to the sacred self we often cannot see for ourselves. Gail yearns to see her bird but not in a selfish way; she does not want the soul-self to disappear, and moves carefully to a place where she can see it for herself. The reflection in the mirror is clear and steady, and she feels confident that she can touch it, which she does. It is hardly surprising that Gail wants to keep something that profoundly beautiful safely sheltered, which makes its message all the more reassuring: it will not fly away, it belongs with her.

Later the same night she had a second dream with implicit spiritual content. She was at a New Year's Eve party where there were two groups of people. The first were rowdy revellers, but in the other, people were serenely celebrating with a song, "so beautiful, with lovely voice harmonization." Gail decided to join the group of celebrants. She described waking up with a peaceful, happy feeling.

Often several dreams in an evening will echo similar themes, though this might be obscured by the story lines of each separate dream. For example, in Gail's dreams there seems to be no connection between the stories of the beautiful bird and of the New Year's Eve party, except for the evocative quality of the sounds themselves. But in both dreams Gail chooses a more spiritual approach: she does not shut up the bird but trusts it to remain with her, and she prefers the singers over the rowdy revellers. She hears and responds to the sacred voices that are calling, which allows the dreams to go further. Perhaps if I had been able to stay asleep in my eagle dream, I might have been carried to more soulful heights as well.

Similar dreams can also occur separated by weeks or months, or even years. When these come in threes I consider them particularly worthy of attention. Such dreams are not the same as recurring dreams, which tend to deal with problem-solving. Instead they have a more spiritual message. In 2000, some months after I had watched two different sand mandalas being created, and had participated in a Buddhist retreat, I had three related dreams that centred on distinctive Asian women, each in a food-related setting. I call these my "Deva Dreams," since the women all felt to me like supernatural figures; devas are divine beings, protective spirits, spiritual nurturers.

In the first dream, my husband and I had gone downstairs to a café in an art gallery but found it full. We went all the way to the back where one small table was available near a large party of Asian people. As I sat down I saw one Asian woman, seemingly a part of the group, sitting by herself near our table. "No room," she said with a smile. Her exquisitely beautiful face was as radiant as the full moon, and when she smiled at me I was entirely filled with a sense of the divine. I offered her a place at our table but she laughed, and said, "We could feed each other." I joked that I was such a slow eater she might regret it, but she was not put off by this. I felt her hands reach around me in readiness, so that we looked like a multi-armed Indian divinity. I awoke feeling cared for and profoundly nourished.

In the second dream some weeks later, my husband and I were again in an eating place, this time a humble cafeteria that had plenty of room at the long tables. We sat down near an older woman, who turned to me and asked, "What are the three important things?" I somehow knew I had to show these rather than speak them, so I pointed to my nose—breath—and to my mouth—nourishment—and then to my heart, indicating the spiritual meaning of these basic needs. She smiled a divine smile and I woke up.

In the last dream some months later, I was in an elegant restaurant without Dan, seated with two Japanese couples at a circular table. We began to talk about Buddhism but then shifted to opera. All four were involved in an opera company in Italy, and I admired the women who were both resplendent, elegantly dressed with elaborately styled hair. They invited me to their opera, telling me that they had also invited the Dalai Lama. I woke up wondering about the connection between Buddhism and opera, and then understood the clever word play. The two women were opera divas—or Buddhist devas.

Only in looking at all three dreams together could I see how similar they were, mundane on the surface but luminous at deeper levels. Each dream, in its own way, underlined the "three important things": sacred breath (singing and speaking), sacred nourishment, and spiritual heart. Dreams like these are so emotionally moving that they are difficult to describe in the bold light of day, where their ambient brilliance, sound, and sensations are hard to recapture. Dreams retain their evocative quality after we wake up because they do not arise merely from thoughts; they are actual experiences, not mental concepts, as we saw in the chapter on lucid dreaming. Joseph Campbell stresses this when he describes such transcendental incidents as "passing beyond even the dream, where all things shine of their own light" (Campbell 1990, 168).

As very young children many of us experienced the world as a mystical, numinous place, waking and sleeping, and perhaps this is one of the inspirations for my "Wise Child" dreams. For people living in societies that encourage such perceptions, visions like those of Black Elk are not unusual. For most of us who live in quite a different sort of place where dreaming is not as respected, those dreams that offer sacred experiences are much rarer. Still, they occur, and can carry over into our wide-awake world as they did when we were children. The free-flowing creativity of the wise child is still available to us, if we keep our channels cleared of silt.

Lucid dreams are particularly silt-free, and in them we can maintain clear vision at least momentarily. In those moments, when we are both creator and created, we can see how our artistic mind actually functions and how this has a touch of the divine. In my blooming flower dream, for example, I see how the hands and the blossom are intimately connected, and that the world quite literally hangs on this balance. In the dream I experienced the abstract Buddhist concept of cause-and-effect in living form, but I did not understand this until I became a practising Buddhist many years later. It was as if lock and key finally came together to reveal a buried treasure, bringing me a deep feeling of release and openness. In an earlier chapter I mentioned a brief Grimm tale, "The Golden Key," that captures this experiences of exhilaration (Zipes 1988, 288-89). Let me repeat it here with more detail:

A boy was sent out to collect firewood in the middle of winter. When he had completed his task he rested, building a small fire to warm his hands. As the snow melted around the fire he saw something gleaming, and discovered that it was a small golden key. He said to himself, "Where there's a key there must be a lock," and he began to dig into the thawed earth around the fire. His hands touched something hard, an ancient metal box, and he lifted it out into the light of the fire. "Now we will see what is inside," he said to himself as he fitted the key into the lock and slowly lifted the lid.

The story ends here, leaving readers to imagine their own treasures. This is what dreams do as well, revealing only so much and no more, and much of this illusive and enigmatic, like the blossoming flower and the hands. While writing this story here, I noticed that yet again there are two elemental mediums of sacred transformation, earth and fire. If the boy were greedy and overly anxious to find a materialistic treasure, the story might well go in another direction. He might find a container full of serpents and toads, as Dark Kate did when she was too hasty. Sacred transformation is a slow process that can be interrupted by impatience and greed. As we saw in the Scottish tale of "The Three Feathers," the story character who expects nothing ends up gaining the truest and most wonderful treasure. Remember, too, that the youngest son in this story finds his three treasures beneath the earth, and that the last treasure is an apparently ordinary frog who becomes a wise human princess with a very fine sense of humour.

As I have already said, our evolving consciousness and mindfulness allows us to reach back through waking and sleeping experiences for new understanding. Dreams and personal memory are amazingly flexible, growing with us as we continue to emerge and bloom. This is the open nature of archetypes. The blossoming flower I dreamed up, for example, has evolved as my spiritual ideas have changed. I remember telling this dream to a friend from India, Rubena Sinha, and having her say with excitement, "Oh, it's a lotus!" I immediately and somewhat defensively rejected her interpretation: "No, it's definitely a rose." Years later I could see how rose and lotus became one, because the flower archetype is open. Archetypal images present forms that you fill with your own unconscious meanings that influence and are influenced by waking life. My flower has transformed itself in my memory.

For me, my brief but profoundly meaningful experience in Grand Central Station and the rose-lotus dream are obviously connected, as are the three "deva" dreams. While these all gain added meaning from my present commitment to Buddhist practice, they stand alone as well. A Christian would see other meanings, as would devotees of any other religion. Someone else can always see other connections in your dreams, and perhaps shed some new light, but you are the only one who has the key to the treasure box.

In many ways being inside a dream is very much like being in a box surrounded by the treasures. A few years ago I dreamed I was standing in a kitchen—a large box—and was challenged by an immense reclining giant who asked me a seemingly nonsensical question that puzzled me. The dream did not seem to have any overt sacred content, but it certainly did have a sense of mystery. I knew there was something more to it, but had no idea what this might be. I remembered not to pry, to let the clam shell of the dream slowly open and reveal itself. I let it rest with me for some time and told it only selectively, sensing that it was more than just oddly interesting.

In this dream I was at a retreat with a group of young people making some kind of music video for which they had asked me to appear in the background as a "wise old woman." A Crone like the ones I dreamed up so many times? I smiled at that. I was guided around the grounds, shown where they were setting up the filming site, and taken to the kitchen where I was left to make my own lunch. I was trying to make a sandwich out of left-over salmon, and I was not going to waste it even though some of it seemed on the edge of spoiling. Even asleep I still responded to my mother's admonition against wasting food. As I worked, a young man from the video group came into the kitchen and said very matter-of-factly, "There's someone at the door for you." I looked down a long hallway to the front door, which stood open, and saw an enormous yellowish face, so huge that I could see only part of a gigantic eye and just small corners of the nose and mouth. This colossus, lying on his left side, must have stretched out down an entire city block. I was too amazed to be terrified, and listened attentively when he asked me in a calm voice, "What is the trash can doing in the kitchen?" I drifted back to awareness still looking wildly around that dream kitchen trying to find a trash can where there did not seem to be one. I awoke more amused than distressed, with no feeling that I had been threatened by the titan.

"What in the world was he asking?" I said to myself. I had heard the message very clearly and sensed its importance, but I still did not understand it. In my experience, the most effective way to keep the potential of a dream alive is to tell it to sympathetic listeners. You gain new perspectives from hearing your own spoken words and listeners' immediate responses. That is how the titan gradually revealed his potential identities.

When I described the dream to my friend and dream-colleague Morgana, she immediately saw the humour in it and dubbed my giant "The Ochre Ogre," acknowledging his earthy colour. Later the same week I told the dream to Phoebe Man, who had been sitting with me for two weeks as we watched four Tibetan monks creating a sand mandala at the Winnipeg Art Gallery. In the mood of the moment she suggested that the ogre was a reclining Buddha. I was sceptical, as I had been with Rubena's suggestion that my rose was a lotus, but I was willing to listen. She offered to bring me a postcard of a reclining Buddha in Thailand, and I went home to find a photograph of another titanic Buddha I suddenly remembered from a book of Asian photographs I had for years. I was stunned by what I found, and by what Phoebe brought the next day. Both figures echoed the size and position of Ochre Ogre, except that they (and all other reclining Buddhas I know about) were lying on their right sides and he was on his left, facing in the opposite direction. Dream characters, and archetypal figure in general, do not have a one-to-one relationship with external forces. That is, dreams are not "true to life" in the rigid fundamental sense, but are always open to interpretation. His import to me was all the greater when I saw his potential spiritual affinity with my Buddhist practice, but this did not limit his character. Someone else dreaming up a similar figure would no doubt have a different personal interpretation, not necessarily spiritual, and it would not necessarily matter to them if he was facing east or west, north or south. A dream invites, it does not proscribe.

Our sacred voices call us to recognize our creative wealth, which is meant to be used and not merely displayed. Even the simple retelling of a dream to a friend invites it out into the light of day. Here dreams can be appreciated for what they have to offer, and we might see how they connect with our waking lives and our artistic interests. I was delighted to hear from my sister-in-law, Elizabeth Stone, who read a draft of this chapter and was very taken with the Ochre Ogre. She asked my permission to actually "use" him in her daily life, and told me why:

> For the past few months I've found work and organization of my daily life quite overwhelming, sorting, cleaning, trying to find things and then losing them again. I often imagine the benign, almost friendly (it seems to me) Ochre Ogre. My instinctive reaction to his question about the trash can in the kitchen is this—what better place for a trash can than in the kitchen, the source of creativity, nourishment, and even excess. The Ogre has often kept me company as I've struggled with my chaos, so I hope you don't mind if I borrow him (letter, June 2002).

I was happy to oblige, and told her that I also felt the benevolent company of the Ogre while working on the chaos in my study, a seven-year project. The Ochre Ogre's presence has added a sacred dimension to this mundane activity—getting one's world together, sorting the trash in our places of nourishment and creativity, for me and for Elizabeth.

In addition to whatever connections a dream might evoke in waking life, I also explore dreams by being aware of similar qualities in a story I am working with at the time of the dream. When I read or hear a story that reverberates deeply, I know I need to begin telling it as soon as possible rather than trying to figure it out, in order to discover why it touches me and how it connects with a dream. Sometimes a story reaches out to grab me with all the force of a powerful but benign ogre, even when I hear it in summary. For example, one of my students was hesitantly describing the bare outline of a Chinese legend she had heard from a tour guide in the city of Wuhan. I knew immediately that this was a special story, and was delighted when she offered to write out what she could remember of it. Here is her own written text of "The Yellow Crane":

This is a Chinese folktale, as told to me on the banks of the Yangtze River in the city of Wuhan.

Once long ago in a faraway land, on the banks of the Yangtze River where now stands the city of Wuhan, a wine merchant had a little shop at the bottom of a hill. The hill was called Snake Hill, perhaps because it had a winding, twisting path which led to the top. The shopkeeper was a kind and generous man who loved to serve his customers and to listen to their stories. One day, just at sunset, an old Taoist monk came to the wine merchant's shop and stopped to rest at a table in the garden. The kindly merchant brought him a refreshing drink of wine, but the monk refused it, saying, "Thank you, but I have no money to pay for wine." The merchant insisted on serving him, saying, "For you there is no charge," and continued to serve the weary monk from his wine pitcher. For two months thereafter, the monk returned to the little shop at sunset, sat at the table in the garden, and continued to receive free wine from the friendly merchant.

At the end of the second month the monk came to speak to the wine merchant, saying, "I must go away now, but before I go I will leave a little gift for you to repay you for your kindness to me." So saying, he stooped down and picked up an old piece of yellowed orange peel, and then proceeded to draw on the wall of the shop. He laboured for several minutes while the puzzled shopkeeper looked on, and then suddenly, the image of a graceful yellow crane appeared. "There," said the monk, "this is my gift. When you wish to entertain your guests, just clap your hands three times. The crane will emerge from the wall to dance for you and your customers." Then the monk went away and the kindly wine shop owner went about serving his guests and sharing in their stories, soon forgetting what the monk had told him.

One day someone asked about the lovely yellow crane on the wall, and the merchant remembered. He thought to himself, "I'll try out the monk's magic," and proceeded to clap his hands three times, as he had been instructed. Sure enough, the crane flew down from the wall and began to dance for the merchant and his guests. All were astonished and awestruck at the beauty of the dancing yellow crane. News soon spread, and travellers from near and far came to the shop of the simple winekeeper to marvel at the performance of the graceful crane. The wine merchant soon had to expand his shop and to serve many different wines to his ever-growing number of customers. He became very rich and famous, but remained a simple and good-hearted man.

When two years had passed, one day at sunset the old Taoist monk reappeared and sat down at the table in the garden. He asked the winekeeper, "Has the gift adequately repaid you for all your generosity?" The grateful merchant bowed at the feet of the monk and said, "You have repaid me many times over. I thank you from the bottom of my heart. Your gift has made me rich and famous." Hearing this the monk said, "That is good. Then I must take back my yellow crane and leave." He summoned the crane with three claps. When it flew down beside him, the monk climbed on its back and away they flew, off into the sky over the city of Wuhan. The grateful merchant, in order to give thanks for the good luck the monk had brought him, set aside part of his fortune to honour the monk. He built a beautiful three-tiered pagoda at the top of Snake Hill beside his shop, and called it The Yellow Crane Pagoda. If you go to the city of Wuhan today, you can climb to the top of Snake Hill and find a pagoda there. At the top of the pagoda you can look out over the city and imagine yourself flying over the city, like the monk on his graceful yellow crane (Donna Cawker, November 2001).

The merchant in this story, like the characters in many of the folktales I have described here, does not lose his balance when his life takes dramatic turns for better and for worse. People I have told this legend to have been delighted when the crane first dances and groan when the monk takes back his gift, but the merchant remains a good-hearted and generous man when fame and fortune surround him and remains humbly grateful to the monk and the crane even when he loses them. Because of this, his life presumably continues to be graced with luck, and he acknowledges this by creating a public tribute to them in the form of the pagoda.

Imagine this merchant as a different story character, one who chose material over spiritual gain: even if the monk had appeared to him in the first place he would never have given him free wine; or, even if he had given him free wine hoping for good fortune (Taoists were known to be workers of magic), he would have been dismayed when the monk picked up a piece of orange peel as a gift; and even if he had allowed the monk to deface his shop wall with a shrivelled orange peel, it is unlikely that the crane would ever have complied to his hand clap and emerged to dance at the man's command. More likely, the greedy merchant would have sneered at the drawing in the first place, and never have learned of its magical potential. I offer these conjectures to show why this is, for me, a sacred story, one in which the numinous, spiritual world is allowed to enter the mundane world; a withered piece of orange peel can create a creature of luminous grace.

A listener involved in such a story does not usually question the peculiar and the unlikely, any more than most of us challenge such incongruities of our dreams. This is not what lucidity is all about. If, for example, I had become lucid in the flower dream and said, "Hey, floating flowers can't bloom, and whose hands are those, anyway," I would have lost the dream. If, on the other hand, I had managed to become fully lucid and accept the dream as a deeper reality, the image might have stayed with me longer. Perhaps I might have seen radiant colours, heard divine music, or seen the blossom transform into something else. I see that I, like the merchant, am trying to build a pagoda to honour spiritual dreams and stories, and it takes the form, metaphorically speaking, of this book. The Ochre Ogre is invited in.

I am often captivated by seemingly small details in dreams and stories, and sense that these contribute to the sacred mystery. It might be the white bone the fox is gnawing on in "The Water of Life," the spots in the linoleum in "The Golden Woman," and the shrivelled orange peel in "The Yellow Crane"—and the missing trash can in "Ochre Ogre." I have learned to trust that in dreams, in stories, and in some waking activities, it is often just exactly those moments of incongruity, surprise, and puzzlement that stop me for a moment and somehow open a space for wonder. It is easy to brush them aside since they seem so inconsequential, or to force an interpretation on them, but such particulars are worth respecting as the mysteries they are. They may offer the key to the treasure, whether it is a blooming flower, a dancing crane, or a moment of new comprehension in the midst of the confusion of everyday living. In waking life as well as dreams, it can be the smallest moment or most insignificant detail that brings us to awareness, as in my small satori in Grand Central Station.

It was such small details that led me on in a dream I had while visiting my friend Norlaine in Maryland, the morning my mother died. If I had failed to notice tiny new leaves on a plant, things might have taken another direction.

In the dream I was in my Winnipeg living room with my husband Dan, and I saw the avocado plant was dying. I was distraught because I had grown the six-foot tree from one of my mother's huge Florida avocados and had kept it alive for several years, and saw it as a vital connection to my mother. I was on my way out to some kind of sacred retreat and did not want to leave the dying plant untended. Dan said, "Call Morgana, she'll take care of it." I did, and her husband Tom assured me that it would be nurtured, so I went off to the retreat with a feeling of deep relief. As I passed the plant on my way out, I noticed minuscule leaves starting to appear on the branches already, and I knew the plant would revive.

I got to the retreat, set in a spacious old building filled with women of all ages and races. I found myself in a large kitchen with dozens of Spanish-speaking women preparing food—again, spiritual nourishment is a theme. I began to help, but then someone called something in Spanish, and I understood the word "missa" as mass. They all stopped what they were doing and began to move in procession out of the kitchen, taking me along with them. We passed through a wide hall and toward broad double doors leading outside. As we approached the door I heard a clear rich voice singing, a sound of utter purity that penetrated directly into my chest and I felt my heart expand. I realized in amazement that it was my friend Morgana who was singing, though I could not see her. All the women began to sing with her, and because I joined them I was able to keep the words in mind as I drifted back to waking state with a deep sense of serenity.

The song stayed with me and I managed to find pencil and paper and struggled to get the melody down while it was still clear in my mind. Since I do not read or write music I had to create my own notation system that would record both tone and timing, and make sure the words I remembered fit the melody. I sat up in bed for almost an hour trying to find a method that would work. I was delighted when my musical husband arrived later that day and was able to hum the tune back to me, amused at my primitive but effective system of notation.

When my younger brother Terry called later in the morning to tell me that my mother had died, I knew immediately that I wanted to use the dream song at her memorial ceremony that I planned to organize with a small group of friends in Winnipeg. Back home, I told the dream to Morgana, who is a professionally trained church organist and choir leader, and showed her my crude notation. She said with a smile, "You've recreated a medieval notation system." She transposed this into a simple modern song and sang it for me. I was in tears listening to her sing and play it:

God is in the air,
God is in the rain,
Earth and fire, Earth and fire.

Later that week a half-dozen women gathered in my living room for my mother's memorial, and we sang the song together. It was an odd and powerful experience to hear a dream song come so fully alive in the waking world, truly a sacred voice calling. It was just the song for my gardening mother, and also for the Golden Woman, who passes through these four elements to arrive at the pure essence of self.

This experience gave me dramatic proof about the living relevance of dreams, especially those with sacred potential. Let me use a friend's dream that echoes and supports my thoughts. It was sent to me by e-mail entirely spontaneously more than a decade later. It, too, touches on dying trees and on wisdom related to the four archetypal elements. I offer it as an example of how we, like this dreamer, can open ourselves to the powerful artistry in our own dreams and perhaps discover our personal spiritual centre:

> Well, I had a dream with you in it last night. We were walking along a beach lined with trees—tall trees with white/gray bark, losing their green leaves because they were dying. You were telling me why the trees were dying and how people could go about saving the trees and bringing the current ill ones back to life. Somewhere in my travels I have actually walked on this beach, but at the moment I can't think of where it was (Cecilia Basic, e-mail communication, October 2002).

When I had commented on her fine sense of detail, she credited it to her long years of training as a scientist (doctoral degree in chemistry), and added more details that she thought might have come from her concerns about the environmental and continuing news reports on issues around the Kyoto Accord. Interestingly, she omits her ongoing interest and informal training in art, particularly leaded glass creations, but she did stress that the dream was very vivid: "It was in colour—the trees were the most amazing grays and greens."

I pushed a bit further, trying to find out if she remembered what the dream Kay was saying, and she responded immediately, and also gave me full permission to use her dream and comments:

> You said that the trees need clean sun and clean air in order to revitalize. Yes, clean sun. Also, the trees closer to the water's edge were more ill than those further inland, implying (though it was not stated) that clean water would do some good too. You also said that this illness in the trees had been seen in past times and that it was everyone's responsibility to make them well again (third e-mail communication, October 2002).

She added, "So there. Clean sun (fire), air, and water. Have we got all the elements there or is there one more?" She has forgotten the earth element, all too easy to miss since earth is so deeply elemental, so much a part of life that we often forget to honour it. Her trees, of course, are depending on clean earth as well as sun, air, and water.

Cecilia reported her dream to me only because I was in it, but found it compelling enough to recall in detail. Let us imagine that another person had the same dream but had not developed their dreaming skills to such a level. They might simply have reported, "I had a dream about you, something about walking along a beach and looking at trees." That would be a beginning. I would ask you more about it, as I asked Cecilia. I might say, "What did the trees look like, what was the colour of the sky and the water, what did it feel like walking on the beach—was it rocky or sandy?" Each question would call forth more detail, and the dream might come to life again. Let me stress here that I am not talking about dream manipulation, trying to prod anyone into creating details that were not there. My experience with my own and others' dreams has given me confidence that if you recall a dream at all, the details are all there whether you can remember them or not. There is no need to "make them up." In fact, this would destroy the integrity of a dream. As with any other art form, dreams benefit from dedication and practice, so if you pay closer attention and begin to ask yourself questions about them, they will most likely open themselves up more fully. It is like working on a challenging passage in writing or composing or choreography, or any other art form. Like the trees Cecilia describes, dreams can be brought back to life, and perhaps it is indeed, building on her words, "everyone's responsibility to make them well again."

Her comments echo those of the authors of the book *Dream Symbol Work* that I mentioned in an earlier chapter. The authors observe that dreams take place in the ever-present timelessness of sacred *chairos* time, in contrast with the clock-ticking *chronos* time of our waking world. Bringing the two together is a delightful challenge, and, they insist, a sacred one as well:

> In this dream-moment outside of *chronos* time, in this dip into *chairos* time, we usually find a gift for our life, a source of energy, an insight, a new alternative, the revelation of an unexpected potential. Dreamwork allows the dreamer to bring the gift of the dream—wisdom, insight, energy—from sacred time into chronological time. Thus, the sacred energies become accessible to the waking ego (Berne/Savary 1991, 95).

The dreamer of "The Child in the Golden Mask," described in chapter 2, found her own sacred experience in this deeply disturbing dream of a trapped child. I was stunned when she described her sacred centre as "liquid gold," no longer a rigid mask but an internalized alchemical transformation: she, too, became a golden woman (Berne/Savary 1991, 86).

Like her, I believe that we can find pure spiritual essences in the interweaving of dreams and waking experiences, our *chronos* and our *chairos* times. Dreams touch our daily interactions with people and the natural artistry that surrounds us, and can be the gift that Berne and Savary describe above. The flowers we carry and the trees on the beach, not to mention the air we breathe and the water we drink, are as vital in our waking lives as in our dreams. Truly, the blooming flower is in our hands. It is all too easy to forget these small miracles in the chaos and challenges of our daily lives, and being reminded by our dreams is, I think, good medicine for our sick world. It might be handy to have your own version of the Ochre Ogre around to remind you not to toss your blooming flower into the trash, and he might also know about cameo pendants that need to be cared for and studied. His voice becomes louder and louder if we ignore our creative impulses, because he is determined to be heard.

Waking Up: The Golden Woman Rises

If you had ever asked me about dreams or told me yours, or if you wondered what they might mean or how you might remember them better, or if you had ever said, "So how's that book going?"—this has been my very long answer to you. One of the joys of working on this book in its many manifestations over several years has been re-experiencing the exhilaration of dreaming as a joy and as an art, not that dreams are always joyful or creative.

I have shown how dreams arise from life experiences in our inner and outer worlds, and how they in turn reflect back on and influence those worlds. I have given examples that demonstrate the wonder and beauty in dreams that are distressing, and the hidden depths of those that seem only superficial. Even in the most mundane, enigmatic, or nonsensical dreams that appear to have not an ounce of significance, there can be glimmers of humour, heroism, passion, colour, movement, and sound. While most dreams are unfinished sketches, a few rare ones are fully resolved creations.

But in the end we do wake up, and what happens then is entirely up to us, the creators as well as the characters of our nocturnal wanderings. Appreciating the dream is enough, but we can go further if we wish by finding ways of bringing it into the waking world. For me this has meant staying with this writing through thick and thin, wading into mental tidal waves and facing monsters that persisted in disrupting my waking world, and most of all, getting past the stony voices of doubt expressed by Nameless Dread and her many sisters. What kept me awake was a pleasant feeling of debt I felt I owed to all those who had taken the trouble to read sections of the book as it evolved, and to everyone who was willing to share some of their own dreams and comments. What we have done together is now out in the waking world.

Obviously, I had to be asleep before I could wake up, and sleeping is something that I do very well. While writing this book I spent a lot of time in bed doing "dream research," using every excuse I could find: comforting my elderly dying cat who took solace in snuggling behind my knees as I read and slept; surviving the very long darkness of short winter days; and of course those occasional naps (all right, frequent) to escape the problems of everyday life in troubled times. My early retirement from academic life, which I had anticipated for too long a time, resulted in a period of dislocation that I responded to with longer naps.

I could not imagine that I would ever tire of napping and dreaming, but I was wrong. A serious fall that put me in bed for several weeks, and then in a rigid back support for three months, compelled me to reconsider. This imposed stagnancy brought new understanding of those story characters who get stuck in enchantments, like the frog who sits at the bottom of the dark well waiting for the golden ball to fall, or the daughter who sleeps for 100 years surrounded by a wall of thorns, and all those people turned to stone on the mountain path in "The Water of Life" who wait for someone to release them from immobility.

In those months there was a lot of paralysis in my dreams, too, and messages to get clear and present and creative. Some of these "stuck" dreams echoed my retreat into my welcoming bed by setting themselves in places of retreat, withdrawals from the daily world. Two particular dreams marked significant turning points in this writing, each pushing me out of retreat and toward creativity.

In the first, late in 1999, I was at a women's retreat with about 30 others of various ages. A guide had been showing me around the buildings, including a huge, ancient, abandoned barn below the main building, where a basement would be. It was very old and dim, but also warm and clean, still with the feeling of all the life it had once held. I could smell that life and it was good. Perhaps that cantankerous horse Lady had been there once.

We left the barn from the inside, climbing old wooden steps up into a large, bright kitchen directly above, and here found several women preparing food for a communal lunch. We all greeted each other warmly, but at that point I felt a cold draft in the room and asked the woman who had showed me around where it was coming from. She pointed to a gap in the kitchen floor down to the barn. A small gleam of light came through even though the barn as we saw it was dark. This seemed significant, but I had no idea why. Waking, I remembered how the gap echoed the passage through the kitchen floor and down through the four elements in "The Golden Woman," but in this new dream it was an incomplete sign, just an echo of possibility. Still, it signalled an opening of sorts.

Suddenly an angry woman burst into the kitchen through a door I had not noticed and began to berate us, yelling loudly, "This is my kitchen and I want you out of it right now!" She seemed to have forgotten, or to have changed her mind, about having given us permission to use it. I was surprised, then somehow embarrassed, as if it was my fault (which it was, as the dream-maker), then angry at her for attacking us and breaking her agreement. But before I could express my anger—as I had with Nameless Dread when I tried to attack her—I decided to make peace with this raging woman. I may even have had a vague sense of her similarity to Nameless Dread. Perhaps because I had made my peace with that crone as a powerful woman in my waking life, I wanted to tell this kitchen woman that I respected her authority and wanted to find out why she was so angry. I even began to feel something spiritual about her and tried to speak to her, but I could not get her to listen. I woke up knowing that the dream was incomplete. Had she failed to get my message, or did I miss hers?

I pondered these things for a while, let them germinate, but nothing much seemed to grow until two years later, in 2001, when I dreamed myself into another kitchen at a retreat. This time my dream messenger, the "Ochre Ogre" whom we met earlier, politely but firmly asked me about the trash in the kitchen, my creative centre. I took his words as a challenge for me to get on with it and stop gathering bits and pieces of ideas and dream examples. If dreams, like these two in particular, seem significant but do not make their import clear, part of the creative task is to explore their deliberately enigmatic nature. My sense was that I was being told, by means of dream-stories, where I needed to do some work.

I could have stopped at the psychological import, that my life at that time was out of balance and that I might be in the wrong kitchen, but I already knew that story and I wanted to see another side of it. So I let these dreams give me some good artistic problems to chew on, keeping in mind the kitchen as an inner place of creation where things go from raw to cooked. Archetypally speaking, if the kitchen is a central place of creativity, any challenges here let us know that we have an artistic problem that will benefit from attention. So the question I asked myself was, "So what's cooking?" Or, in the words of the cartoon trickster Bugs Bunny, "What's up, Doc?" I kept on cooking.

The first challenger, the enraged Kitchen Woman who reminded me of Nameless Dread, seemed to be trying to throw me out, but she was also challenging me to see her other side even if she seemed to neglect it herself. I, dreamer-as-artist, am sending myself a poetic message to get clear on what I am doing in that kitchen, getting my act together in this drama so I can stake my claim to it as my rightful territory and negotiate with the cook, who is yet another aspect of me. And then there is that gap in the floor to consider, the crack that reveals light coming up from the old barn, pure and luminous, not the flames of the inferno. Like the linoleum I passed through in "Golden Woman," it suggests another passage down into darkness to the depths of bright wisdom.

Part of the art of dreaming is remembering as much as possible about how a dream flowed, and the other part is letting it go on flowing in the waking world. Perhaps because I allowed these reflections to come into conscious thought, both Kitchen Woman and Ochre Ogre could push me to figure out what I want to cook, and to get the trash out of my kitchen. As in any other artistic form, I had to dump what I did not need, and stop using leftovers—the spoiled salmon in the dream echoed old and repetitious ideas in my writing, going over old material again and again, rethinking, rewriting, endlessly rereading what I had already written.

While I was engaged in cleaning my metaphorical kitchen to make it a more creative space for imaginative nourishment, I received a cheerful dream by e-mail from my friend Gail Beck, painter and skilled cook in waking life:

> I am at some sort of family gathering and I am putting food on the table when I realize I've done a painting on the wall of a table with food, especially bread, which is spread all around the

> sides of the table I'm setting. This table we're going to eat on is against the wall, so that you can't tell where the real food ends and the painting begins. I say to my father [no longer living in actual life], "What do you think of this, I can make it so it looks like the table is ready to eat from all of the time." He thinks it's a clever idea and I'm pleased. The painting was colourful and realistic, so much so that when it first came to me I couldn't tell where the painting ended and the "real" table began (e-mail correspondence, February 2002).

In waking life, this dreamer strives to achieve convincing realism in all of her paintings, so for her the dream is a great artistic success. She cleverly uses her cherished father as a witness to the effectiveness of the painting and of her skill as a cook and hostess, able to provide a table that will always look ready for guests because it is backed by the culinary wall mural. As an artistic expression, this dream is a fine example of multiple layers of creativity—Gail as painter and cook who creates a dream that brings painting and food presentation together in a colourfully seamless way that becomes an illustrated story when brought back intact to the waking world, where it becomes part of this book.

Neither dreams nor artistic expressions of any sort are always simple and light as Gail's dream. In fact, more often it is enigmatic ones that offer stiffer challenges to that petty inner critic who carps and censures: "Why bother to remember that silly thing, it's just a dream, and it doesn't even make any sense." In waking life you can hear snarky voices saying with a sneer at art exhibits, dance programs, or musical events, "A three-year-old could have done that!" Maybe so. Dreamers and artists can be as persistent as any three-year-old at getting enigmatic messages up into consciousness, sometimes in a form that might seem like a three-year-old's creation. And why not? Three-year-olds are right in the middle of roiling creative energy, they just do not have the technical or verbal skills to get it out to us yet.

I listen to children when I have the chance, knowing that I will always learn something new. Some years ago I was in an elementary school class telling folktales. One of the stories seemed particularly dream-like, and the children spontaneously began talking about dreams they had that frightened them, made them laugh, or even foretold a future event—as had a dream in the folktale they had just heard. One boy sat in thoughtful silence while the others enthusiastically reported their dreams. He waited until they had all gone out to recess and stayed behind to talk to me: "I think dreams are things that happened to us when we were babies but we couldn't talk about them." Then he tried to recreate a dream-memory that expressed this non-verbal experience of "lying in a thing with other things standing up (bars) and someone (his mother) leaning over with something (a bottle)." He found a place where waking and sleeping experiences come together in fine ambivalence, and the key to bringing these to consciousness—language of some sort. All those unnamed "things" he had no words for as a baby become named later, and he now has a way to recreate a small but significant adventure in imagination. I was reminded of my own dream that seemed to me a symbolic reliving of the birth experience, an event that was obviously pre-verbal but still rememberable.

And speaking of birth, our original creative experience, let me introduce a very reflective Sikh cab driver I met at the Toronto airport in the late 1980s. I had come in to visit friends and to attend the annual storytelling festival and had missed the last bus, so had to take a taxi. When the driver heard that I was interested in stories he said, "Sit up here and we can tell stories." Of all the folktales, legends, and sacred narratives that flowed like a river as we drove through the night, the most evocative was one he modestly introduced as "not really a story, but something we believe." He described the prenatal experience of being able to communicate directly with God when we are in the womb, who shares with us the sacred nature of the world and all things in it. "But," he said, "the world we are in grows too small and we beg to be freed. God agrees, but asks us to promise that we will remember everything we've heard. Of course we promise, who would want to forget such things? But we do not know how difficult the passage is into the next world, and because we must use all our energy to be born, we do forget everything except for one thing—that we once knew something very beautiful." He thought that we spend the rest of our lives trying to remember what we had forgotten, and in his opinion this was how religions came into being. And, I would add, dreams. They offer one way of waking up to such lost wisdom. Perhaps this is the source of the Wise Child who appears in my dreams, the one who still remembers divine connections.

Imagine for a moment that, as dreamers, we are like those lively children recalling dreams, like the boy re-experiencing infancy or me reliving my own birth, or the Sikh cab driver finding his way back to a sacred centre through a story. We are each finding our own ways of translating all that imaginative energy into something meaningful for our lives as we are in the process of living them. If we keep saying "no" to the kid who wants to play, we might have to deal with dream messengers who get bigger and louder in order to get and hold our attention. They all have something to say, whether we understand it or not. My own creatures go from that polite but distressing rat at age five to a huge yet compliant buffalo at age eleven, and then to the titanic Ochre Ogre, still calm and patient but larger and more insistent. My angry crones, far less polite, get madder and louder and more aggressive, impatient with not being heard. One of them even tries hiding my car keys so I cannot escape. And then there are the tidal waves, culminating in the wave that stretches across the horizon and waits for me to do something, at the very least to acknowledge its awesome radiance.

Here is another splendid gift of dreams: they can make us more alert to the marvels of waking life. For example, my various wise child dreams surely contributed to my appreciation of a living example of an elfin two-year-old girl with a halo of dark hair, almost uncanny in her resemblance to my dream children. I was wading on the shore of Lake Winnipeg when this child came dashing fearlessly past me into the shallow water and began, with amazing balance, to lift her tiny legs and step over each in-coming wave, which for her were waist-high. I stopped and watched her (as did her mother), noting her pure delight and wondering if she might do better than I did with a tidal wave. I plan to try her method when I revisit that dream.

When we are open to dreaming as our private art and can keep any specific dream in the back of the mind, like wise children, for example, everything around us has the possibility of offering associations. The three Tidal Wave dreams rested in the back of my mind as I was reading a book on Tai Chi Chuan, in which the words of Taoist master Lao-Tze are cited:

> There is nothing under heaven that's more yielding and more resilient than water, yet when it attacks stronger things, it always overcomes them (Lowenthal 1991, 28).

As I allowed that simple and brilliant insight to settle in, I saw that it was appropriate not only for all the watery dreams I had ever had, but perhaps for dreams in general. Their first approach might be gentle and resilient, but if barriers are raised against them—from fear, from avoidance, or from misunderstanding—they will flow around these and reform in other dreams, perhaps even threatening to sweep away whatever is erected against them. Our rickety towers will not suffice if the artist in us really wants to have fun. Unlike an actual tidal wave or fast-moving river or deep water held back by a dam, our dream waters cannot literally drown us, but they can inspire us to learn to swim in new ways.

Why, then, does the Golden Woman surround herself in a hard cocoon as she passes through the water? Did this protection arise from my fears of water, my misunderstanding of transformation, or perhaps from avoidance of going through the life-changing process of metamorphosis? My instinctual response, both inside the dream and later when reliving it awake and aware, was that this cocoon did not seem to have any defensive connotations at all. It was a slow accretion that seemed to be fully a part of the process of the downward movement and it did not block me—the "me" in the dream—from feeling the water's temperature and flow, nor from seeing and hearing the four people who rolled the cylinder out into the fire. Like the membrane-caul of actual birth (those born with it still intact have been thought to have special powers), the cylinder was a part of the birthing experience. In this particular dream, it was literally the mold for a golden figure. How could the Golden Woman have been born without it? She is not imprisoned, she is encased while the fire does its alchemical work; she is ready for new life.

I imagine her sitting up and looking around. If she had spoken in the dream, she might have said, "Aha. A new world. Here I go," as she stepped out of the fire. She surely would have appreciated the enthusiastic exhortations of Brenda Ueland, the spirited writer I cited much earlier in this book, who asked, "Why should we use our creative power and write or paint or play music, or whatever it tells us to do?" Her answer was optimistically eloquent: "Because," she says, "there is nothing that makes people so generous, joyful, lively, bold and compassionate, so indifferent to fighting and the accumulation of objects and money" (Ueland 1987, 179). In addition to the pure joy of creation, we can certainly use some strong antidotes to the ills of these hard times of fighting and global greed. We all have the resilience and the strength of living water, the water of life.

The Golden Woman stands up and steps out of the flames.

Epilogue: An Empty Suitcase

There will always be another dream, and of course there was, but it had to be the last if this book was ever going to be finished. My endlessly recurring dream of trying to get all my things in order offered a fitting conclusion here.

I was also spurred on by my annoyingly relevant horoscope for March 11, 2003, which said:

Gemini, you can no longer continue to ignore the project that's been left undone. Try to remember the original spark that got you so excited.

The original spark, my excitement about dreaming as an art, was a simple notion that managed to burn on through the periods of undoneness, part of this hanging on, the difficulties of letting go of any creative project that has to be just right. This clearly echoes my ongoing dreams about getting stuck because I cannot manage to get all my stuff together. I suppose I am trying to get too many ducks in a row. Just the other night I was almost caught on an island in a dream hurricane because I was still bundling up things in my favourite bright shawls while my friends were getting on the escape boat. In my favour, my dreaming artist has at least replaced suitcases with beautiful shawls.

My musical friend Morgana pointed out that I am in good company with composers who might seem to be struggling to let go as they weave a series of codas into a dramatic conclusion. Each promised ending builds to the next, until the last musical wave breaks through. With my tidal wave dreams in mind, my own wave-like codas seem an echo in reverse, the aftermath of a receding tsunami in which each wave is more gentle than the last until there is only a tranquil swell on the ocean surface, while the depths are still alive and moving. My March horoscope set off my last small inner wave and the dream carried it further.

I had not had a memorable dream for months, just flotsam and jetsam that floated randomly. The night after being amused by my horoscope (and, by the way, doing nothing about it), I had a very small dream that gave me a way of relighting the spark for the last time here. In it my husband and I were preparing for a trip, and I began yet again to gather things for the suitcase that cannot be packed. But there were significant differences. First, I had taken out a good-sized suitcase instead of the usual small, wheeled carry-on that was easy to handle but hard to cram with everything I thought I might need—clothes, underwear, shoes, toothbrush and other toiletries (don't forget the dental floss), books and little reading lights, and on and on. There was always something else I needed and couldn't find.

The bag I chose this time was large enough to put lots of things in, as much as I might want. It was a nondescript old black bag, plain but sturdy. I felt its rough fabric texture, picked it up by its comfortably padded handle to test its weight, then put it flat to begin to pack it. As I opened the bag, hearing that satisfying *zzzzhhhh* of the zipper, my husband came into the room and said, "You don't have to put anything in that, you know." Of course. I realized that I could buy whatever was needed wherever we were going, so I really didn't have to pack anything at all. I immediately felt exhilarated, light, free of burdens. I did put one thing in, though, a smaller bag that also seemed, by its light weight, to be empty. It was an elegant soft black leather carry-on with a very new, fresh smell. I had no plans to fill it with anything either, it just seemed to belong inside the larger suitcase.

I woke up just after I set this black bag inside the older one, wondering if perhaps it might contain a still smaller case, and inside that one another, and another, each one smaller than the last, like Chinese puzzle boxes or Russian Matrioshka dolls.

The dream had made its point. I could travel as light as I wished, appreciating the weightless potential of an empty suitcase possibly filled with even more emptiness in each smaller bag. But why carry anything at all? In the logic of the waking world this question makes sense, of course, but a dream has its own logic. As in any other satisfying work of art, dreams do not create things that have no use or meaning. So as I lay there imagining the empty suitcases within empty suitcases, I marvelled at the potent symbolism of an empty vessel. For one thing, there is the very essence of dreams themselves as symbolic containers, particularly apt in the case of recurring dreams as a series of puzzle-box containers waiting to be solved. Containers of what? Whatever we put into them as spontaneous dream artists, filling them with countless people and other creatures, events and adventures, sights, senses, and sounds—like laughter, swooshing waves, a blustery wind, wolves howling, birds singing, and my husband's dream voice telling me I don't have to pack anything.

As a metaphor for dreaming, then, what is this symbolic suitcase empty of? Empty of burdens. Empty of anxiety. Empty of heaviness. Empty of anything that is not needed. Paradoxically, my sense was that it was not, in fact, empty at all. It was full of potential, and that inspired my exhilaration. Because my dream-persona was no longer the anxiety-filled packer trying to shove in all the things she thought would make her safe, the suitcase was free to fill itself entirely spontaneously. This dream hovered just on the edge of lucidity. If I had recognized its dream-nature and said, "Oh yes, a dream. What would you like to carry?" My case might have responded by filling itself with unexpected gifts. Perhaps poetry or music or a clear vision.

Folktales abound with such magical objects that fill themselves up—with diamonds or toads, salt or porridge, any number of things, sometimes dangerous and sometimes valuable. Such objects can be burdensome if the story characters, like my anxious dream-packing self, try to keep too much control over the objects, if they misuse them in some way, if they are greedy, or if they are simply too practical. In one story a man loses his mystical wife because he opens her forbidden basket and finds nothing inside, unable to see the beauty she has placed there. In other stories the sea is filled with salt or the village is inundated with porridge because the greedy character cannot recall the magic words that stop the flow. Or the covetous older sister chooses the larger, fancier box and gets toads instead of diamonds.

A folktale builds on the nature of the character who possesses the magical object, like a Vietnamese story I had been working on the week of my suitcase dream. In "The Jar of Gold" a poor rice farmer finds a jar full of gold buried in his rice field. Because it's heavy the man leaves it on the narrow path between fields, telling his wife that if heaven wants them to have the gold no one else will steal it. Two thieves who happen to be listening outside retrieve the jar and take it to their hideout, but when they open it, find it full of poisonous snakes. They maliciously carry it to the farmer's hut thinking that he'll be attacked by the snakes. In this way the honest couple get their jar back and find it filled with gold. "And naturally, they lived happily ever after," the story concludes (SGI Canada 2002, 46).

Imagine this jar, or my suitcase, as a metaphor that opens out as we explore it. The suitcase can be symbolic for a dream itself, available for ongoing interpretation, full of potential for continual reviewing. Depending on how one looks at it, there is potential for gold as well as for snakes. Good dreams and bad are all the skilful creations of our dreaming minds, and their interpretation is always open, always ready to be packed with new meaning, even when we encounter snakes. Unless, of course, we are as dark-hearted as the thieves.

As a potent symbol, an empty suitcase is easier to transport into the waking world, bringing with it the possibility that it is ready to be filled. As my daughter Rachel put it more simply, "If your dream suitcase is empty you can bring something back." In part, the "something back" is this epilogue.

I am reminded of the flash of a dream that began this book: an empty pail dips into a well and rises with water from the depths of the unconscious, making the unseen visible and the unknown comprehensible. The pail, like the suitcase, can only bring something back if it is empty to begin with. I was startled by a comment in the book *Dream Symbol Work* that echoed this exact image:

> As a bucket winds its way down into the deep well and serves as a container to bring a gift of water to the surface, so the dream and its symbols serve as containers that can hold and bring to the surface for you gifts of insight, inspiration, information, energy, and all that comes from your deepest sources of wisdom and guidance (Berne/Savary 1991, 102-03).

I am reminded, too, of the dream in which my old friend Katy Simons presents me with a glass box in which the contents are obscure. This leaves the treasure open to possibility, an apt symbol, in this case, for the work of her valuable memoir that I had left undone and have since completed, spurred on by her dream appearances.

To extend the metaphor further, this book itself is an empty suitcase, a dipping pail, a glass box. It is as empty as I have been able to make it in order to allow for your own views and reactions and interpretations, yet sturdy enough to provide a trusty container that holds untold treasures you might not have considered. I understand that someone who has no interest in dreams might find little meaning in my metaphorical suitcase, seeing it as merely empty, and that is entirely fair. But for others, dreams have more promise. My initial spark was to offer you something that might carry your own artful treasures back into the waking world.

Bon voyage.

Dream Mandala

Mandalas are sacred circles with the essence of power in the centre and guardian spirits around the periphery. My own dream mandala is inspired by the work of Patricia Garfield (Garfield 1989), who created a mandala of her significant dreams based on a Tibetan Buddhist model. I was already familiar with Tibetan sand mandalas, a highly developed sacred art, and used two different sources to develop my own dream mandala (Till 2000; Watts 2002). I was fortunate to have first-hand experience with mandalas when I watched two separate mandala creations in Manitoba. Each of these exceptional events guided me as I worked.

In the spring of 2000, the Winnipeg Art Gallery sponsored four Tibetans from the Zongkar Choede monastery in southern India, who spent two weeks creating an intricate design in coloured sand. The centre of this mandala was compassion, symbolized by the Bodhisattva Avalokitesvara. The head monk began the circle from the centre, using an ordinary compass and ruler, on the wooden platform that would hold the mandala. It had to be geometrically precise from the start in order for the design to be accurate, and thus spiritually effective. Almost at the end of the two weeks, when the exquisite mandala was almost complete, one of the younger monks dropped his sand-tool in the section he was working on. There was no sign at all of any problem, except that all four monks immediately went into a quiet consultation. When I returned the next day, the entire section had been wiped away and the monk was beginning again, with no hint of impatience or dismay. Their calm precision was a strong inspiration for me. According to information available at the gallery, mandalas are alternately described as visual prayers or visual meditations. They are both, and much more. When the intricate sacred circle is completed, it is ceremonially swept up and poured reverently into moving water, in this case the nearby Assiniboine River. Watching this entire "visual prayer" from beginning to end was a deep meditation.

Later that year I spent another two weeks at a ruined Trappist monastery south of Winnipeg, where one monk created the "Circle of Life" mandala, centred on the Three Poisons (greed, anger, and ignorance) and surrounded by tiny figures in each section of the six lower worlds of existence (Hell, Hunger, Animality, Anger, Heavenly Rapture, Humanity). This, too, was swept up carefully and poured into the nearby La Salle River.

As I worked on my dream mandala over a few months, not in a hurry, I had a small taste of the spiritual experience that arises from placing appropriate figures in their proper places with careful attention. I deliberately did not begin the mandala until I had finished the last of my writing, because I did not want to be biased about which dreams would be brought to life in a new way. I reread Garfield's various chapters on her own dream mandala more than once, studied the other mandala sources, and finally began a rough practice piece in pencil, using kitchen plates and pots for my circles. Over the next several days I inked in and coloured these circles, pencilled in which dreams might be symbolized in the central spaces, and then let this rest in the kitchen over a period of weeks as other dreams suggested themselves. I was bemused to realize that my kitchen was the place of creation, as it had been in my dreams.

When all dreams were ready, I began work in earnest on a second practice piece, using compass and ruler and careful to have each segment properly placed and each dream figure carefully drawn and coloured. Three months later I began work on the final mandala, as you see it here.

There was never any doubt that The Golden Woman would be at the centre, but I was surprised to see how her presence in the midst of all the other dreams evoked a sense of the spiritual in each one. I could see how the dream was so full that it embodied the qualities of all the others—the equanimity of the east, the modesty of the south, the compassion of the west, and the generosity of the north. Because The Golden Woman touches on each dream symbol depicted in the mandala, I see more clearly how it is the true centre of my dreaming world. Looking at the mandala as a whole gives me new perspectives on how our dreams are telling us one great story of our own sacred lives.

ENTERING THE MANDALA: We will pass through the circular border representing the four elements, and then through symbolic walls enclosing a sacred structure that houses various dream figures. Guardian figures protect the four directional entryways on the path to The Golden Woman at the sacred centre.

I use Garfield's mandala as a model for the challenges of the four directions. We begin in the east, which in the Tibetan tradition sits at the bottom of the circle, and we move sunwise around the sacred structure as we spiral inward.

EAST: The challenge is overcoming fear/anger, epitomized by "The Caged Puma" represented by the small ape's hands enclosing the life-giving symbol. In the inner circle above are Buffalo and Rat, other challengers of fear/anger. We pass to the southern gate through bright sunlight from the "Red Emergency Door."

SOUTH: The challenge is conquering our pride, epitomized by proud "Lady the Horse," who confronts my own pride. In the inner circle above is the watchful eye of the "Ochre Ogre." We move through a star-filled sky, suggesting several night sky dreams, on to the western doorway.

WEST: The "Blooming Flower" exemplifies the shift from passion to compassion, the challenge here. In the circle above, a floating tree exemplifies both tree dreams that challenged me to view them with dispassion rather than with passionate emotion. A glowing full moon leads us on to the north.

NORTH: Bear is an apt symbol for meeting the challenge here; conquering greed and envy with strength, generosity and openness, my task in "Bear in the Tree." Above Bear is Eagle, a generous rescuer in several dreams. Moving on, we pass through a cloud-filled blue sky and begin our journey into the inner circle.

THE INNER CIRCLE: On the other side of the red path we meet four more guardians: in the southeast, the changeable faces on the Cameo Pendant greet us; in the southwest a dark hag with keys for unlocking mysteries represents Nameless Dread and her sisters; in the northwest a glowing woman with silver cups suggesting "The Water of Life" embodies women in the Deva dreams; and finally, a gleaming tidal wave rises in the northeast.

THE FINAL CIRCLE: Passing through a last circle of blood red, a symbolic umbilical cord, we arrive at the heart of the mandala. Here The Golden Woman stands in front of the yin-yang symbol that represents the ultimate equilibrium between polar opposites. In Garfield's dream mandala, this central figure conquers delusion and ignorance. This was the triumph of the Golden Woman, with her clear gaze into the mirror from the dream that is the heart of this book.

ACKNOWLEDGEMENTS

I am grateful for the generosity and creativity of the honours students and English department colleagues who took part in two years of classes, especially Gerri Cooper and Richard Pound who allowed me to adapt their work for this book, and Tanis MacDonald whose poetry brought new perspectives. The book also benefits immeasurably from the dreams and comments of friends: Gail Beck, Morgana Graham, Christel Kraft, Gwenda LedBetter, Tanis MacDonald, Lilith Quinlan, and Kira Van Deusen. Gordon and Mary Toombs, dream guides extraordinaire, were generous with insightful critiques and encouragement.

Obviously, this book would not be in your hands now without the good work of a publisher. I am grateful for the encouragement and good humour of Gord Shillingford, whose initial phone message was, "This sounds like fun. Let's do it!" And so we have.

My seemingly endless mistakes were caught by copy editor Heidi Harms, and by Amy Stone in New York. I blame Trickster for any that slipped by their eagle eyes.

My two families, the Mitchells (Allen, Janet, Jolene, Lois, Terry) and Stones (Daniel, Nathaniel, Rachel, Elizabeth), are also an integral part of the book in many ways, and I thank them for being there. And to you, Miss Kitty, I would sing the blues if I had your talent.

works cited

Aarne, Antti and Stith Thompson. (1973) *The Types of the Folk-Tale: A Classification and Bibliography*, Folklore Fellows Communications No. 184. Helsinki: Academia Scientiarum Fennica.

Afanas'ev, Aleksander. (1945, 1973) Trans. Norbert Guterman. *Russian Fairy Tales*. New York: Pantheon.

Andrews, Jan. (2000) *Out of the Everywhere: New Tales for Canada*. Toronto: Groundwood Books/Douglas & McIntyre.

Ashliman, D. L. (1987) *A Guide to Folktales in the English Language: Based on the Aarne-Thompson Classification System*. New York: Greenwood Press.

Barrie, J.M. (1911) *Peter Pan*. London: Hodder & Stoughton.

Bayles, David and Ted Orland. (1993) *Art & Fear: Observations on the Perils (and Rewards) of Artmaking*. Santa Barbara: Capra Press.

Berne, Patricia H. and Louis M. Savary. (1991) *Dream Symbol Work: Unlocking the Energy from Dreams and Spiritual Experiences*. New York: Paulist Press.

Blacker, Thetis. (1973) *A Pilgrimage of Dreams*. London: Turnstone Books Ltd.

Briggs, Katharine. (1970) *A Dictionary of British Folktales (Vols. I and II)*. London: Routledge and Kegan Paul.

Campbell, Joseph. (1971) *The Portable Jung*. New York: Penguin Books.

_____. (1972) *The Hero with a Thousand Faces*. Princeton: Princeton UP.

_____. (1986) *The Inner Reaches of Outer Space*. New York: Alfred van der Marck.

_____. (1988) *The Power of Myth*. New York: Doubleday.

_____. (1990) *The Flight of the Wild Gander: Explorations in the Mythological Dimensions of Fairy Tales, Legends, and Symbols.* New York: Harper Collins.

Campbell, Marie. (1958) *Tales From The Cloud Walking Country.* Bloomington: Indiana University Press; reprinted by Greenwood Press, 1976.

Chase, Richard. (1943) *The Jack Tales.* Boston: Houghton Mifflin Company.

_____. (1948) *The Grandfather Tales.* Boston: Houghton Mifflin Company.

Cooper, Gerri. (1996) "What I Didn't Know That I Knew." Unpublished English honours essay, University of Winnipeg.

Dorson, Richard. (1975) *Folktales Told Around the World.* Chicago: U. of Chicago Press.

Epel, Naomi. (1993) *Writers Dreaming.* New York: Vintage Books.

Fanua, Tupou Posesi. (1975) *Po Fananga: Folktales of Tonga.* Tonga: Tofua Press.

Franz, Marie-Louise von. (1970) *Introduction to the Interpretation of Fairy Tales.* New York: Spring.

Garfield, Patricia. (1989) *Pathways to Ecstasy: The Way of the Dream Mandala.* New York: Prentice Hall Press.

Harris, Joel Chandler. (1974) *Uncle Remus.* New York: Schocken Books (originally published in 1880).

Heilbrun, Carolyn H. (1997) *The Last Gift of Time: Life Beyond Sixty.* New York: The Dial Press.

Jacobs, Joseph. (1967) *English Fairy Tales.* New York: Dover (reprinted from 1898 edition).

_____. (n.d.) *More English Fairy Tales.* New York: G.P. Putnam's Sons.

Jung, Carl G. (1964) *Man and His Symbols.* London: Aldus Books Limited.

_____. (1969) *The Phenomenology of the Spirit in Fairy Tales.* Collected Works. Trans. R. F. C. Hull. 20 vols. Princeton, NJ: Princeton University Press, Vol. 9, 207-53.

_____. (1984) *Dream Analysis: Notes on the Seminar Given in 1928-1930.* Princeton, N.J.: Princeton Univ. Press, Bollingen Series XCIX (originally published in 1938).

_____. (1989) *Memories, Dreams, and Reflections.* (Ed. Aniela Jaffe.) New York: Vintage Books.

Kennard, Edward A. (1977) *Field Mouse Goes to War: Tusan Homichi* Tuwvota. Palmer Lake, Colo.: The Filter Press. (Originally published by U.S. Bureau of Indian Affairs, 1944).

LaBerge, Stephen. (1985) *Lucid Dreaming: The Power of Being Awake & Aware in Your Dreams*. New York: Ballantine Books.

Lang, Andrew. (1967) *The Pink Fairy Book*. New York: Dover. (Originally published in 1897.)

_____. (1968) *The Lilac Fairy Book*. New York: Dover. (Originally published in 1910.)

Lowenthal, Wolfe. (1991) *There Are No Secrets: Professor Cheng Man-ch'ing and his Tai Chi Chuan*. Berkeley, California: North Atlantic Books.

Lüthi, Max. (1976) *Once Upon A Time*. Bloomington: Indiana University Press.

_____. (1985) *The Fairytale As Art Form and Portrait of Man*. Bloomington: Indiana University Press.

_____. (1986) *The European Folktale: Form and Nature*. Bloomington: Indiana University Press.

MacDonald, Margaret Read. (1982) *The Storyteller's Sourcebook: A Subject, Title, and Motif Index to Folklore Collections for Children*. Detroit: Gale Research Company.

MacDonald, Tanis. (2000) *holding ground*. Toronto: Seraphim Editions.

Maguire, Jack. (1985) *Creative Storytelling*. New York: McGraw-Hill Book Company.

McCarthy, William. (1994) *Jack in Two Worlds*. Chapel Hill, N.C.: University of North Carolina Press.

Metayer, Maurice. (1972) *Tales from the Igloo*. New York: St. Martin's Press.

Ming, Justin Wu Ho. (n.d.) *One Hundred Chinese Stories Retold*. Hong Kong: The English Language Publishing Company.

Mooney, James. (1992) *History, Myths, and Sacred Formulas of the Cherokees*. Reprinted from 1891 and 1900 editions. Asheville, North Carolina: Historical Images/Bright Mountain Books.

Neihardt, John G. (1961) *Black Elk Speaks: Being the Life Story of Holyman of the Oglala Sioux*. Lincoln, Nebraska: University of Nebraska Press.

Pound, Richard. (1996) "Jack at Earl's." Unpublished English honours essay, University of Winnipeg.

Radin, Paul. (1956) *The Trickster: A Study in American Indian Mythology*. New York: Schocken Books.

_____. (1975) "The Trickster." *Literature of the American Indians: Views and Interpretations*. (Ed. Abraham Chapman). New York: New American Library.

Roberts, Leonard. (1969) *Old Greasybeard: Tales from the Cumberland Gap*. Detroit: Folklore Associates.

_____. (1955) *South of Hell-fer-Sartin: Kentucky Mountain Folktales*. Lexington, Ken: University of Kentucky Press.

Roberts, Warren. (1958) *The Kind and the Unkind Girls*. Berlin: De Gruyter.

Sargent, Helen Child and George Lyman Kittredge. (1932) *English and Scottish Popular Ballads*. Boston: Houghton Mifflin Company.

SGI Canada (Soka Gakkai International). (2000) "The Dragon Gate." *New Century Magazine* (October, No. 241). 28-33.

_____. (2002) "The Jar of Gold." *Read Me a Story!* Toronto, Ontario: Soka Gakkai International Association of Canada, 46-47.

Stevens, H. C. (trans.). (1967) *Russian Folk Tales*. London: Paul Hamlyn.

Stone, Kay. (1975) "Romantic Heroines in Anglo-American Folk and Popular Literature." Unpublished doctoral dissertation, Indiana University.

_____. (1994a) "Jack's Adventures in Toronto." *Jack in Two Worlds*. (Ed. William McCarthy.) Chapel Hill, North Carolina: University of North Carolina Press, 250-71.

_____. (1994b) "The Curious Girl." *Next Teller: A Book of Canadian Storytelling*. (Ed. Dan Yashinsky.) Charlottetown, P.E.I.: Ragweed Press, 8-14.

_____. (1997) "Inside Out: Folktale and Personal Story." *Marvels & Tales: Journal of Fairy-Tale Studies*, Vol. 11 nos. 1-2, 13-23.

_____. (1998) *Burning Brightly: New Light on Old Tales Told Today*. Peterborough, Ontario: Broadview Press.

_____. (1998) "The Water of Life." *At the Edge: A Book of Risky Stories*. (Ed. Dan Yashinsky.) Charlottetown, P.E.I.: Ragweed Press, 1998, 211-216.

_____. (2000) "Fire and Water: A Journey into the Heart of a Story." *Marvels & Tales: Journal of Fairy-Tale Studies*, Vol. 14 nos. 1, 136-151.

Storm, Hjemeyohsts. (1972) *Seven Arrows*. New York: Ballantine Books.

Thompson, Stith. (1968) *Tales of the North American Indians*. Bloomington, Indiana: Indiana University Press.

_____. (1975) *One Hundred Favorite Folktales*. Bloomington, Indiana: Indiana University Press.

Till, Barry. (2000) *The Tibetan Mandala and Tibet's Sacred Art*. Victoria, British Columbia: Art Gallery of Greater Victoria.

Ueland, Brenda. (1987, 1938) *If You Want To Write: A Book About Art, Independence and Spirit*. St. Paul, Minn.: Graywolf Press.

Van de Castle, Robert L. (1994) *Our Dreaming Mind*. New York: Ballantine Books.

Van Deusen, Kira. (1996) *Shyaan am!: Tuvan Folktales*. Bellingham, Washington: Udagan Books.

_____. (1998) "The Man Who Wintered in a Bear's Den." *At the Edge: A Book of Risky Stories*. (Ed. Dan Yashinsky). Charlottetown, P.E.I.: Ragweed Press, 227-329.

_____. (1999) *Raven and the Rock: Storytelling in Chukotka*. Seattle: University of Washington Press.

_____. (2001) *The Flying Tiger: Women Shamans and Storytellers of the Amur*. Montreal and Kingston: McGill-Queen's University Press.

_____. (2003) *Singing Story, Healing Drum: Shamans and Storytellers of Turkic Siberia*. Montreal: McGill-Queen's University Press, 2003.

Watts, Laura J. (2002) *Mandalas: Spiritual Circles for Harmony and Fulfillment*. London, England: Hermes House.

Weinreich, Beatrice (ed.) and Leonard Wolf (trans.). (1988) *Yiddish Folktales*. New York: Pantheon.

Yashinsky, Dan. (1990) *Tales for an Unknown City*. Montreal and Kingston: McGill-Queen's University Press.

_____. (1994) *Next Teller: A Book of Canadian Storytelling*. Charlottetown, P.E.I.: Ragweed Press.

_____. (1998) *At the Edge: A Book of Risky Stories*. Charlottetown, P.E.I.: Ragweed Press.

Yolen, Jane. (1986) *Favourite Folktales from Around the World*. New York: Pantheon Books.

Yu, Anthony C. (trans. & ed.) (1980) *The Journey to the West*. Chicago: University of Chicago Press.

Zipes, Jack, translator. (1988) *The Complete Fairy Tales of the Brothers Grimm*. New York: Bantam Books, 1988.

General Index

Dream titles are not in quotation marks, to set them apart from story titles. Aarne-Thompson Tale Type numbers are listed for folktales.

Index of Aarne-Thompson Tale Types